T0219982

Lecture Notes in Artificial Intelligence 10798

Subseries of Lecture Notes in Computer Science

LNAI Series Editors

Randy Goebel
University of Alberta, Edmonton, Canada
Yuzuru Tanaka
Hokkaido University, Sapporo, Japan
Wolfgang Wahlster
DFKI and Saarland University, Saarbrücken, Germany

LNAI Founding Series Editor

Joerg Siekmann
DFKI and Saarland University, Saarbrücken, Germany

More information about this series at http://www.springer.com/series/1244

Graçaliz Pereira Dimuro · Luis Antunes (Eds.)

Multi-Agent Based Simulation XVIII

International Workshop, MABS 2017
São Paulo, Brazil, May 8–12, 2017
Revised Selected Papers

 Springer

Editors
Graçaliz Pereira Dimuro ⓘ
Universidade Federal do Rio Grande
Rio Grande
Brazil

Luis Antunes ⓘ
Universidade de Lisboa
Lisbon
Portugal

ISSN 0302-9743   ISSN 1611-3349   (electronic)
Lecture Notes in Artificial Intelligence
ISBN 978-3-319-91586-9   ISBN 978-3-319-91587-6   (eBook)
https://doi.org/10.1007/978-3-319-91587-6

Library of Congress Control Number: 2018944268

LNCS Sublibrary: SL7 – Artificial Intelligence

© Springer International Publishing AG, part of Springer Nature 2018
This work is subject to copyright. All rights are reserved by the Publisher, whether the whole or part of the material is concerned, specifically the rights of translation, reprinting, reuse of illustrations, recitation, broadcasting, reproduction on microfilms or in any other physical way, and transmission or information storage and retrieval, electronic adaptation, computer software, or by similar or dissimilar methodology now known or hereafter developed.
The use of general descriptive names, registered names, trademarks, service marks, etc. in this publication does not imply, even in the absence of a specific statement, that such names are exempt from the relevant protective laws and regulations and therefore free for general use.
The publisher, the authors and the editors are safe to assume that the advice and information in this book are believed to be true and accurate at the date of publication. Neither the publisher nor the authors or the editors give a warranty, express or implied, with respect to the material contained herein or for any errors or omissions that may have been made. The publisher remains neutral with regard to jurisdictional claims in published maps and institutional affiliations.

Printed on acid-free paper

This Springer imprint is published by the registered company Springer International Publishing AG
part of Springer Nature
The registered company address is: Gewerbestrasse 11, 6330 Cham, Switzerland

Preface

The Multi-Agent-Based Simulation (MABS) Workshop series aims to bring together researchers engaged in modeling and in analyzing multi-agent systems, and those interested in applying agent-based simulation techniques to real-world problems. Its scientific focus lies in the confluence of socio-technical-natural sciences and multi-agent systems, with a strong application/empirical vein. Lately, its emphasis has been placed on (a) exploratory agent-based simulation as a principled way of undertaking scientific research in the social sciences, and (b) using social theories as an inspiration to new frameworks and developments in multi-agent systems.

The 2017 International Multi-Agent-Based Simulation Workshop was held in conjunction with the 16th Autonomous Agents and Multi-Agent Systems Conference (AAMAS) in São Paulo (Brazil) during May 8–12, 2017.

This volume represents the 18th in a series that began in 1998. In total, 15 papers from 10 countries were submitted to the workshop. We selected 13 papers for long presentation and three papers for short presentation (around 62% acceptance). The papers presented at the workshop were extended and revised, incorporating points from the discussions held at the workshop with their original ideas, resulting in 15 papers about architectures, methods, simulations methodologies, and MABS applications.

In this MABS edition, two papers, the most "visionary" and the "best" papers, had already been published by Springer in the *Lecture Notes in Artificial Intelligence* (LNAI) series and the *Communications in Computer and Information Science* (CCIS) series, respectively.

The workshop could not have taken place without the contribution of many people. We are very grateful to Jaime Simão Sichman, who gave a very interesting invited talk in homage to Rosaria Conte, and to all the participants who took part in a lively debate during the presentation of the papers. We are also very grateful to all the members of the Program Committee for their hard work. Thanks are also due to Juan Antonio Rodríguez-Aguila and Gita Sukthankar (AAMAS 2017 workshop chairs), to Kate Larson and Michael Winikoff, (AAMAS 2017 general co-chairs), to Sanmay and Ed Durfee (AAMAS 2017 program co-chairs), and again to Jaime Simão Sichman (AAMAS 2017 local arrangements chair).

March 2018

Graçaliz Pereira Dimuro
Luis Antunes

Organization

General and Program Chairs

Graçaliz Pereira Dimuro   Universidade Federal do Rio Grande, Brazil
Luis Antunes   Universidade de Lisboa, Portugal

MABS Steering Committee

Frédéric Amblard   Université Toulouse 1 Capitole, France
Luis Antunes   University of Lisbon, Portugal
Paul Davidsson   Malmö University, Sweden
Nigel Gilbert   University of Surrey, UK
Scott Moss   University of Koblenz-Landau, Germany
Keith Sawyer   University of North Carolina, USA
Jaime Simão Sichman   University of São Paulo, Brazil
Keiki Takadama   University of Electro-Communications, Japan

Program Committee

Diana Francisca Adamatti   Universidade Federal do Rio Grande, Brazil
Fred Amblard   IRIT - University Toulouse 1 Capitole, France
Luis Antunes   Universidade de Lisboa, Portugal
Joao Balsa   Universidade de Lisboa, Portugal
Raquel Barbosa   Instituto Federal do Rio Grande do Sul, Brazil
Cleo Billa   Universidade Federal do Rio Grande, Brazil
Cristiano Castelfranchi   Institute of Cognitive Sciences and Technology, Italy
Helder Coelho   Universidade de Lisboa, Portugal
Paul Davidsson   Malmö University, Sweden
Frank Dignum   Utrecht University, The Netherlands
Graçaliz Pereira Dimuro   Universidade Federal do Rio Grande, Brazil
Bruce Edmonds   Manchester Metropolitan University, UK
Benoit Gaudou   CNRS, IRIT, Université de Toulouse, France
Gustavo Giménez-Lugo   Federal University of Technology-Paraná, Brazil
Nick Gotts   Independent Researcher, UK
Wander Jager   University of Groningen, The Netherlands
Marco Janssen   Arizona State University, USA
Satoshi Kurihara   The University of Electro-Communications, Japan
Bill Kennedy   George Mason University, USA
Eder Mateus Gonçalves   Universidade Federal of Rio Grande, Brazil
William Griffin   Arizona State University, USA
Laszlo Gulyas   Eotvos Lorand University, Hungary
Rainer Hegselmann   Bayreuth University, Germany

Ulf Lotzmann	University of Koblenz-Landau, Germany
Ruth Meyer	Manchester Metropolitan University Business School, UK
Jean-Pierre Muller	CIRAD, France
Luis Gustavo Nardin	Brandenburg University of Technology, Germany
Emma Norling	Manchester Metropolitan University, UK
Paulo Novais	University of Minho, Portugal
Mario Paolucci	Institute of Cognitive Sciences and Technology, Italy
Juan Pavón	Universidad Complutense de Madrid, Spain
Gary Polhill	The James Hutton Institute, UK
William Rand	North Carolina State University, USA
Fernando Santos	Universidade Federal do Rio Grande do Sul, Brazil
Keiki Takadama	The University of Electro-Communications, Japan
Gennaro Di Tosto	The Ohio State University, USA
Jan Treur	Vrije Universiteit Amsterdam, The Netherlands
Klaus G. Troitzsch	University of Koblenz-Landau, Germany
Stephen John Turner	King Mongkut's University of Technology Thonburi, Thailand
Harko Verhagen	Stockholm University, Sweden

Sponsors

Contents

Architectures, Methods and Simulation Methodologies

NATYASASTRA: A Dramatic Game for the Self-Regulation of Social Exchange Processes in MAS

Renata Gomes Wotter[1], Nelson de Farias Traversi[1], Lucas Tubino Costa[1], Graçaliz Pereira Dimuro[1,2], and Diana Francisca Adamatti[1(✉)]

[1] Centro de Ciências Computacionais, Universidade Federal do Rio Grande, Av. Itália km 08, Campus Carreiros, Rio Grande 96201-900, Brazil
dianaada@gmail.com

[2] Institute of Smart Cities, Universidad Publica de Navarra, Campus Arrosadía, 31006 Navarra, Spain

Abstract. This paper presents a dramatic game for the self-regulation of social exchange processes in multi-agent systems, called Natyasastra, based on the concepts of Drama Theory. The model has five phases of dramatic resolution, which involve feelings, emotions, trust and reputation. Agents with different social exchange strategies interact among each other in order to maximize their strategy-based fitness functions. The objective is to obtain a more natural model than the ones existing in the literature, which are based either on (partially observable) Markov decision processes or in game theory, so that it can be applied in real-world applications. We aim at promoting more balanced and fair multi-agent interactions, increasing the number of successful social exchanges and, thus, promoting the continuity of social exchanges. The simulations showed that there is an improvement of fitness along time, as result of the self-regulation of the interactions. The agents have evolved their social exchange strategies, and other strategies, different from the original ones, have emerged in the society, so contributing to this evolution. This game was implemented in NetLogo.

Keywords: Regulation of social exchange processes · Drama theory Emotions

1 Introduction

Piaget's Social Exchanges Theory [18] has been used as the basis for the analysis of interactions in Multiagent Systems (MAS), where the interactions are understood as services exchanges, which are evaluated by the agents themselves while interacting, creating the concept of social exchange values, that are qualitative and subjective values [4]. A fundamental problem that has been discussed in the literature is the regulation of social exchanges [3,5,6,14,17,22,26], in order to allow, for example, the emergence of balanced exchanges along time, leading to social equilibrium and stability [18] and/or fairness behaviour [19,28]. In

© Springer International Publishing AG, part of Springer Nature 2018
G. P. Dimuro and L. Antunes (Eds.): MABS 2017, LNAI 10798, pp. 3–17, 2018.
https://doi.org/10.1007/978-3-319-91587-6_1

particular, this is a difficult problem when the agents, adopting different social exchange strategies, have incomplete information on the other agents' strategies. This is a crucial problem in open agent societies (see [5,6]).

Dimuro et al. and Pereira et al. [3,5,6], introduced different models for the social exchange regulation problem, some based in hybrid agent models BDI[1] and (partially observable) Markov decision processes. On the other hand, in [14], Macedo et al. introduced the Game of Self-Regulation of Social Exchange Processes (GSREP), where the agents, possessing different social exchange strategies, considering both the short and long-term aspects of the interactions, evolve their exchange strategies along the time by themselves, in order to promote more equilibrated and fair interactions, guaranteeing the continuation of the exchanges. In [26], Von Laer et al. analysed the problem of the self-regulation of social exchange processes in the context of a BDI-based MAS, adapting the GSREP game to Jason [2] agents and introducing a cultural aspect, where the society culture, aggregating the agents' reputation as group beliefs, influences directly the evolution of the agents' exchange strategies, increasing the number of successful interactions and improving the agents' outcomes in interactions.

In Game Theory [13], usually, a game is defined by fixing the preferences and opportunities of the players. In 1991, Nigel Howard created the Drama Theory [9,11], a game theory extension, where the preferences and choices of the characters (players) may change under the pressure of the pre-game negotiations. Game theory tries to predict the outcome of a game with "rational" players. However, drama theory shows how aspiring players, communicating each other before a game, build not only the game that they will play, but also the result that they expect of it, without the need to predict an outcome. Furthermore, drama theory challenges the theoretical concept of "rational" game. After analysing the pre-game communication, it is discarded the hypothesis that the players know what they want, what the others want, and what they and others can do about it, and that all these things are fixed [11].

The objective of this paper is to introduce a dramatic game model for the self-regulation of social exchange processes, applying the concepts of drama theory to GSREP, adding feelings and expressions of emotions based on the OCC model [16], in order to obtain a natural model that approximates the reality.[2] In this model, called Natyasastra[3], the agents may adopt different social exchange strategies, e.g., altruism, selfishness and rationality. Unlike GSREP, Natyasastra has the pre-game stage, the strategies are not fixed and can be changed throughout the interactional process among the characters. The proposed drama considers the five stages of dramatic resolution, and may or may not generate some emotions, depending on the strategy chosen and whether or not the exchange are balanced. The agents evolve their social exchange strategies based on their

---

[1] BDI stands for "Beliefs, Desires, Intentions", a cognitive agent model introduced in [20].

[2] A very initial proposal of this model was presented in [27].

[3] Natyasastra is a text on the theatre, written between 200 BC and 200 AC in India, by a prophet, Bharata, which manifests itself in sensitivities, reasons and feelings.

fitness functions, which take into account the adopted strategies, the emotions involved and the agents' reputation.

The paper is organized as follows. Section 2 summarizes its theoretical basis. Section 3 presents Natyasastra. The simulation are in Sect. 4. Section 5 is the Conclusion.

2   Social Exchanges Theory and Drama Theory

This sections briefly discusses the theoretical basis of this work, namely, the social exchange process and the drama theory.

Social Exchanges in MAS. According to Piaget [18], a social exchange process is any sequence of actions among two agents, such that one of them, to realize his/her actions, provides a service to another, with the immediate individual qualitative evaluation of the services provided. That is, the agent assigns a value to its investment in the realization of a service to another agent and the latter assigns a value of satisfaction for having received such a service. Such values are called material exchange values. In a social exchange process, debt and credit values are also generated, which allow the realization of future exchanges. Debt and credit are called virtual values.

A social exchange is analysed individually among agents and involves at least two agents, X and Y, in two exchanges steps/stages. In **Step I** the agent X performs a service to the agent Y, generating the following exchange values: r_X (*Investment* value of agent X), s_y (*Satisfaction* value of agent Y), t_y (*Debit* value of agent Y) and v_x (*Credit* of agent X). In **Step II**, the agent X requests to the agent Y a payment for the service previously performed for it, and the values generated are analogous. A social exchange process is a sequence of these steps exchanges, in any order. A balanced exchange happens when the sum of the investment and satisfaction of an agent is around zero, after the two steps of an exchange process had occured between a pair of agents. A society is in equilibrium if the exchanges among pair of agents are balanced for both agents after a sequence of exchange processes.

Drama Theory. Differently from Game Theory, which considers that a game is defined by previously fixed preferences and opportunities for the players, Drama Theory [8–11] shows under which conditions the game itself may change. The game transformations result from the fact that the players may put pressure on the others during the pre-game negotiations, since they exchange threats, promises, emotional persuasion and rational arguments. Then, Drama theory helps to identify the transformations caused by the internal dynamics of the pre-game negotiations. Such transformations describe rational and irrational processes of human development and self-realization, rather than just the rational choice of a given end.

While game theory exposes the rational behaviour, based on goals, drama theory shows how, in the course of an interaction, people change and evolve. Rationality is still important, but no longer dominates. Then, Drama theory depends on the fact that, only if there are no paradoxes of rationality, the agents solve their problem totally convincingly. Specifically, in Phase 2 (see next Section), when the agents decide on a group of positions, they are confronted with paradoxes. If there is just one position, there is a strict and strong balance [10]. The phases of Drama Theory are explained in Sect. 3.

3   The Natyasastra Drama Model

The dramatic model of self-regulation of social exchange processes is based in the five phases of the dramatic resolution of drama theory, which are represented in Fig. 1.

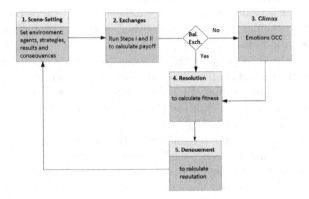

Fig. 1. Phases of the dramatic resolution

3.1   Phase 1: Scene-Setting

At this phase, the environment is defined with the actors (agents), agents' social exchange strategies, results and consequences. The agents' social exchange strategies that are considered in this paper are: altruism, weak altruism, selfishness, weak selfishness and rationality. For example, an agent with selfishness strategy is more likely to undervalue the received service and overvalue an offered service, which impacts on debt and credit values; the rational agent plays just for the Nash Equilibrium[4].

A social exchange strategy of an agent $\lambda = i, j$, is defined by the tuple:

$$(r_\lambda^{max}, r_\lambda^{prop}, r_\lambda^{efect}, s_\lambda^{min}, s_\lambda^{exp}, k_\lambda^{\rho t}, k_\lambda^{\rho v}), \tag{1}$$

where $r_\lambda^{max} \in [0, 1]$ and $s_\lambda^{min} \in [0, 1]$ are the maximal investment value that the agent λ is willing to have for a service performed for another agent, and the minimal satisfaction that the agent λ is willing to accept for a received service,

---

[4] See [14] for a discussion on the Nash Equilibrium of the Game of Social Exchange Processes.

respectively; $r_\lambda^{prop} \in [0,1]$ and $s_\lambda^{exp} \in [0,1]$ are the proposed investment that the agent λ will have for this service and the expected satisfaction value of the another agent, respectively; $r_\lambda^{efect} \in [0,1]$ is the effective investment that the agent λ actually has, since depending on the chosen strategy by the agent, this investment may be higher, lower or equal to the proposed; $k_\lambda^{\rho t}, k_\lambda^{\rho v} \in [0,1]$ are, respectively, the factors of depreciation ($\rho = d$) or overvaluation ($\rho = o$) of debit and credit values that define each exchange strategy.

In the dramatic model, the result of an agent is represented by the proposed investment (r^{prop}) (i.e., the future it proposes to other agents) and the expected satisfaction (s^{exp}) (i.e., the desire, a particular future that it would like to achieve).

3.2 Phase 2: Exchanges

At this phase, a determinate frame $F = (Q, P)$ is selected, where, Q is the result set of each agent and $P = (P_i | i \in C)$ is a family of preference relations, one for each character or agent i at casting C, defined along of results set X. In this game, $(x, y) \in P_i$ means that "the agent i prefers the strategy x to strategy y".

After selecting the frame, the steps **I** and **II** of the social exchange process are executed, as shown in Sect. 2. Observe that an important parameter is (s_{efect}), which represents the effective satisfaction that another agent actually has for the received service. This parameter is not part of the social exchange strategy of an agent, and is calculated during the exchange as follows:

$$s_{ij}^{efet}(r_{ji}^{prop}, r_{ji}^{efet}) = \begin{cases} \min\{r_{ji}^{prop} + 0.05, 1\} & \text{if } r_{ji}^{efet} \geq r_{ji}^{prop} \\ \max\{r_{ji}^{prop} - 0.05, 0\} & \text{otherwise,} \end{cases}$$

where 0.05 is an step value, the minimum value that does change the strategy.

After performing Steps I and II of a social exchange, we calculated the Supposed Payoff (*SupPayoff*) and the Effective Payoff (*EffectPayoff*) of the social exchange between the agents i and j:

$$(r_i^{max}, r_{ij}^{prop}, r_{ij}^{efect}, s_i^{min}, s_i^{exp}, s_i^{efect}, k_i^{\rho t}, k_i^{\rho v}),$$

$$(r_j^{max}, r_{ji}^{prop}, r_{ji}^{efect}, s_j^{min}, s_j^{exp}, s_j^{efect} k_j^{\rho t}, k_j^{\rho v})$$

The *SupPayoff* obtained by an agent i in this interaction is evaluated by function $p_{ij}^{sup} : [0,1]^4 \to [0,1]$, defined by:

$$p_{ij}^{sup}(r_{ij}^{prop}, r_i^{max}, s_{ji}^{exp}, s_j^{min}) = \begin{cases} \dfrac{1 - r_{ij}^{prop} + s_{ij}^{exp}}{2} & \begin{array}{l} \text{if } (r_{ij}^{prop} \leq r_i^{max} \wedge s_{ji}^{exp} \geq s_j^{min}) \\ \wedge (r_{ji}^{prop} \leq r_i^{max} \wedge s_{ij}^{exp} \geq s_i^{min}) \end{array} \\[2ex] \dfrac{1 - r_{ij}^{prop}}{2} & \begin{array}{l} \text{if } (r_{ij}^{prop} \leq r_i^{max} \wedge s_{ji}^{exp} \geq s_j^{min} \\ \wedge (r_{ji}^{prop} > r_j^{max} \vee s_{ij}^{exp} < s_i^{min}) \end{array} \\[2ex] 0 & \text{if } (r_{ij}^{prop} > r_i^{max} \vee s_{ji}^{exp} < s_j^{min}) \end{cases}$$

$$(2)$$

The *EffectPayoff* obtained by an agent i in this interaction is evaluated by function $p_{ij}^{efect} : [0,1]^4 \rightarrow [0,1]$, defined by:

$$
p_{ij}^{efect}(r_{ij}^{efect}, r_j^{max}, s_{ji}^{efect}, s_j^{min}) = \begin{cases} \dfrac{1 - r_{ij}^{efect} + s_{ij}^{efect}}{2} & \text{if}\,(r_{ij}^{efect} \leq r_i^{max} \wedge s_{ji}^{efect} \geq s_j^{min}) \\ & \wedge(r_{ji}^{efect} \leq r_j^{max} \wedge s_{ij}^{efect} \geq s_i^{min}) \\ \dfrac{1 - r_{ij}^{efect}}{2} & \text{if}\,(r_{ij}^{efect} \leq r_i^{max} \wedge s_{ji}^{efect} \geq s_j^{min}) \\ & \wedge(r_{ji}^{efect} > r_j^{max} \vee s_{ij}^{efect} < s_i^{min}) \\ 0 & \text{if}\,(r_{ij}^{efect} > r_i^{max} \vee s_{ji}^{efect} < s_j^{min}) \end{cases}
\tag{3}
$$

In the Eqs. (2) and (3), the first line represents a complete social exchange (both Steps I and II are executed), the second line is an incomplete social exchange (only Step I is executed) and the third line represents that no social exchange occurs (Step 1 is not executed and, thus, there is no Step 2). The *SupPayoff* and the *EffectPayoff* of j agent are defined analogously.

Considering an environment composed of the cast $C = 1, \ldots, m$ of m agents, each agent $i \in C$ interacts with the others $m - 1$ neighbours agents $j \in C$, such that $j \neq i$. In every interaction cycle, each agent i evaluates its material results of local social exchange with each neighbour agent j, using the local *SupPayoff* and *EffectPayoff* functions, given in the Eqs. (2) and (3). Then, the full *SupPayoff* and *EffectPayoff* received by each agent are calculated after each agent has performed the two-step exchange with all its neighbours. For p_{ij}^{sup} and p_{ij}^{efect} calculated by Eqs. (2) and (3), the allocation of total *SupPayoff* and *EffectPayoff* of a neighbourhood of m agents, is given by:

$$
X^{sup} = x_1^{sup}, \ldots, x_m^{sup}, \text{ where } x_i^{sup} = \sum_{j \in C, j \neq i} p_{ij}^{sup}
\tag{4}
$$

$$
X^{efect} = x_1^{efect}, \ldots, x_m^{efect}, \text{ where } x_i^{efect} = \sum_{j \in C, j \neq i} p_{ij}^{efect}
\tag{5}
$$

After calculating the effective payoff of exchanges, the balance of these exchanges is analysed. Ideally, a balanced exchange is when the difference between the payoffs of all exchanges is zero. However, in practice, this divergence occurs around zero. This divergence between the payoffs are calculated according to:

$$
D_i = \frac{1}{(m-1)} \sum_{\substack{i \neq j}}^{j = [1..m]} |x_i - x_j|
\tag{6}
$$

where m is the total number of agents. The exchanges are considered balanced when $D_i \leq \alpha$, for all exchanges, for $\alpha = 0$

3.3   Phase 3: Climax

If, in phase 2, all the exchanges occur in a balanced way, the phase 3 is ignored and the drama moves on to the phase 4, where the emotions will have null weight in the calculus of the *fitness* value, denoted by $F_i(X^{efect})$ of an agent i. If the exchanges are not balanced, all agents migrate to the phase 3.

We consider four types of emotions of the OCC model [16], namely, gratification, gratitude, regret and anger, represented by the factors $a_\lambda, b_\lambda, c_\lambda$ and d_λ, respectively. Observe that in the OCC model there are three aspects that change the world reactions: events, agents and objects. The events are interesting because we may analyse the consequences, the agents because we may analyse their actions, and objects because the aspects and properties of those objects are analysed. The chosen emotions are part of a group that focuses on the action of an agent and the consequences of the events [1].

A *spatial social exchange strategy* of an agent λ, $\lambda = 1, \ldots, m$ is defined by:

$$(r_\lambda^{prop}, r_\lambda^{efect}, s_\lambda^{exp}, s_\lambda^{efect}, a_\lambda, b_\lambda, c_\lambda, d_\lambda, k_\lambda^{\rho t}, k_\lambda^{\rho v}), \tag{7}$$

where $a_\lambda, b_\lambda, c_\lambda, d_\lambda$ reflect the influence of the emotions in the fitness value $F_i(X^{efect})$ of an agent i, in the following way:

- **Gratification (a_i):** $F_i(X^{efect}) = x_i^{efect} + \frac{a_i}{(m-1)} \sum_{i \neq j} \max(x_j^{efect} - x_j^{sup}, 0)$, where X^{efect} is the total effective payoff allocation of agent i. *Gratification* is a positive feeling generated in the agent itself who proposed the exchange when the *effective payoff (EffectPayoff)* of the agent that received the service (x_j^{efect}), obtained by effective investment, is greater than the *supposed payoff (paypffSup)* it was supposed to receive (x_j^{sup}). This means that practising a value greater than the promised value, the agent feels more confident, also generating a reciprocal gratitude feeling on the other agent.

- **Gratitude (b_i):** $F_i(X^{efect}) = x_i^{efect} + b_i \max(x_i^{efect} - x_i^{sup}, 0)$, where X^{efect} is the total effective payoff allocation of agent i. Gratitude is a positive feeling generated in the agent that received the service when the *effective payoff (EffectPayoff)* of the agent that has done the exchange (x_i^{efect}) is greater than the *supposed payoff (SupPayoff)* it was supposed to receive (x_i^{sup}). When receiving a greater value than the one promised, the agent is grateful to the agent who performed the service, generating a good reputation of this agent, since it complies with what it has previously promised.

- **Regret (c_i):** $F_i(X^{efect}) = x_i^{efect} - \frac{c_i}{(m-1)} \sum_{i \neq j} \max(x_j^{sup} - x_j^{efect}, 0)$, where X^{efect} is the total effective payoff allocation of agent i. *Regret* is a negative feeling generated in the agent itself who proposed the exchange when the *effective payoff (EffectPayoff)* of the agent that received the service (x_j^{efect}) is less than the *supposed payoff (SupPayoff)* that it was supposed to receive (x_j^{sup}). This feeling generates a reciprocal feeling of anger in another agent, and consequently it will get a bad reputation of this other agent, since it did not comply with what it has previously promised.

- **Anger (d_i):** $F_i(X^{efect}) = x_i^{efect} - d_i max(x_i^{sup} - x_i^{efect}, 0)$, where X^{efect} is the total effective payoff allocation of agent i. *Anger* is a negative feeling generated in the agent who received the service when the *effective payoff (EffectPayoff)* of the agent who practised the exchange (x_i^{efect}) is less than the *supposed payoff (SupPayoff)* it was supposed to receive (x_i^{sup}).

Therefore, it is clear that an equilibrated balance is achieved when the antagonistic emotions are annulled.

3.4   Phase 4: Resolution

After execution of the steps **I** and **II** of the social exchange process in the build up phase, if there is an equilibrated balance, the game progresses to phase 4. At this phase, considering the payoff obtained in phase 2, the agent i calculates its adaptation degree through its *fitness* function $F_i : [0,1]^m \rightarrow [0,1]$, defined by $F_i(X^{efect}) = x_i^{efect}$, where X^{efect} is the total payoff effective allocation of agent i.

If the phase 3 has been executed, the generated emotions are considered in the fitness function, representing the influence of these emotions on the results of the total effective agents' payoff. Let X be the allocation of total *EffectPayoff* of a neighbourhood of m agents. The general definition of the fitness function, based on exchange strategy of an agent i, is given by:

$$F_i(X^{efect}) =$$
$$x_i + \frac{a_i}{(m-1)} \sum_{i \neq j} \max(x_j^{efect} - x_j^{sup}, 0) + b_i \max(x_i^{efect} - x_i^{sup}, 0)$$
$$- \frac{c_i}{(m-1)} \sum_{i \neq j} \max(x_j^{sup} - x_j^{efect}, 0) - d_i \max(x_i^{sup} - x_i^{efect}, 0). \qquad (8)$$

3.5   Phase 5: Denouement

After obtaining the value of the *fitness* function, the phase 5 is executed. At this phase, the reputation of agents is calculated. For the social sciences, reputations are defined as a collective of beliefs and opinions that influence the actions of individuals in relation to their peers. The reputation can still be seen as a social tool in order to reduce uncertainty to interact with individuals of unknown attributes. To [15], reputation is generally defined as the amount of confidence inspired by a particular person in an environment or specific area of interest. Trust and Reputation may be used for the search for partners. The reputation has the power to propagate trust and can prevent unnecessarily agent interactions. See also [12, 24, 25, 29].

Rodrigues et al. [21] developed a reputation model based on models such as REGRET [23] and Hübner et al. [7]. The analysis of the reputation is divided into three dimensions: Social Dimension, Single Dimension and Ontological Dimension, as proposed in REGRET model. In the Social Dimension it is analysed the effectiveness of the agent to its social group. In the Single Dimension it is analysed the direct exchanges among agents. Finally, there is the Ontological Dimension, where social and individual dimensions are combined for a final analysis.

In our dramatic model, inspired by the initial reputation model proposed in [21], we consider only the single dimension at the moment. At this phase 5, the *payoffs* obtained in phase 3 through social exchanges between the agents i and j is stored in a list of size v. The calculation of the reputation is then given by $Rep = \frac{\sum_{j \in C, j \neq i} p_{ij}}{size(v)}$.

With the obtained information in the denouement phase, the game return to phase 1 and a new *fitness* (F') is calculated by $F' = F - / + (Rep.\beta)$, where F is the *fitness* calculated in the phase 4, and β is the setting value in percent. This means that, if the agent's reputation is greater than or equal to the average of the total payoffs, then it is considered a good reputation, and the resulting value of $(Rep.\beta)$ is added to the previous *fitness* value. Otherwise, we subtract it from the previous *fitness* value.

The agents analyse the results of their previous *fitness* and actual *fitness*, adjust their strategies according to an adjustment vector of 27 probabilities, increasing, decreasing, or keeping constant the investment values they want to achieve, maximum investment which it intends to offer and the lowest acceptable satisfaction, r^{efet}, r^{max} and s^{min}, respectively. This process is repeated in each cycle of the simulation.

Before starting the a new cycle, the agent evaluates its *fitness* comparing its current *fitness* with the previous one: if it exceeds the value of the previous *fitness*, then the current strategy is better than the previous one, and the agent makes an adjustment in the vector of 27 probabilities, increasing the probability of the current strategy to be chosen again, increasing/decreasing the parameters of its strategy. So, the agent will redefine the environment from new strategies, i.e., the agents will choose new partners to execute the social exchange, and start the second cycle.

4   Simulation and Results

Each agent has its social strategy determined by its behaviour in relation to the exchanges proposed by other agents, by the investment values it intends to perform and by the degree of the emotions generated in the social exchange. Agents become regulators of the exchange processes, as the overall results emerge in the evolution of time.

Each strategy is defined by the following characteristics: maximum investment value that the agent intends to perform, investments values that the agent proposes and that it effectively performs, minimum satisfaction value accepted by the agent, and the expected satisfaction value, both when receiving the service. These characteristics are determinant in the evolution process of the agents. The parameters adopted, which define each exchange strategy, are in the Table 1. The feelings generated when performing a exchange are null for the rational agent, so the values a, b, c and d are set to zero.

Each agent plays with its neighbours seeking the best strategy, finding a combination of values (Table 1) that provide the increment of the number of successful exchanges, the decrement of the unsuccessful interactions and the increment of its *fitness*.

Table 1. Parameters of social exchange strategies

Strategy	r^{max}	r^{prop}	r^{efect}	s^{min}	s^{exp}	a	b	c	d	$k^p t$	$k^p v$
Altruism	1	[0.75; 1]	[0.75; 1]	0.51	[0.51; 0.61]	0.8	0.8	0.2	0.2	0.2, $\rho = o$	0.2, $\rho = d$
Weak altruism	0.8	[0.68; 0.75]	[0.68; 0.79]	0.6	[0.62; 0.75]	0.6	0.6	0.4	0.4	0.1, $\rho = o$	0.1, $\rho = d$
Selfishness	0.6	[0.55; 0.55]	[0.4; 0.55]	0.8	[0.85; 1]	0.2	0.2	0.8	0.8	0.2, $\rho = d$	0.2, $\rho = o$
Weak self	0.7	[0.55; 0.67]	[0.55; 0.69]	0.7	[0.75; 0.85]	0.3	0.3	0.7	0.7	0.1, $\rho = d$	0.1, $\rho = o$
Rationality	0.5	[0; 0.5]	[0; 0.5]	0.5	[0; 0.5]	0	0	0	0	0	0

Given a game between an agent i and an agent j, the number of exchanges is defined as follows: agent i makes a proposal according to its strategy defined in Table 1. The agent j analyses if the proposal performed is greater than the minimum satisfaction value defined in its strategy. If so, then the game moves on to the next stage. Otherwise, it is defined that no exchange occurs between i and j.

In a second moment of the game, i charges such investment made, according to the credit that i believes to have with j. The agent j analyses his debt and makes an investment proposal for i, which analyses if the proposal made by j is greater than the minimum satisfaction value defined in its strategy. If positive, then the two exchanges between the agents i and j occur. Otherwise, it just an exchange occur between agents i and j, the exchange that j accepted the investment made by i.

We have analysed 5 different simulation scenarios. However, for the lack of space, in this paper, we chose an heterogeneous scenario to be presented, i.e., with the five defined strategies. In this scenario, each strategy was allocated to 30 agents. Thus, there are 150 agents (30 altruist, 30 weak altruist, 30 selfish, 30 weak selfish and 30 rational agents). The simulations were performed with 1000 cycles, in a total of 10 simulations.

In some cases, the system stabilizes before 1000 cycles. However, in most simulations, there was no such stability, even at the end of 1000 cycles. To achieve stability, an adjustment factor of 0.1 was used for 50 consecutive cycles, i.e., strategies should maintain a difference between values of at least 0.1 for a minimum period of 50 cycles.

Three aspects were analysed: amount of performed social exchanges, fitness value at the beginning and end, and evolution of each agent's strategy. The *fitness* is the individual gain of each agent during the game; increase of successful exchanges is the gain of society. Evolution means the adaptation of agents in the proposed scenario.

Through the simulations, we observed the evolution of the strategy of each agent. New ranges for the maximum investment and minimum satisfaction values of each strategy were determined (see the Table 2). The agents that during the evolution process did not have their values belonging to these new intervals were classified as "unclassified".

The objective of this scenario is to show a heterogeneous environment, more conductive to obtain successful exchanges, as can be seen in the Table 3. In

Table 2. Parameters of strategies after evolution

	Altruist	Weak Alt.	Selfish	Weak Self.	Rational
r^{max}	[0.86; 1]	[0.76; 0.85]	[0.56; 0.65]	[0.66; 0.75]	[0.45; 0.55]
s^{min}	[0.51; 0, 55]	[0.56; 0.65]	[0.76; 0.85]	[0.66; 0.75]	[0.45; 0.5]

this scenario, there was an increase in the number of complete exchanges (2 exchanges) and incomplete (1 exchange) in the last stage (cycle 1000) in relation to the first one (cycle 1).

Table 3. Number of exchanges in cycles 1 and 1000

	Cycle 1			Cycle 1000			Exchange gain		
	0	1	2	0	1	2	0	1	2
Sim. 1	4708	4150	2317	1809	6214	3152	−2899	2064	835
Sim. 2	4574	3838	2763	1641	6054	3480	−2933	2216	717
Sim. 3	4484	4147	2544	1589	6159	3427	−2895	2012	883
Sim. 4	4368	4122	2685	1866	6248	3061	−2502	2126	376
Sim. 5	4384	4278	2513	1558	6515	3102	−2826	2237	589
Sim. 6	4378	4127	2670	1451	5864	3860	−2927	1737	1190
Sim. 7	4827	4098	2250	1355	6180	3640	−3472	2082	1390
Sim. 8	4468	4152	2555	2306	6367	2502	−2162	2215	−53
Sim. 9	4544	3865	2766	2166	6242	2767	−2378	2377	1
Sim. 10	4699	3978	2498	1470	6398	3307	-3229	2420	809
Media	4543.40	4075.50	2556.10	1721.10	6224.10	3229.80	-2822.30	2148.60	673.70
S. D.	158.26	138.67	174.07	314.34	182.90	403.82	388.43	204.58	489.54

Table 4 presents the behaviour of the *fitness* value of each kind of strategy agent in the initial (cycle 1) and final (cycle 1000) stages of the simulations.

As the number of exchanges increased, the *fitness* value also increased for all strategies. A greater increase of *fitness* is observed for the agents Selfish, Weak Selfish and Rational, which in cycle 1 presented a very low value, and over time, due to the evolution, it increased considerably, reaching more than an average of 90% of gain.

The evolution of the strategies of this scenario is presented in Table 5. It can be seen that, although most of the strategies have evolved into an unclassified strategy, the exchanges continued to increase, as well as the game adaptation factor (*fitness*).

This scenario, in relation to the others, proved to be the most favourable to exchange processes, presenting a greater gain in exchanges and *fitness*. In this environment, selfish, weak selfish and rational agents obtained the highest gain at the end of the 1000 cycles, almost 100% in the value of *fitness*.

Table 4. Fitness value in cycles 1 and 1000, and the obtained gain.

	Fitness cycle 1					Fitness cycle 1000					Fitness gain				
	Alt	W. Alt	Self	W. Self	Rat	Alt	fW. Alt	Self	W. Self	Rat	Alt	W. Alt	Self	W. Self	Rat
Sim. 1	30	25.75	0.89	1.28	0	90.32	44.50	20.91	74.35	49.05	60.08	18.75	20.02	73.07	49.05
Sim. 2	32	26.80	0.76	1.400	0	81.88	67.96	15.96	45.18	37.82	50.38	41.15	15.20	43.78	37.82
Sim. 3	29	24.80	0.64	1.20	0.66	84.19	71.77	22.24	41.84	38.38	54.83	46.97	21.59	40.63	37.71
Sim. 4	31	26.359	0.795	1.141	0.42	89.70	75.61	20.217	40.02	39.40	58.28	49.25	19.42	38.88	38.98
Sim. 5	31	27.56	0.94	1.42	0	83.72	73.66	23.98	48.19	39.19	52.47	46.10	23.04	46.76	39.19
Sim. 6	30	23.94	0.82	1.10	0.79	93.11	67.15	25.86	32.29	57.50	63.40	43.20	25.04	31.18	56.70
Sim. 7	31	23.39	0.82	1.30	0	93.39	76.04	31.79	51.00	41.65	61.99	52.64	30.97	49.70	41.65
Sim. 8	28	22.35	1	1.09	0	93.88	72.85	22.38	36.19	47.12	65.66	50.50	21.46	35.09	47.12
Sim. 9	28	21.61	0.71	1.03	0	98.62	78.71	18.38	48.83	44.79	71.03	57,098	17.67	47.80	44.79
Sim. 10	30	26.37	0.82	1.46	0	88.87	77.09	30.71	52.74	34.14	58.63	50.72	29.88	51.28	34.14
Media	30.09	24.89	0.81	1.24	0.18	89.77	70.53	23.24	47.06	42.90	59.67	45.64	22.43	45.82	42.72
S.D.	1.38	2.01	0.09	0.15	0.32	5.28	9.88	5.05	11.61	6.85	6.23	10.51	5.02	11.55	6.74

Table 5. Evolution of strategies at the end of simulations

	Altr.	W. Alt.	Self.	W. Self.	Rat.	Unclassified
Sim. 1	1		1	2	2	144
Sim. 2		2			1	147
Sim. 3	2					148
Sim. 4	1	2				147
Sim. 5	2		1	1		146
Sim. 6	1	2	1	2		145
Sim. 7	1		1	1	1	146
Sim. 8	1					149
Sim. 9	3		1	1		145
Sim. 10	3			1	2	144

In this presented scenario, it was observed that agents with altruistic strategy evolved into egoistic strategies, selfish weak and rational, and selfish agents became altruistic and rational. In relation to the other scenarios, this was what most had agents evolving into non-classified strategies.

5   Conclusion

This paper introduced a dramatic game of self-regulation of social exchange processes.

In the real world, the social exchanges do not happen exclusively in a rational way, frequently involving feelings and emotions. In this way, the possibility of applying the drama theory to the game of self-regulation of social exchange processes has emerged.

Applying the concepts of drama theory and improving the trust and the reputation model to the developed dramatic model, we aim at the application in a simulation game of social exchanges in an environment that approximates the real world, that is, a world where the exchanges relations are based on emotions, feelings, trust and reputation.

The model was implemented in NetLogo, and simulations with different compositions of the agent society and scenarios were conducted to study the development of the strategies and social exchange processes through time.

In most simulations there was no stability in the exchanges, but this is due to the fact that the adjustment factor contains 243 possibilities, causing the agents to require more cycles to achieve stability. In spite of this, the results showed that in all scenarios there was a gain of *fitness*, especially in the simulations of the scenario presented in this article, composed of agents of all strategies, which obtained a gain of almost 100%. It was observed that, in all scenarios, the agents evolved, contributing to the evolution of society.

In addition to the strategies defined in Natyasastra, other strategies emerged from the evolution of these strategies. Analysing the simulations, it was possible to verify which agents evolved. Most were classified as "unclassified", but some maintained their strategies and others progressed to one of the classified. Depending on the configuration of the environment, these unclassified strategies obtained, in the end, values very close to 1 or zero, reaching the extreme limits. For example, maximum investment value close to 1 and minimum satisfaction value also close to 1. That is, the agent while offering a high value, also has its minimum high satisfaction.

Future work will consider a more complex evaluation of reputation and examples of simulation in real-world applications.

Acknowledgments. Thanks to CNPq (Proc. No. 306970/2013-9).

References

1. Adamatti, D.F., Bazzan, A.: Afrodite - ambiente de simulação baseado em agentes com emoções. In: Proceedings of ABS 2003 - Agent Based Simulation, Montpellier (2003)
2. Bordini, R.H., Hübner, J.F., Wooldrige, M.: Programming Multi-agent Systems in AgentSpeak Using Jason. Wiley Series in Agent Technology. Wiley, Chichester (2007)
3. Pereira Dimuro, G., da Rocha Costa, A.C., Vargas Gonçalves, L., Hübner, A.: Centralized regulation of social exchanges between personality-based agents. In: Noriega, P., Vázquez-Salceda, J., Boella, G., Boissier, O., Dignum, V., Fornara, N., Matson, E. (eds.) COIN -2006. LNCS (LNAI), vol. 4386, pp. 338–355. Springer, Heidelberg (2007). https://doi.org/10.1007/978-3-540-74459-7_22
4. Dimuro, G.P., Costa, A.C.R., Palazzo, L.: Systems of exchange values as tools for multi-agent organizations. J. Braz. Comput. Soc. **11**, 27–40 (2005)
5. Dimuro, G.P., Costa, A.R.C., Gonçalves, L.V., Pereira, D.: Recognizing and learning models of social exchange strategies for the regulation of social interactions in open agent societies. J. Braz. Comput. Soc. **17**, 143–161 (2011)

6. Dimuro, G.P., da Rocha Costa, A.C.: Regulating social exchanges in open MAS: the problem of reciprocal conversions between POMDPs and HMMs. Inf. Sci. **323**, 16–33 (2015)
7. Hübner, J.F., Vercouter, L., Boissier, O.: Instrumenting multi-agent organisations with artifacts to support reputation processes. In: Hübner, J.F., Matson, E., Boissier, O., Dignum, V. (eds.) COIN -2008. LNCS (LNAI), vol. 5428, pp. 96–110. Springer, Heidelberg (2009). https://doi.org/10.1007/978-3-642-00443-8_7
8. Howard, N.: Soft game theory. Inf. Decis. Technol. **16**, 215–227 (1990)
9. Howard, N.: Drama theory and its relation to game theory. Part 1: dramatic resolution vs. rational solution. Group Decis. Negot. **3**(2), 187–206 (1994)
10. Howard, N.: Drama theory and its relation to game theory. Part 2: formal model of the resolution process. Group Decis. Negot. **3**(2), 207–235 (1994)
11. Howard, N.: Oedipus, decision-maker: theory of drama and conflict resolution (2006). http://aconflict.ru/wp-content/uploads/oedipus_chap1.pdf. Acessed Jan 2016
12. Huynh, T.D., Jennings, N.R., Shadbolt, N.R.: An integrated trust and reputation model for open multi-agent systems. JAAMAS **13**(2), 119–154 (2006)
13. Leyton-Brown, K., Shoham, Y.: Essentials of Game Theory: A concise, Multidisciplinary Introduction. Morgan & Claypool, California (2008)
14. Macedo, L.F.K., Dimuro, G.P., Aguiar, M.S., Coelho, H.: An evolutionary spatial game-based approach for the self-regulation of social exchanges in MAS. In: Schaub, T., Friedrich, G., O'Sullivan, B. (eds.) ECAI 2014–21st European Conference on Artificial Intelligence, Proceedings. pp. 573–578, no. 263 in Frontier in Artificial Intelligence and Applications, IOS Press, Netherlands (2014)
15. Marsh, S.: Formalising trust as a computational concept. Ph.D. thesis, University of Stirling (1994)
16. Ortony, A., Clore, G.L., Collins, A.: The Cognitive Structure of Emotions. Cambridge University Press, Cambridge (1988)
17. Pereira, D.R., Gonçalves, L.V., Dimuro, G.P., Costa, A.C.R.: Towards the self-regulation of personality-based social exchange processes in multiagent systems. In: Zaverucha, G., da Costa, A.L. (eds.) SBIA 2008. LNCS (LNAI), vol. 5249, pp. 113–123. Springer, Heidelberg (2008). https://doi.org/10.1007/978-3-540-88190-2_17
18. Piaget, J.: Sociological Studies. Routlege, London (1995)
19. Rabin, M.: Incorporating fairness into game theory and economics. Am. Econ. Rev. **86**(5), 1281–1302 (1993)
20. Rao, A.S., Georgeff, M.P.: Modeling rational agents within a BDI-architecture. In: Fikes, R., Sandewall, E. (eds.) Proceedings 2nd International Conference on Principles of Knowledge Representation and Reasoning, pp. 473–484. Morgan Kaufmann, San Mateo (1991)
21. Rodrigues, H.D.N., Adamatti, D.F., Dimuro, G.P., Dimuro, G., de Manuel Jerez, E.: Simulating reputation with regulatory policies: the case of San Jerónimo Vegetable garden, Seville, Spain. In: Demazeau, Y., Ito, T., Bajo, J., Escalona, M.J. (eds.) PAAMS 2016. LNCS (LNAI), vol. 9662, pp. 195–206. Springer, Cham (2016). https://doi.org/10.1007/978-3-319-39324-7_17
22. Rodrigues, M.R.: Social techniques for effective interactions in open cooperative systems. Ph.D. thesis, University of Southampton, Southhampton (2007)
23. Sabater, J., Sierra, C.: Regret: A reputation model for gregarious societies. In: Proceedings of the Fourth Workshop on deception Fraud and Trust in Agent Societies, pp. 61–70 (2001)

24. Sabater, J., Sierra, C.: Reputation and social network analysis in multi-agent systems. In: Proceedings of AAMAS 2002, pp. 475–482. ACM (2002)
25. Sabater, J., Sierra, C.: Review on computational trust and reputation models. Artif. Intell. Rev. **24**(1), 33–60 (2005)
26. Von Laer, A., Dimuro, G.P., Adamatti, D.F.: Analysing the influence of the cultural aspect in the self-regulation of social exchanges in MAS societies: an evolutionary game-based approach. In: Pereira, F., Machado, P., Costa, E., Cardoso, A. (eds.) EPIA 2015. LNCS (LNAI), vol. 9273, pp. 673–686. Springer, Cham (2015). https://doi.org/10.1007/978-3-319-23485-4_68
27. Wotter, R.G., Adamatti, D.F., Dimuro, G.P.: Self-regulation of social exchange processes: a model based in drama theory. In: Bajo, J., et al. (eds.) PAAMS 2016. CCIS, vol. 616, pp. 161–172. Springer, Cham (2016). https://doi.org/10.1007/978-3-319-39387-2_14
28. Xianyu, B.: Social preference, incomplete information, and the evolution of ultimatum game in the small world networks: an agent-based approach. JASSS **13**, 2 (2010)
29. Yu, H., Miao, C., An, B., Shen, Z., Leung, C.: Reputation-aware task allocation for human trustees. In: Proceedings of AAMAS 2014, pp. 357–364. IFAAMAS/ACM, New York (2014)

A Variable Dimensional Fuzzy Logic-Based Reputation Model for MAS

Henrique Donâncio N. Rodrigues[1], Graçaliz P. Dimuro[1,2], and Diana F. Adamatti[1(✉)]

[1] Centro de Ciências Computacionais, Universidade Federal do Rio Grande, Av. Itália km 08, Campus Carreiros, Rio Grande 96201-900, Brazil
dianaada@gmail.com
[2] Institute of Smart Cities, Universidad Publica de Navarra, Campus Arrosadía, 31006 Navarra, Spain

Abstract. Reputation may be understood as representing beliefs or opinions about someone or something, and it is recognized as a mechanism of social control. Reputation mechanisms are largely applied in online marketplaces, multiagent systems (MAS), P2P networks and other applications that require distributed and known information about agents. The process of evaluating agent's reputation clearly involves imprecision, ambiguity and incompleteness. In this paper, we introduce a fuzzy logic-based reputation model for social exchange processes in MAS. We consider a variable dimensional system evaluation, using weighted aggregation functions in order to aggregate the fuzzy information of agent's experiences (related to all considered dimensions) continuously, giving greater weight to more recent information. Some case studies are presented to analyse the behavior of the model. For that, we consider a MAS scenario in the context of online marketplace. We adopt the JaCaMo framework for the implementation, which uses BDI (Believe, Desires and Intentions) agent architecture and artifacts.

Keywords: MAS-based social simulation · Reputation · Fuzzy systems

1 Introduction

It is well known the importance of computational models of trust and reputation for multiagent systems (MAS). In fact, the relation trust-reputation is recognized as an implicit form of social control. The information extracted from such models contributes to MAS interactions in the form of cooperation, exchanges, formation of coalitions, choice of partners, among others [11].

The definition of trust, on one hand, is related to reliability, truth or ability of someone or something. On the other hand, reputation is defined as beliefs or opinions about someone or something. Pinyol and Sabater [11] have discussed about the boundaries of current models proposed over such definitions. This paper does not argue about this discussion and it is assumed that the model is an information provider of the reputation of the agents involved.

© Springer International Publishing AG, part of Springer Nature 2018
G. P. Dimuro and L. Antunes (Eds.): MABS 2017, LNAI 10798, pp. 18–32, 2018.
https://doi.org/10.1007/978-3-319-91587-6_2

The information about the reputation of an agent can be stored in a centralised way, which is commonly used in e-commerce web sites, or in a distributed form, as in MAS, where very often the agents are responsible for storing the results of their own experiences [11,17]. Then, besides e-commerce, MAS is another context in which the concept of reputation is frequently approached. In particular, in cognitive MAS [11], agents have to rely in the other agents since they frequently need cooperation of them in order to accomplish their tasks and achieve individual or collective goals.

Observe that the process of evaluating an agent's reputation clearly involves imprecision, ambiguity and incompleteness [19], in which context fuzzy sets and logic [21,22] can provide more suitable results [3,8], since they allows an interpretable model, with a similar behavior to a human-being reasoning, and offer theoretical support for modeling the aggregation of group information about the social interactions of the elements of the group. Besides that, the use of linguistic terms for modeling the problem domain allows these systems to be easily applied and understood by the final users of real world applications.

The objective of this paper is to introduce a fuzzy logic-based reputation model for social exchange process in MAS. For that, besides the fuzzy modeling of individual evaluation of agent's reputation, we consider a variable dimensional system evaluation, using weighted aggregation functions in order to aggregate the fuzzy information of agent's interactions (related to all dimensions) continuously, giving greater weight to more recent information. A case study is presented to analyse the behavior of the model. We consider a MAS scenario in the context of online marketplace. For the implementation, we adopt JaCaMo [1] framework, which uses BDI (Believe, Desires and Intentions) agent architecture and artifacts.

This paper is organized as follows. Section 2 discusses related work. Section 3 explains our motivation. The proposed model is introduced in Sect. 4. The fuzzy evaluation method is in Sect. 5. The case study is in Sect. 6. Section 7 is the Conclusion.

2 Related Work

Reputation models can be divided into two groups: (i) centralized reputation models, where all information is calculated and stored in a repository and to which all agents have access; and (ii) decentralized models, where the information is not stored in a repository, but each agent stores its own experiences individually [11,17].

The centralized reputation model is commonly used in online e-commerce systems, where all information about the reputation is managed centrally, such as the SPORAS model [20]. In SPORAS model, new users receive a minimum value of reputation, building their reputation during their activities in the system. This might discourage the entry of new users, but it prevents users with a bad reputation leave the system and come back with a better reputation than the last.

The decentralized reputation model gives each agent the power to make its own evaluation about the others's reputations, without relying on a central unit.

Some examples of models adopting this approach are: Jurca and Faltings [7], ReGreT [16] and TRAVOS (Trust and Reputation model for Agentbased Virtual OrganisationS) [19].

The ReGreT model [16] is a completely decentralized mechanism, where each agent classifies others at the end of each interaction (-1 = absolutely negative, 1 = absolutely positive and 0 = neutral), and these classifications have weights according to the time. ReGreT also divides the evaluation into three dimensions, where the Individual Dimension examines only the direct interactions between the involved agents; the Social Dimension, in which, on some occasions, it is possible to obtain information about the target agent based on reviews of other agents in the society; the Ontological dimension, which combines the Individual and the Social Dimension in a single one.

TRAVOS [19] adopts a binary classification (1 for successful interaction, and 0 for failure). After interacting with the target agent itself, the evaluator compares the report of witnesses with its own observations.

In [24], fuzzy logic is used for self evaluation and evaluation of third party recommendations for the composition of confidence. As will be presented in this paper, this model is based on expectations, that is, the evaluation is obtained through the relation of an initial expectation of the service and its effective realization. The model also offers a dynamic confidence update function. Basically the model consists of the following steps: search of partners (contractor's agents), choice of partner and finally update of trust. As it is a trust model, the model does not worry about storing the history of interactions cumulatively, but modifies it dynamically.

PATROL-F (comPrehensive reputAtion -based TRust mOdel with Fuzzy subsystems) [23] is a fuzzy version of the PATROL [26] model. Just as [24], PATROL and PATROL-F use of third-party information to compose a reputation for value about a particular agent. PATROL addresses the idea of "First Impression," a period in which the agent is tested until the information about the reputation is stabilized. Beside this, the information obtained by third parties is based on Similarity (Sim), Activity (Act), and Popularity (Pop). In the PATROL-F model, the result of an interaction is based on satisfaction of interaction (good or bad), time (more than expected or less than expected) and monetary value, where high monetary values express valuable services and low monetary values express low valuable services.

In [25] model, just as PATROL-F, uses decay factors to qualify information according to the time frame. Another important factor is that both models use *support* agents to obtain information about the target agent, that is, agents that provide some kind of information about previous experiences of the target agent, being these agents of the system itself (as is the case of [24]), or participating agents playing roles of the same hierarchy (as is the case of [23]).

In [5], the Reputation Artifact [5,13,14] works as a centralized unit that stores the performance or competence of the agent, visible to other agents. This model works with competence measures, which can be quantified in a binary form, in this case 0 or +1. Beside that, the model provides an architecture capable of taking into account social aspects of the agent, such as its role(s) and the implemented policies.

3   Motivation

Virtual communities have arisen in recent decades and changed the way we view human relationships. Some examples, such as e-commerce and virtual multi-player games, bring together several people in different places on an unprecedented scale in the physical world [9]. E-commerce, for example, offers the user a wide search on different products and salesmen in search of the best deal, but, at the same time, demand confidence that the virtual agreement will be realized, and, for this reason, reputation and trust are important social factors. Mui [9] presents some aspects of virtual interactions:

- Members of virtual communities often overpass geopolitical boundaries, where formal mechanisms that guarantee trust are difficult to establish.
- Virtual interactions do not have direct physical cues, such as tone of voice, body language, handshakes, store-front etc., which are often used as first impression to measure reliability in everyday interactions.
- The members are often anonymous and can get in and out of a community easily.
- Members often interact with strangers that the others members and even their friends had not met before.

Virtual communities, even with these limitations, have been booming and they are part of everyday life, such as the web sites Ebay (http://www.ebay.com/) and Amazon (http://www.amazon.com/). They aggregate a large community as well as move an entire economy. To address these limitations, trust and reputation mechanisms have been adopted in order to provide more security to their participants.

Cognitive MAS are usually populated by a few agents, due to the high degree of specification of these agents. Cognitive agents are able to represent and observe the environment where they act, manage to keep a history of their actions, organize themselves socially and have their own goals. For these reasons, the community of agents need a mechanism of control so that agents can choose their partners based on some information. However, a reputation value can not be analysed under a crisp approach, due to its imprecision, ambiguous and incomplete nature, as other kinds of values that are imbedded in contexts of imperfect information [22]. The performance of reputation systems has always been a concern for the users due to the existence of unfair/unrealistic ratings [8].

Then, a reputation model based on fuzzy logic [21] aims to provide a more realistic approach for evaluating and aggregating qualitative, uncertain, subjective, imprecise and/or ambiguous information, closer to human relationships, thinking and reasoning. Such approach presents an interpretable character, using linguistic terms and variables, so can be trustworthy to those adopting roles in the social organization.

4   The Proposed Model

The reputation model is inspired in the structure adopted by ReGreT model [16], where the evaluation of the reputation is based on a composition of different dimensions. In the case of the ReGreT model, there are three dimensions: Individual Dimension, Social Dimension and Ontological Dimension.

The Individual Dimension is the result of direct interactions between the agents. In [16], this dimension is treated as the most reliable, because it expresses results of direct interactions with the target agent, i.e., an assessment given by the result of the interaction between the involved agents. Direct interactions are not exclusive of the agents involved in the process, but can also be caused from a direct observation of the agents involved, however this kind of information is less common.

The Social Dimension is related to group relationship [16]. In this dimension, the agents can get information about a particular agent when there was no direct interactions with it, based on information provided by other agents, thus constituting an initial expectation for the agent's reputation. When this dimension is adopted, agents can increase their network of relationships in a safer manner, having initial information about their future partners. Therefore, the system can relate the ability of an agent to provide any information about other agents (the information provider agent - IPA), thus providing higher compatibility in the exchange of information and evaluations. Table 1 shows the fuzzy rule base for qualifying the IPA. Observe that the farther away the information received by the IPA is from the real interaction, the worse it should be qualified.

Table 1. Fuzzy rule base for qualifying the IPA

IPA qualification	Provided information		
Interaction	Bad	Regular	Good
Bad	good	regular	bad
Regular	normal	good	regular
Good	bad	regular	good

The Ontological Dimension is able to combine the concepts of Social Dimension and Individual Dimension into a single dimension.

The proposed model extends the ReGreT model assuming that there are several possible dimensions necessary to generate a reputation, evaluating different aspects with their respective weights or influences. The use of other kinds of dimensions, different from just the Individual and Social dimensions, also appeared in other works. For example, in [10,15,18], the authors adopt a dimension called Normative Dimension, where agents with certain roles should fulfil certain obligations, and regulator agents are able to insert information about the agent's obedience in a centralized unit, allowing all other agents to verify the performance of the others in relation to the normative policy.

Moreover, agents can assume multiple reputation values with the same agent, because an agent can assume different roles in the same organization, so the evaluation of each role played by the agent must be different. When an agent performs more than one role it may have distinct performances exercising the different roles.

In our approach, the Ontological Dimension is the combination of all dimensions and their respective weights. The weights are used to assign importance to dimensions, that is, the relevance of a particular aspect in the formation of the opinion. We point out that the direct interactions (Individual Dimension) should always have greater weight in relation to the others, because they are more reliable.

Then, the fuzzy evaluation of an agent α is given by the weighted n-ary aggregation function $evaluation_{(\alpha)} : [0, 1]^n \to [0, 1]$, for $n > 0$, defined by:

$$evaluation_{(\alpha)}(ID_{(\alpha)}, SD_{(\alpha)}, \ldots, Dn_{(\alpha)}) = \frac{\gamma ID_{(\alpha)} + \delta SD_{(\alpha)} + \ldots \epsilon Dn_{(\alpha)}}{\gamma + \delta + \ldots + \epsilon} \quad (1)$$

for all $ID, SD, \ldots, Dn \in [0, 1]$, where $ID, SD, \ldots, Dn$ are the fuzzy evaluations of the Individual, Social, $\ldots$, Dn dimensions, respectively, and the factors γ, δ, $\ldots$, ϵ define the importance of such dimensions. This aggregation function is an called a weighted mean whenever the weights are fixed. When the weights are given differently accordingly to the different agents, then this function is called a mixture operator [4].

5   Fuzzy Evaluation

Each aspect evaluated for the constitution of an image must be defined in any fuzzy function, with its respective linguistic terms, rule bases and defuzzification methods. An image is the evaluation that the agent perceives of a single interaction with an agent.

In e-commerce, for example, the evaluation of a product could be based on its price, delivery time and quality. The relationship between the expected satisfaction at the time of purchase, and the reception of the product can be used in order to generate feedback.

In a fuzzy rule base, the factors used for the product evaluation combine themselves to provide some information extracted from the fuzzy membership functions. Given such fuzzy inferences, we can aggregate this information and extract a defuzzified value, using an appropriate defuzzification method, which will be used to compose an agent's reputation. For basic information about fuzzy systems, see [21].

Consider that the history of information is allocated in a list V corresponding to the occurred interactions. In the proposed model, the aggregate of images, i.e., the information about the agent, is done by the a weighted aggregation mapping I, where assigning greater weights to the most recent interactions, defined by:

$$I(size(V), V) = \sum_{i=1}^{size(V)} \frac{v_i * a_i}{size(v)}, \quad (2)$$

where $a_i = a_1 + (i - 1) * \beta$, being β given by $\beta = \frac{a_1+1}{size(V)+1}$ and $a_1 = 0.1$

Assigning higher weights to the most recent interactions allows agents to recognize a possible change in the behavior of their partners more quickly.

5.1 Service Evaluation Attitudes

The service evaluation attitude refers to the possibility that the agent can combine several aspects observed to form an image of the interaction being evaluated. For example, in e-commerce, the agent could evaluate only the time of delivery in a commodity, or even the quality of the same, even combine delivery time and product quality to form an evaluation. This combination is done through fuzzy rules tables, such as those presented in Tables 2 and 3. The attributes of the services are represented by linguistic variables, whose value is expressed qualitatively by linguistic terms and quantitatively by membership functions.

Some considerations about the model: (1) if there is a need to define an initial reputation value this should be the initial value for new agents in the system; (2) each agent can have different service evaluation attitudes in relation to different agents and services; (3) Individual Dimension and Social Dimension may or may not coexist; (4) agents assuming different roles should be evaluated individually for each role; (5) the maximum and minimum reputation values reached by the agents are related to the definition of the membership functions, fuzzy base rules besides the used defuzzification method; (6) the lowest reputation value should be attributed to new agents according to [20], because it inhibits agents who have a bad reputation from leaving and entering the system with a better reputation than the previous one; this may discourage interactions with new agents because in some cases the information about them may be unknown.

6 Case Study

In this section, we present a case study related to online markets. We adopted the JaCaMo [1] platform, which is a framework for MAS programming consisting of three tools: Jason, CArtAgO and MOISE+. Jason [2] is an AgentSpeak(L) [12] language interpreter based on the BDI architecture.

6.1 Online Marketplaces

E-commerce communities illustrate direct relationships between agents. Usually this relationship happens among sellers and buyers who can take one or both roles, depending on the dynamics of the community. Information is usually centrally placed so that all participants have access to an agent's reputation. This type of system, although simple, is able to guide the choice of agent's partners, i.e., a Social Dimension that provides an overview of the attitudes of a given agent taking into account their interactions with a varied number of agents.

For this case study, we consider the individual side, i.e., the Individual Dimension that expresses the interactions between pairs of seller and buyers agents, because a Social Dimension in this case is nothing more than a broad consideration of Individual Dimensions of various agents.[1]

The fuzzy membership functions associated with this experiment are shown in Fig. 1. A product is composed of three linguistic variables: price, delivery time and quality. The price varies between 0 and 10, the delivery time and the quality range from 0 to 100. Price is associated with the linguistic terms *low*, *medium* and *high*. Delivery time is associated with the linguistic terms *quickly*, *normal* and *slow*. Quality is associated with the linguistic terms *bad*, *regular* and *good*.

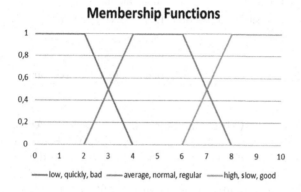

Fig. 1. Membership functions used in the online marketplace experiment

The relationship between expected satisfaction and actual satisfaction corresponding to the feedback is the image of each interaction. Feedback is associated with the linguistic terms *bad*, *regular* and *good*. Agents who exceed expectations tend to have larger image values than those who disappoint their buyers.

The fuzzy rule bases that compose this system are presented in Tables 2, 3 and 4.

Table 2. Satisfaction based on arrival time and quality

Satisfaction	Quality		
Arrival time	Low	Average	high
Slow	low	low	average
Normal	low	average	high
Quickly	average	high	high

---

[1] The construction of the simulation scenarios was based on scenarios found in the literature related to e-commerce, social simulation experiments, JaCaMo platform and MAS applications.

Table 3. Satisfaction based on just the arrival time (quality)

Arrival time (quality)	Satisfaction
Slow (low)	low
Normal (average)	average
Quickly (high)	high

Table 4. Feedback based on expected satisfaction and real satisfaction

Feedback	Real satisfaction		
Expected satisfaction	Low	Average	High
low	regular	good	good
Average	bad	regular	good
High	bad	bad	regular

Experiment 1 - Analyzing the Service Evaluations Attitudes. Agents can evaluate the service in different ways according to their service evaluation attitudes in order to reach their individual interests. According to the Tables 2 and 3, agents can evaluate a service taking into account a combination of delivery time and product quality, or either just quality or just delivery time. This experiment aims to demonstrate how the evaluation service attitude influences the composition of a reputation. For this purpose, we performed simulations in order to evaluate the same product with unchanged values and with different service evaluations of only two agents (buyer and seller) (Fig. 3).

The product in question has a price value of 8, an estimated delivery time of 30 days and an expected quality of value 25. When the service is actually delivered, the delivery time exceeds the expected expectations in 3 days, this means a slight improvement compared to the estimated. Quality, however, exceeds the expectations, taking the value of 64. In this way, the agent takes into account only the quality of the product, creates images of larger values and computes a better reputation in relation to the selling agent than that taken into account delivery time and quality or only the delivery time.

Experiment 2 - Deeper Analysis of Expectations. In this experiment, we demonstrate how the fuzzy rule base is determinant for the construction of an image. In this case study, there are three distinct situations in simulations: the first is when the agent fully meets expectations (Simulation 1); the second is when the agent exceeds expectations (Simulation 2); and the third is when the agent disappoints the buyer by delivering a product with a delivery time much larger than the combined and a lower quality (Simulation 3) (see Fig. 2). For the evaluation of the product we used the service evaluation attitude that takes into account delivery time and quality.

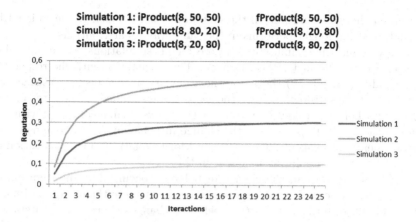

Fig. 2. Experiment 1: results of the analysis of expectation simulation

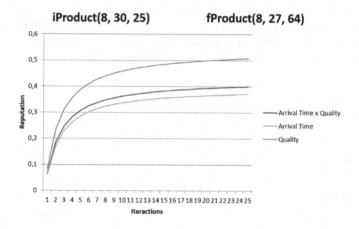

Fig. 3. Experiment 2: results for different service evaluation attitudes

Experiment 3 - Behavior Changes. The goal is to evaluate how much a change in the agent's behavior affects the reputation of the agent. For that, negative variation was chosen, i.e., the agent in determined time changes its strategy offering a service or product with low values than it has been performing or offering. The model is not only capable of evaluating negative changes as well as positive behavior changes too.

The evaluation of a behavior change is relative because the generation of images of the interactions is related to the fuzzy functions and their rule bases. The objective of this experiment is to demonstrate that the model is able to take into account the history of interactions among the agents, as well as to identify, even taking into account this history, a possible change in an agent behavior in a satisfactory way. A very deep change in the reputation of an agent due to its change of behavior would disregard all its history of interactions and a little accentuated change would put all the system at risk, not being able to identify that that agent no longer performs in the same way its attributions.

We have done three simulations where for all simulations the initial value of the service are Product (Price, Delivery Time, Quality), with the respective values Product (8, 50, 50), both for the calculation of expected satisfaction, as for the actual satisfaction, i.e., the agent corresponded exactly to all the expectations, being analyzed by the buyer the delivery time combined with the quality of the product. To analyze the change in behavior, it was assumed that at certain periods the agent altered its behavior in relation to the generation of real satisfaction, disappointing its client in this case.

In the first simulation, the change of behavior occurred in the iteration of number 26. In the second iteration, the change occurred in the iteration of number 51, and in the third simulation the behavior change occurred in the iteration of number 76, i.e., after 76 iterations corresponding to the expectations, the agent starts to "disappoint" the expectations of its client, and the same happened to the other simulations in their respective interactions. This behavior change occurred when in fact the agent provides the service and for this the attributes for the final product fProduct (8, 80, 20) were defined. The expected satisfaction calculated by the agent was not changed (Fig. 4).

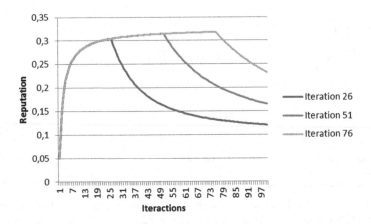

Fig. 4. Experiment 3: analysis of behavior change taking into account the history of interactions

The variations in the reputation value of the agents in simulation 1, simulation 2 and simulation 3, in the first 10 iterations starting from the first service rendered after the behavior has changed are shown in the Table 5. In this table, it is possible to notice that the amount of interactions accumulated, i.e., the history of interactions, influence in fact on future reputation values, as expected in the model proposal. It is important to note that the maximum and minimum reputation values reached by agents are related to the fuzzy definition of the problem as well as the defuzzification method used.

Table 5. Variation in ten first interactions after the behavior has changed

Iteration number 26	0.104414896
Iteration number 51	0.076104129
Iteration number 76	0.058774847

Experiment 4 - Centralized Reputation. Online Marketplaces generally group information centrally, combining user ratings to form an agent's reputation. In this experiment, we aggregate the various evaluations of three agents that evaluated based on the initial expectation values iProduct (8, 50, 50) and final product fProduct (8, 80, 80), and with the evaluation rates: Delivery Time And Quality, Delivery Time only and Quality only, each agent assumed one of these attitudes independently.

In Jason [2], the execution of a multi-agent environment is no-deterministic and distributed. In this way, it is not possible to specify a prior order for which agent inserted an image in the Reputation Artifact, which gives a higher degree of realism in this experiment, because in a virtual e-commerce environment, agents can receive feedback at any time, including out of order of the purchase.

Figure 5 shows the result of this experiment for the simulations. Series 1 combines 10 interactions of each agent, totalizing 30 interactions. In this series, each agent after interacting with the seller inserted the image into the Reputation Artifact. In Series 2, 3 and 4 interactions were simulated between pairs of agents, a seller and a buyer interacting for 30 times. Each series presents a great difference since they all used different service evaluation criteria. In Fig. 5, the concern was about how this no-determinism of interactions influenced the reputation results of an agent. For this purpose, we simulated 10 times the scenario, series 1 already presented and the results are shown in Fig. 6.

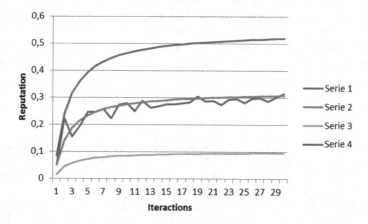

Fig. 5. Experiment 4: reputation stored centrally and no-deterministically

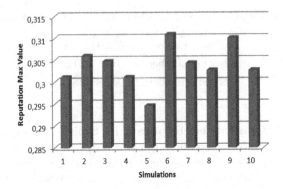

Fig. 6. 10 simulations for centrally nondeterministically reputation

7 Conclusion

After the analyzes made in this paper, some aspects should be considered. The first aspect is that reputation models can be used as implicit social control mechanism, giving support to its users about information about the agents involved, helping to build networkings, guiding agents to achieve the expected objectives.

The second aspect is the use of fuzzy logic in a reputation model. As presented, fuzzy logic is able to represent the ambiguity, incompleteness and subjectivity of information, such as human behavior tends to represent it. This is an important tool if it is a mechanism that has all its information-based functioning.

The third aspect is about the applicability of the model. The results presented are a simulation using BDI agents. The model can be efficient in MAS applications, in an e-commerce scenario, P2P networks or distributed systems in general. Its efficiency is related to the fuzzy definition of the problem. In addition, consideration of the history of interactions as well as the attribution of weights is useful in the sense that agents are sensitive to behavioral changes without disqualifying the history of their partners.

For future work will consider other kinds of dimensions in order to apply in other contexts and to be able to a fully comparative analysis of the presented model in relation to other models in different applications.

References

1. Boissier, O., Bordini, R.H., Hübner, J.F., Ricci, A., Santi, A.: Multi-agent oriented programming with JaCaMo. Scie. Comput. Program. **78**(6), 747–761 (2013)
2. Bordini, R.H., Hübner, J.F., Wooldridge, M.: Programming MAS in AgentSpeak using Jason. Wiley, London (2007)
3. Farias, G.P., Dimuro, G., Dimuro, G., Jerez, E.D.M.: Exchanges of services based on Piaget's theory of social exchanges using a BDI-fuzzy agent model. In: 2013 BRICS Congress on Computational Intelligence and 11th Brazilian Congress on Computational Intelligence (BRICS-CCI & CBIC), pp. 653–658. IEEE, Los Alamitos (2013)

4. Grabisch, M., Marichal, J., Mesiar, R., Pap, E.: Aggregation Functions. Cambridge University Press, Cambridge (2009)
5. Hübner, J.F., Boissier, O., Kitio, R., Ricci, A.: Instrumenting multi-agent organisations with organisational artifacts and agents. Auton. Agent. Multi-Agent Syst **20**(3), 369–400 (2010)
6. Hübner, J.F., Sichman, J.S., Boissier, O.: Developing organised multiagent systems using the MOISE+ model: programming issues at the system and agent levels. Int. J. Agent-Oriented Softw. Eng. **1**(34), 370–395 (2007)
7. Jurca, R., Faltings, B.: Towards incentive-compatible reputation management. In: Falcone, R., Barber, S., Korba, L., Singh, M. (eds.) TRUST 2002. LNCS, vol. 2631, pp. 138–147. Springer, Heidelberg (2003). https://doi.org/10.1007/3-540-36609-1_11
8. Liu, S., Yu, H., Miao, C., Kot, A.C.: A fuzzy logic based reputation model against unfair ratings. In: Proceedings of AAMAS 2013, pp. 821–828. IFAAMAS/ACM, New York (2013)
9. Mui, L.: Computational models of trust and reputation: agents, evolutionary games and social networking. Ph.D. thesis, Massachusetts Institute of Technology (2002)
10. dos Santos, F.P., Adamatti, D., Rodrigues, H., Dimuro, G., Jerez, E.D.M., Dimuro, G.: A multiagent-based tool for the simulation of social production and management of urban ecosystems: a case study on san jerónimo vegetable garden - seville, spain. J. Artif. Soc. Soc. Simul. **19**(3), 12 (2016)
11. Pinyol, I., Sabater, J.: Computational trust and reputation models for open multi-agent systems: a review. Artif. Intell. Rev. **40**, 1–25 (2013)
12. Rao, A.S.: AgentSpeak(L): BDI agents speak out in a logical computable language. In: Van de Velde, W., Perram, J.W. (eds.) MAAMAW 1996. LNCS, vol. 1038, pp. 42–55. Springer, Heidelberg (1996). https://doi.org/10.1007/BFb0031845
13. Ricci, A., Piunti, M., Viroli, M.: Environment programming in multi-agent systems: an artifact-based perspective. Auton. Agent. MAS **23**(2), 158–192 (2011)
14. Ricci, A., Viroli, M., Omicini, A.: Give agents their artifacts: the A&A approach for engineering working environments in MAS. In: Durfee, E., Yokoo, M., Huhns, M., Shehory, O. (eds.) 6th International Joint Conference Autonomous Agents and Multi-Agent Systems (AAMAS 2007), pp. 601–603. IFAAMAS, Honolulu (2007)
15. Rodrigues, H.D.N., Adamatti, D.F., Dimuro, G.P., Dimuro, G., de Manuel Jerez, E.: Simulating reputation with regulatory policies: the case of San Jerónimo vegetable garden, Seville, Spain. In: Demazeau, Y., Ito, T., Bajo, J., Escalona, M.J. (eds.) PAAMS 2016. LNCS (LNAI), vol. 9662, pp. 195–206. Springer, Cham (2016). https://doi.org/10.1007/978-3-319-39324-7_17
16. Sabater, J., Sierra, C.: REGRET: a reputation model for gregarious societies. In: Proceedings of the Fourth Workshop on deception Fraud and Trust in Agent Societies, pp. 61–70 (2001)
17. Sabater, J., Sierra, C.: Review on computational trust and reputation models. Artif. Intell. Rev. **24**(1), 33–60 (2005)
18. dos Santos, F.C.P., et al.: Analyzing the problem of the modeling of periodic normalized behaviors in multiagent-based simulation of social systems: the case of the San Jerónimo vegetable garden of Seville, Spain. In: Kamiński, B., Koloch, G. (eds.) Advances in Social Simulation. Advances in Intelligent Systems and Computing, vol. 229, pp. 61–72. Springer, Heidelberg (2014). https://doi.org/10.1007/978-3-642-39829-2_6
19. Teacy, W.T.L., Patel, J., Jennings, N.R., Luck, M.: Coping with inaccurate reputation sources: experimental analysis of a probabilistic trust model. In: Proceedings AAMAS 2005, pp. 997–1004 (2005)

20. Zacharia, G., Maes, P.: Trust management through reputation mechanisms. Appl. Artif. Intell. J. **14**, 881–907 (2000)
21. Zadeh, L.A.: Fuzzy sets. Inf. Control **8**, 338–353 (1965)
22. Zadeh, L.A.: Is there a need for fuzzy logic? Inf. Sci. **178**(13), 2751–2779 (2008)
23. Tajeddine, A., Kayssi, A., Chehab, A., Artail, H.: Fuzzy reputation-based trust model. Appl. Soft Comput. **11**(1), 345–355 (2011)
24. Chen, G., Li, Z., Cheng, Z., Zhao, Z., Yan, H.: A fuzzy trust model for MAS. Adv. Natural Comput. (2005)
25. Schmdit, S., Steele, R., Dillon, T.S., Chang, E.: Fuzzy trust evaluation and credibility development in multi-agent systems. Appl. Soft Comput. **7**, 492–505 (2007)
26. Tajeddine, A., Kayssi, A., Chehab, A., Artail, H.: PATROL: a comprehensive reputation-based trust model. Int. J. Internet Technol. Secur. Trans. **1**, 108–131 (2007)

Stable Configurations with (Meta)Punishing Agents

Nathaniel Beckemeyer[✉]⑩, William Macke, and Sandip Sen

The Tandy School of Computer Science, The University of Tulsa, Tulsa, OK, USA
{nate,william-macke,sandip}@utulsa.edu

Abstract. We consider an adaptation of Axelrod's metanorm model, where a population of agents choose between cooperating and defecting in bilateral interactions. Because punishing incurs an enforcement cost, Axelrod proposes using metanorms, to facilitate the stability of a norm of punishing defectors, where those who do not punish defectors can themselves be punished. We present two approaches to study the social effects of such metanorms when agents can choose their interaction partners: (a) a theoretical study, when agent behaviors are static, showing stable social configurations, under all possible relationships between system parameters representing agent payoffs with or without defection, punishment, and meta-punishment, and (b) an experimental evaluation of emergent social configurations when agents choose behaviors to maximize expected utility. We highlight emergent social configurations, including anarchy, a "police" state with cooperating agents who enforce, and a unique "corrupt police" state where one enforcer penalizes all defectors but defects on others!

Keywords: MABS workshop · Multi-agent systems · Cooperation
Norm emergence · Network topologies · Metanorm · Metapunishment
Punishment

1 Introduction

With the burgeoning of participation and activities in online social networks, there is increasing interest in understanding how interactions between individuals can give rise to emergent social structure and phenomena [3,4,10], such as information cascades [7], as well as the influence individuals have on others [9]. Concomitantly, researchers have used agent-based models and simulations to study how behavioral traits and interaction decisions can shape the dynamics of social networks. The goal of these research is to understand the dynamics of network connections and topologies [13,15,18], information flow [5,19], or to characterize the emergence of conventions or norms [1,11,12,17,21] or cooperative

This paper has already been published in: © Springer International Publishing AG 2017 G. Sukthankar and J. A. Rodriguez-Aguilar (Eds.): AAMAS 2017 Visionary Papers, LNCS 10643, pp. 31–44, 2017. https://doi.org/10.1007/978-3-319-71679-4_2

© Springer International Publishing AG, part of Springer Nature 2018
G. P. Dimuro and L. Antunes (Eds.): MABS 2017, LNAI 10798, pp. 33–46, 2018.
https://doi.org/10.1007/978-3-319-91587-6_3

behavior [14,16]. While some of these research analytically prove convergence or equilibrium or formally derive rational agent behaviors [8,16,18], others use extensive experimental evaluations to understand the nature of emerging behaviors and topologies in networks of self-interested agents [1,14,15].

A number of these studies investigate scenarios where the network topology changes based on strategic or exploratory rewiring of connections by agents seeking more beneficial partnerships [15,17,18]. Interaction between neighbors on networks are often represented as a stage game [11,12]. Some of these studies on norm emergence have also considered agents who use punishments and sanctions to facilitate convergence to social welfare maximizing outcomes for these games [14,20]. The use of punishments to facilitate norm emergence goes back to the work of Axelrod [2] who observes *"A norm exists in a given social setting to the extent that individuals usually act in a certain way and are often punished when seen not to be acting in this way."* Axelrod observes that punishing norm violators can be costly and hence free riders, who do not punish violators but rely on others to do so, may proliferate. He then suggested the use of a *metanorm*, a norm to punish those who do not punish norm violators (we refer to this as *metapunishment*)! Mahmoud *et al.* [14] have used resource-aware, adaptive use of metanorms to promote cooperation in peer-to-peer resource sharing networks, when individuals may have incentives to defect.

Our goal in this paper is to investigate how the ability to rewire as well as the use of punishment and metapunishment can result in the emergence of different network topologies between different types of agents. We consider the following agent types connected in a network: *cooperators* who always cooperate with their neighbors, *defectors* who defect against all neighbors, *punishers (corrupt)* who are cooperating (defecting) agents that also punish, and metapunish if that option is available. A link is created between two agents if any one of them wants to interact with the other. Each agent interaction is represented as a stage game with a payoff matrix representing a social dilemma: mutual cooperation is preferable to mutual defection but there is incentive to defect against a cooperator. When punishment is allowed, the situation corresponds to an extensive form game, where an agent has the option to punish a defecting neighbor. When metapunishment is allowed, an agent can metapunish a neighbor who do not punish its defecting neighbors. Punishment and metapunishment have costs to the enforcer, which are less than the corresponding costs to the recipient.

In the present study, we make the two following assumptions: Only one agent is necessary to choose another as a neighbor, or, equivalently, both agents must agree to cease interacting; and agents, once having selected a strategy, do not change their behavior. We assume the former following initial work in [6], wherein only one agent must choose to interact in order to connect to the other agents. Additionally, one can imagine a variety of real world scenarios corresponding to bilateral agreement, such as a group in a social network where leaving brings a substantial cost to the user, reputation or otherwise, which forces the user to interact with others he or she may not like. This formulation of the problem also allows for an interesting new aspect of the game: oppression. With mutual consent required to terminate a link, one party can defect and enforce norms upon another without this parties permission. Additionally, we find the choice of static strategies a reasonable formation because people tend to maintain a mostly constant persona when interacting with their neighbors.

Similar work was performed by Galán *et al.* in [13]. We note, however, that their work focused on stable norms resulting from static topologies; our paper considers the converse question of the stable topologies that result from rewiring connections while agents follow static behaviors. The network characterizations that they present are also unsuitable for our model due to the fact that, in our work, the networks either initialize as fully connected or links can be added as agents deem rational, as opposed to constant topologies. For example, since all agents of a particular type behave in the same manner in our model, they will all make the same decisions as to which other agents to connect to or attempt to disconnect from—contrasting the probabilistic behaviors used in their work. Consequently, analyses of the resultant clustering coefficients, numbers of triples, or other metrics are uninteresting. Another key difference between the two works is that the agents in their work change strategies by the genetic forces of selection and mutation; in our work, however, behaviors only change in the experimental analysis due to rational choice, and are constant in the theoretical analysis.

The paper is organized as follows. In Sect. 2, we present the configurations that will result when agents cannot change their type but can change their connections. These situations are amenable to algebraic solutions and we can precisely derive the network topologies that will arise by the rewiring process. We consider all possible game scenarios conforming with the social dilemma mentioned above and for various cost of making a new connection. We highlight interesting resultant networks for situations where there is (a) no punishment, (b) punishment but not metapunishment, and (c) metapunishment. In Sect. 3, we present experimental results showing converged network topologies where in addition to rewiring their connections, agents can also myopically change their types to maximize the utility they expect to receive given their current neighbors (these scenarios do not lend them to similar algebraic analysis as in the case of fixed agent types). We find interesting converged topologies such as a *police state* where few punishing agents keep other agents from defecting, as well as an oddball *corrupt police state* where a lone (meta)punishing agent prevents others from defecting but itself defects against all others! An associated interesting observation is the relative frequency with which the different converged topologies result when punishment is used with or without metapunishment. We conclude with a brief discussion of future work.

2   Theoretical Analysis

2.1   Specification

Game Mechanics. Starting with an initial network of fully connected agents, the game proceeds in many rounds. In each round, an agent interacts with each of its neighbors. An agent, *Player A*, can either choose to cooperate or defect against its neighbor, *Player B*. Choosing to defect gives *Player A* the temptation reward and *Player B* the hurt value, and choosing to cooperate gives the baseline reward to both players. When the punishment option is present, each interaction has a second stage, wherein, if *Player A* chooses to defect against *Player B*, then *Player B* has the opportunity to punish *Player A*.

Finally, if the metapunishment option is present, each round has a second phase. Each player, *Player A*, observes the interactions of each other agent, *Player B*—specifically, whether *Player B* chose to punish. If *Player B* chose not to punish a defector, then *Player A* has the opportunity to metapunish *Player B*. Metapunishment enables agents to encourage other agents to punish those agents who defect.

An agent has to pay a linking cost r for each of its link to a neighbor. If a link to a neighbor brings negative utility, then an the agent will try to cut that link at the end of a round. If both agents in a linked pair attempt to cut a link, the link will be eliminated. If only one agent, however, attempts to cut that link, then the link will remain.

Agent Strategies. For a description of the payoffs used in this game, see Table 1.

Table 1. Glossary of Payoffs. If a payoff contains the letter on the left, then the payoff includes the reward for the interaction on the right (the payoffs are additive). For instance, dh indicates that the agent both defected and was defected against.

b	The baseline—the reward for cooperation on both sides
d	Defecting
h	Being defected against (harmed)
dp	Defecting and being punished
he	Being defected against and enforcing
m	Being metapunished
M	Metaenforcing

Each agent type in the population has a type or strategy which cannot be changed. Without punishment, there are two agent types: *cooperator* types always cooperate and *defector* types always defect.

In the case of basic punishment, the *cooperator* type agents cooperate but do not enforce punishment. The *defector* type agents defect but do not enforce. There are two additional types: The *punisher* and *corrupt*. The *punisher* type agents cooperate and enforce punishment. The *corrupt* type agents defect and enforce punishment.

In the case of metapunishment, the agent types are the same as those in the basic punishment case, but the *punisher* and *corrupt* types both metapunish as well while other agent types do not.

2.2 Payoff Topologies

No Punishment. We first examine the case of no punishment. Table 2 represents the payoff matrix for this scenario.

Table 2. Payoffs without punishment

	cooperator	defector
cooperator	(b, b)	(h, d)
defector	(d, h)	(dh, dh)

Because there is no punishment, the only options are passivity and defection. b is simply the baseline. d is the baseline plus the temptation reward, which is included to incentivize agents to defect. h is b plus the hurt value, included to incentivize agents to punish. So, we make the following assumptions:

1. The temptation reward is greater than 0, or equivalently, $d > b$
2. The hurt value is less than 0.

From these assumptions, we can conclude that $d > b > h$ and, furthermore, that $d > dh > h$, since dh is simply $b + hurt\ value + temptation\ reward$

These conditions lead to six meaningful placements of the linking cost, r, and five unique topologies:

1. $r > d$: The network is empty because the linking cost is higher than the maximum possible reward from a link.
2. $d > r \geq dh, b$: The defecting agents form links with the passive agents in order to gain the temptation reward, d.
3. $d, dh > r > b$: The defecting agents form links with themselves (for dh) and the passive agents (for d).
4. $b > r \geq dh, h$: The defecting agents connect to the passive agents, and the passive agents connect to themselves.
5. $b, dh > r > h$: A complete network is formed (the defecting agents will forcibly connect to the passive agents).
6. $h > r$: A complete network is formed.

Punishment. In this section, we examine the case of basic punishment. Table 3 represents the payoff matrix for this scenario.

In addition to the assumptions made in the previous section, we assume that enforcing and being punished cost the agent, and that it is worse for an agent to be punished after defecting than for an agent to enforce after being defected against:

1. The enforcement cost is less than 0.
2. The punishment cost is less than the enforcement cost.
3. $he > dp$: Total payoff for the punisher is greater than that of the punished.

Table 3. Payoffs with basic punishment

	cooperate	punish	defect	corrupt
cooperate	(b,b)	(b,b)	(h,d)	(h,d)
punisher	(b,b)	(b,b)	(he,dp)	(he,dp)
defector	(d,h)	(dp,he)	(dh,dh)	(dhp,dhe)
corrupt	(d,h)	(dp,he)	(dhe,dhp)	$(dhpe,dhpe)$

From these assumptions, we can conclude that $d > b > h > he > dp > dhp > dhpe$, that $d > dh > h$, and that $dh > dhe > he$. These orderings suggest 13 possible placements for the linking cost, which lead to 10 different topologies. An interesting few selected results follow.

Agents who punish can, in some configurations, prevent defecting agents from connecting to themselves. Figure 1(a) shows a sample configuration wherein the *punisher* agents are not connected to defecting agents, but the *cooperator* agents are. An interesting note about Fig. 1(a) is its similarity to a hub network, where the *cooperator* agents are the hub, and the other agents do not interact outside of their own groups.

In general, punishment is a highly effective method for agents to defend themselves against defection. Figure 1(b) represents the most connected network wherein agents who defect, *corrupt* and *defector* agents, still connect to the *punisher* agents.

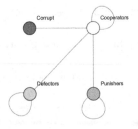

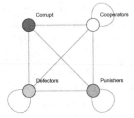

(a) $d, b, dh > r \geq dhe,$ $he, dp, dhp, dhpe$
This is an example of a network where punishers are safe from defection.

(b) $d, b, dh, h, dhe, he > r \geq dp, dhp, dhpe$
This topology is the most connected network wherein agents still defect against punishers.

Fig. 1. Interesting topologies from basic punishment.

Metapunishment. In this section, we examine the case of metapunishment. Table 4 represents the payoff matrix for this scenario. In this section, similarly to the case of basic punishment, we assume additionally that it costs to meta-enforce and to be metapunished, and that being metapunished for neglecting to punish is worse for an agent than for an agent's meta-enforcing. That is,

1. The meta-enforcement cost is less than 0.
2. The metapunishment cost is less than the meta-enforcement cost.
3. $M > m$: Being metapunished is worse than meta-enforcing.

Table 4. Payoffs with metapunishment

	cooperate	punish	defect	corrupt
cooperate	(b, b)	(m, M)	(h, d)	(hm, dM)
punish	(M, m)	(b, b)	(eM, dpm)	(he, dp)
defect	(d, h)	(dpm, eM)	(dh, dh)	$(dhpm, dheM)$
corrupt	(dM, hm)	(dp, he)	$(dheM, dhpm)$	$(dhpe, dhpe)$

From these assumptions, we can conclude that $d > b > h > he > dp > dhp > dhpe$, that $d > dM > M > m > hm > dpm > dhpm$, that $M > eM > dpm > hm$, that $d > dh > h$, that $dh > dhe > he$, that $dhe > dheM$, and that $dM > dheM > dpm$.

These constraints imply 113 possible placements for the linking cost, which lead to 73 unique topologies. In the following paragraphs, we highlight notable results.

Metapunishment can destabilize previously stable topologies. Figure 2(a) shows one circumstance in which *punisher* agents will not connect to *cooperator* agents in contrast to the case of basic punishment. Specifically, the *cooperator* and *punisher* agents used to receive b when they interacted; however, in this case, metapunishment reduces the payoffs below the linking cost.

Additionally, metapunishment can entirely cease interactions between *punisher* agents and nonpunishing agents. As an example, Fig. 2(b) contains no connections between the *punisher* agents and the *defector* agents nor the *cooperator* agents. This topology is also remarkable because the temptation reward is sufficient to offset the meta-enforcement cost, as evidenced by the connection from the *corrupt* agents to the nonpunishing ones. This phenomena is interesting because the *corrupt* agents are punishing agents for not punishing the *corrupt* agents.

An interesting side effect of metapunishment is that the *defector* strategy may actually present a way for agents to defend themselves. In Fig. 2(c), the *defector* agents are not connected to the *punisher* agents. The *cooperator* agents also are connected to the *punisher* agents. This connections implies that the meta-enforcement cost is, alone, insufficient to prevent *punisher* agents from linking to *cooperator* agents. Additionally, the *corrupt* agents are, connected to the *punisher* agents. This connection implies that the hurt value and enforcement cost are insufficient to prevent a link from forming. Therefore, it is the combination of hurt value, enforcement cost, and meta-enforcement cost that does prevent the link from the *punisher* to the *defector* agents from forming—a combination that can only occur with agents using the *defector* strategy.

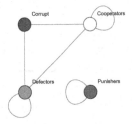 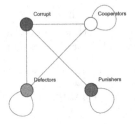 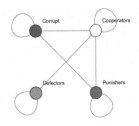

(a) d, b, dh, dhe, dM, $dheM > r > h$, he, dp, dhp, $dhpe$, M, m, hm, eM, dpm, $dhpm$

This topology demonstrates metapunishment can halt agents connected with only basic punishment from connecting now.

(b) d, b, dh, h, dhe, he, dp, dhp, dM, $dheM$, $> r > dhpe$, M, m, hm, eM, dpm, $dhpm$

A topology wherein the meta-enforcement cost prevents *punisher* agents from connecting to nonpunishing agents.

(c) d, b, dh, h, dhe, he, dp, dhp, $dhpe$, dM, $M > r > m$, hm, eM, $dheM$, dpm, $dhpm$

This topology shows the power of *defector* agents to thwart metapunishment.

Fig. 2. Interesting topologies from including metapunishment

3 Experimental Analysis

The above analysis assumed agent types were static. To understand the emergent topologies when agents could myopically adapt their types to optimize payoff given their neighbors types, we ran simulations varying various parameters. During rounds, agents would follow this algorithm:

```
procedure AGENT_BEHAVIOR()
maxUtility = Utility(currentStrategy)
maxStrategy = currentStrategy
for strategy in Strategies do
  if Utility(strategy) > maxUtility then
    maxUtility = Utility(strategy)
    maxStrategy = strategy
  end if
end for
if maxStrategy != currentStrategy then
  currentStrategy = maxStrategy
  return
end if
for link in CurrentLinks do
  if Utility(link)<0 then
    removeLink()
    return
  end if
end for
LinkToRandomAgent()
```

Where the utilities of links are defined by the values in the payoff matrices given in Sect. 2, and the utility of a strategy is simply the sum of all of the links of an agent, assuming that the agent adopts that strategy. In a round agents make their decisions sequentially. The order of turns was decided randomly at the beginning of each round. Simulations were run with both simple punishment and meta-punishment and with various numbers of agents. Each simulation ran for 1000 rounds. Only simple graphs were used; i.e., if Agent 1 connected to Agent 2, then Agent 2 could not connect to Agent 1. Each agent was assigned a random strategy at the beginning of the game.

3.1   Observed Stable Configurations

All experiments produced one of three stable configurations: *Anarchy* indicates all agents are defecting, *Police State* refers to a few punishing agents and the rest neutral, and *Corrupt Police State* refers to exactly one agent defecting and punishing while the rest are neutral.

The three stable configurations mentioned above could form different topologies: *Complete Network, Empty Anarchy, One way corrupt police*. In the complete network, all agents linked with all other agents. Any of the three configurations could form with this topology. Empty anarchy was an anarchy network without any agent linking to any other agent. The one way Corrupt Police was the most interesting of the three topologies. It was a corrupt police state, but none of the cooperators were willingly linked to the corrupt police officer. Thus we had one group of agents that would link to only agents of their own type, but were being stabilized and exploited simultaneously by an outside agent. See Fig. 3.

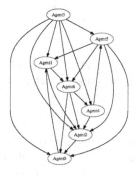

Fig. 3. One way corrupt police (red-*cooperator*, violet-*corrupt*). (Color figure online)

3.2   Conditions for Network Development

An important goal of the experimental analysis was to observe what conditions were required for each of the three stable configurations to emerge.

Figure 4 shows the relative frequency of emergence of different stable configurations as we vary the number of agents in the network. Without metapunishment, as the number of agents increases, the number of configurations that result

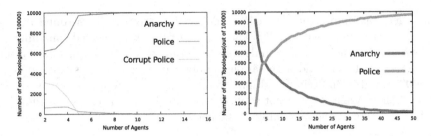

Fig. 4. End topologies with different # of agents: punishment only (left), metapunishment included (right). Parameters: Base 0, Defection Reward 3, Defection Hurt 1, Punishment Cost 2, Punishment Hurt 9, Linking Cost 0.

in anarchy also increases. We will discuss this phenomena in detail below. With metapunishment, increasing the number of agents increases the likelihood of a police state emerging. Presence of more metapunishers force non-punishers to start punishing; thus with more agents present there is an increase in frequency of the emergence of police states.

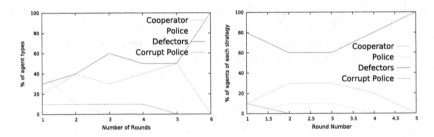

Fig. 5. % of agent types as anarchy develops, 10 agents: punishment only (left), with metapunishment (right). Parameters: Base 10, Defection Reward 1, Defection Hurt 3, Punishment Cost 3, Punishment Hurt 12, Linking Cost 0.

Anarchy. Due to the randomness of allocation of initial agent types, the initial number of agent types may not be equal. The initial agent type distribution is likely to be more skewed particularly for small agent populations. If there were too many defectors at the beginning, anarchy developed from large numbers of agents defecting. When a punisher links with a defector, one of two things happen: the defector stops defecting or the punisher stops punishing. When there are far more defectors than there are punishers, it becomes much more likely that the punisher will have to back down and stop punishing at some point. For small populations there are more chances of very few defectors in the initial population, whence the network may evolve to a state different from anarchy. With larger populations, there are more agents that can defect in the early rounds of the game and it becomes harder for the punishing agents to maintain order. With large enough numbers of agents, the end topology is almost always anarchy.

Hence, all figures of networks developing are shown with 10 agents. Anarchy was by far the most common of the three stable configurations that formed without metapunishment. When metapunishment was included, the frequency of anarchy networks drastically decreased because of reasons listed below. The percentage of different agent types in sample runs that evolved Anarchy networks, with or without metapunishment, are shown in Fig. 5. Modified parameters are used when observing network developments to reduce the anarchy development rate.

Police. The convergence to a police state was facilitated by an initial state of a large number of punishers. These punishers would have to immediately link with each other in order for the police state to form, because otherwise the punishers would want to become defectors. If two punishers link with each other, neither will defect to avoid being punished by the other. However if a punisher is linked only with non-punishing agents, then it will become a defector for the Utility boost. From there they would force all defecting agents to become neutral as they connected to them. When metapunishment is included, punishers gain the ability to force other agents to become punishers. This aides the development of police networks and increases their relative frequency. Sample runs that evolved the Police state are presented in Fig. 6.

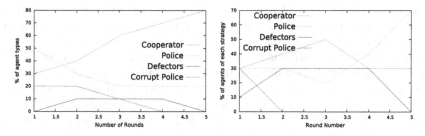

Fig. 6. % of agent types as police state evolves, 10 agents: punishment only (left); with Metapunishment (right). Parameters: Base 10, Defection Reward 1, Defection Hurt 3, Punishment Cost 3, Punishment Hurt 12, Linking Cost 0.

Corrupt Police. The corrupt police state developed from an initial state of a large number of agents who were defecting and punishing. As these agents linked with others, they forced those agents to become neutral to avoid punishment. When two of these agents connect, one will back down and become neutral while the other will remain a defector and punisher. A sample run that evolved a Corrupt Police network is shown in Fig. 7.

This demonstrates one of the more interesting outcomes of the game: Corruption will not tolerate company while non-corruption requires it. In the corrupt police network, all corrupt police officers will eliminate each other until only one remains, while the police network requires multiple interacting officers. The corrupt police network was only stable without metapunishment. If metapunishment exists, then the corrupt police officer will have to punish neutral agents for not punishing it. This in turn forces the neutral agents to become punishers, and hence the corrupt police network does not emerge with metapunishment.

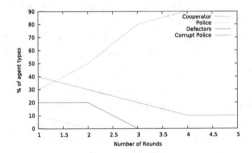

Fig. 7. % of agent types as corrupt police configuration develops (simple punishment); 10 agents. Parameters: Base 10, Defection Reward 1, Defection Hurt 3, Punishment Cost 3, Punishment Hurt 12, Linking Cost 0.

4   Conclusions

We investigated the effect of rewiring and behavior adoptions on the emergent topology of networked self-interested agents interacting in a social dilemma scenario with and without punishment and metapunishment options. When agent types were fixed, we identify, using algebraic calculations, interesting topologies that result under various relationships between agent interaction payoffs and rewiring costs. Such derivations are not forthcoming when agents can change their types myopically to maximize payoffs given their neighborhood. We run a suit of experiments and observe the emergence of different classes of network topologies. Particularly interesting are the police and corrupt police states and their relative abundance with and without the option of metapunishment.

We plan to investigate unilateral elimination of links which should allow for cooperators to thrive more frequently. We will analyze mixed, rather than pure strategy types, where agents defect with some probability $0 < p < 1$. We will also study a broader class of social dilemmas, including the prisoner's dilemma and the Hawk-Dove game. In Sect. 2, we assumed all types are present in equal numbers; we will analyze non-uniform distribution of agent types. Finally, we intend to perform analyses similar to those done by Galán et al. in [13]: Allowing for nondeterministic behavior could lead to some highly intriguing resultant social networks and network properties. Combining all of these future directions, characterizing networks with unilateral links could additionally prove fascinating.

Acknowledgments. We would like to thank the University of Tulsa and in particular the Tulsa Undergraduate Research Challenge (TURC) for financial support of this project.

References

1. Airiau, S., Sen, S., Villatoro, D.: Emergence of conventions through social learning. Auton. Agents Multi-agent Syst. **28**(5), 779–804 (2014)
2. Axelrod, R.: An evolutionary approach to norms. Am. Polit. Sci. Rev. **80**, 1095–1111 (1986)
3. Baetz, O.: Social activity and network formation. Theor. Econ. **10**(2), 315–340 (2015)
4. Barabasi, A.: Network Science. Cambridge University Press, Cambridge (2016)
5. Belardinelli, F., Grossi, D.: On the formal verification of diffusion phenomena in open dynamic agent networks. In: Proceedings of the 2015 International Conference on Autonomous Agents and Multiagent Systems, AAMAS 2015, pp. 237–245. International Foundation for Autonomous Agents and Multiagent Systems, Richland (2015)
6. Berninghaus, S., Vogt, B.: Network formation and coordination games, March 2003
7. Borge-Holthoefer, J., Baos, R.A., Gonzlez-Bailn, S., Moreno, Y.: Cascading behaviour in complex socio-technical networks. J. Complex Netw. **1**(1), 3–24 (2013)
8. Brooks, L., Iba, W., Sen, S.: Modeling the emergence and convergence of norms. In: IJCAI, pp. 97–102 (2011)
9. Cha, M., Haddadi, H., Benevenuto, F., Gummadi, K.P.: Measuring user influence in Twitter: the million follower fallacy. In: Proceedings of International AAAI Conference on Weblogs and Social in ICWSM 2010 (2010)
10. David, E., Jon, K.: Networks, Crowds, and Markets: Reasoning About a Highly Connected World. Cambridge University Press, New York (2010)
11. Delgado, J.: Emergence of social conventions in complex networks. Artif. Intell. **141**(1–2), 171–185 (2002)
12. Epstein, J.M.: Learning to be thoughtless: social norms and individual computation. Comput. Econ. **18**(1), 9–24 (2001)
13. Galán, J.M., Latek, M.M., Rizi, S.M.M.: Axelrod's metanorm games on networks. PLOS ONE **6**(5), 1–11 (2011)
14. Mahmoud, S., Miles, S., Luck, M.: Cooperation emergence under resource-constrained peer punishment. In: Proceedings of the 2016 International Conference on Autonomous Agents & #38; Multiagent Systems, AAMAS 2016, pp. 900–908. International Foundation for Autonomous Agents and Multiagent Systems, Richland (2016)
15. Peleteiro, A., Burguillo, J.C., Chong, S.Y.: Exploring indirect reciprocity in complex networks using coalitions and rewiring. In: Proceedings of the 2014 International Conference on Autonomous Agents and Multi-agent Systems, AAMAS 2014, pp. 669–676. International Foundation for Autonomous Agents and Multiagent Systems, Richland (2014)
16. Ranjbar-Sahraei, B., Bou Ammar, H., Bloembergen, D., Tuyls, K., Weiss, G.: Evolution of cooperation in arbitrary complex networks. In: Proceedings of the 2014 International Conference on Autonomous Agents and Multi-agent Systems, AAMAS 2014, pp. 677–684. International Foundation for Autonomous Agents and Multiagent Systems, Richland (2014)
17. Savarimuthu, B.T.R., Cranefield, S., Purvis, M., Purvis, M.: Norm emergence in agent societies formed by dynamically changing networks. In: Proceedings of the 2007 IEEE/WIC/ACM International Conference on Intelligent Agent Technology, IAT 2007, pp. 464–470. IEEE Computer Society, Washington (2007)

18. Sina, S., Hazon, N., Hassidim, A., Kraus, S.: Adapting the social network to affect elections. In: Proceedings of the 2015 International Conference on Autonomous Agents and Multiagent Systems, AAMAS 2015, pp. 705–713. International Foundation for Autonomous Agents and Multiagent Systems, Richland (2015)
19. Tsang, A., Larson, K.: Opinion dynamics of skeptical agents. In: Proceedings of the 2014 International Conference on Autonomous Agents and Multi-agent Systems, AAMAS 2014, pp. 277–284. International Foundation for Autonomous Agents and Multiagent Systems, Richland (2014)
20. Villatoro, D., Andrighetto, G., Sabater-Mir, J., Conte, R.: Dynamic sanctioning for robust and cost-efficient norm compliance. In: Proceedings of the Twenty-Second International Joint Conference on Artificial Intelligence - Volume Volume One, IJCAI 2011, pp. 414–419. AAAI Press (2011)
21. Villatoro, D., Sen, S., Sabater-Mir, J.: Topology and memory effect on convention emergence. In: IAT (2009)

Developing Multi-agent-based Thought Experiments: A Case Study on the Evolution of Gamete Dimorphism

Umit Aslan[✉], Sugat Dabholkar, and Uri Wilensky

Northwestern University, Evanston, IL, USA
{umitaslan,sugatdabholkar2020}@u.northwestern.edu, uri@northwestern.edu

Abstract. Multi-agent modeling is a computational approach to model behavior of complex systems in terms of simple micro level agent rules that result in macro level patterns and regularities. It has been argued that complex systems approaches provide distinct advantages over traditional equation-based mathematical modeling approaches in the process of scientific inquiry. We present a case study on how multi-agent modeling can be used to develop thought experiments in order to push theory forward. We develop a model of the evolution of gamete dimorphism (anisogamy), for which there are several competing theories in the evolutionary biology literature. We share the outcomes of our model and discuss how the model findings compare with, and contribute to previous work in the literature. The model clarifies mechanisms that can result in the evolution of anisogamy and offers a much simpler structure that is easier to understand, test, modify and extend.

1 Introduction

The most commonly used approach to model behavior of biological systems involves equational modeling with a focus on describing population-level changes based on population level descriptor variables [9]. Unfortunately, this modeling approach is limited when it comes to adding new variables or incorporating new assumptions because entirely new equations might be needed to capture even small changes [25]. In contrast, multi-agent-based modeling is a powerful approach to model complex natural and social phenomena in terms of simple micro-level agent rules that result in the emergence of macro-level patterns and regularities [22]. In this paper, we draw on Wilensky and Papert's Restructuration Theory and argue that multi-agent-based modeling can be used to develop thought experiments on complex scientific questions for novices to learn scientific domain knowledge easily, as well as domain experts to verify, modify, and even extend these models [25].

This paper has already been published in: © Springer International Publishing AG 2017 G. Sukthankar and J. A. Rodriguez-Aguilar (Eds.): AAMAS 2017 Best Papers, LNCS 10642, pp. 51–65, 2017. https://doi.org/10.1007/978-3-319-71682-4_4

© Springer International Publishing AG, part of Springer Nature 2018
G. P. Dimuro and L. Antunes (Eds.): MABS 2017, LNAI 10798, pp. 47–61, 2018.
https://doi.org/10.1007/978-3-319-91587-6_4

We present a multi-agent-based model about the evolution of gamete dimorphism (anisogamy) to make a case for our argument. Anisogamy is the phenomenon of males producing large numbers of small sperm cells and females producing small numbers of large egg cells for reproduction [4]. We believe this topic is a good fit for developing a multi-agent-based thought experiment for two primary reasons: (1) there is no universally accepted theory or model in the literature [4,6,17], (2) the bulk of research in this area has been done through equation-based modeling (e.g., [5,12,14,15]). We begin by reviewing Restructuration Theory in detail. Then, we describe anisogamy and review the literature related to the evolution of anisogamy, as our multi-agent-based thought experiment incorporates and builds on the ideas from the existing evolutionary biology literature. We describe our model's assumptions and agent rules in detail and then present our findings. We demonstrate that our model achieves similar results to those achieved in the literature while increasing access to underlying ideas.

2 Restructuration of Scientific Domain Knowledge Through Multi-agent-based Modeling

Restructuration Theory, as proposed by Wilensky and Papert, describes how disciplinary knowledge can be re-encoded using new representational technologies in a way that can have powerful implications for science, culture and learning [25]. Many such historical restructurations are presented including the restructuration of Roman numerals to Hindu-Arabic numerals. Wilensky and Papert argue that computation offers many new opportunities for powerful restructurations and that multi-agent-based modeling can be used to create many such restructurations [25].

A good example is Wilensky and Reisman's restructuration of models of predation [23]. Traditionally, predator-prey relationships are modeled through differential equations. An example of such models is the Lotka-Volterra models that offer two equations that describe the rate of change in the densities of the predator and prey populations over time [11,20]:

$$\frac{dN_1}{dt} = b_1 N_1 - k_1 N_1 N_2 \tag{1}$$

$$\frac{dN_2}{dt} = k_2 N_1 N_2 - d_2 N_2 \tag{2}$$

In these equations, N_1 is the density of the prey population, N_2 is the density of the predator population, b_1 is the birth rate of the prey, d_2 is the death rate of the predators, and k_1 and k_2 are constants. These equations specify the dependence of the density of each population to one another. When plotted, the model shows cyclical fluctuations between the two populations: increases in the prey population will result in rising predator birth rates and increases in the predator population will result in rising prey death rates. Wilensky and Reisman's attempt to *restructurate* this problem through multi-agent-based modeling focuses on considering prey and predator as agents and describing the agent rules that emerge as population level patterns:

Rule set for wolves *(at each clock-tick)*:
1. move randomly to an adjacent patch which contains no wolves.
2. decrease energy by E_1
3. if on the same patch as a sheep, then eat the sheep and increase energy by E_2
4. if energy < 0 then die
5. with probability R_1 reproduce

Rule set for sheep *(at each clock-tick)*:
1. move randomly to an adjacent patch and decrease energy by E_3
2. if on grassy patch, then eat grass and increase energy by E_4
3. if energy < 0 then die
4. with probability R_1 reproduce

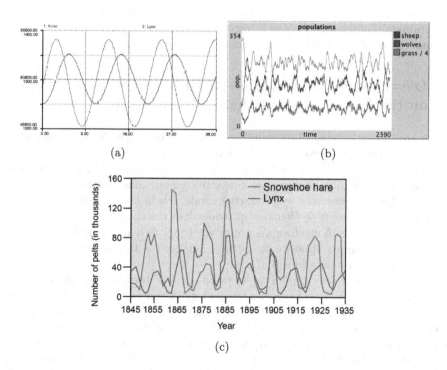

(a)

(b)

(c)

Fig. 1. Two models of predation compared to real world observations: (a) the Lokta-Volterra equational models [11, 20], (b) the Wilensky-Reisman multi-agent-based model (middle) [23], and (c) real world data from a lynx-hare population in Northern Canada [16].

Rule set for grass *(at each clock-tick)*:
1. if green, then do nothing
2. if brown, then wait E_4 clock-ticks and turn green

Wilensky and Papert theorize that multi-agent-based restructurations of such natural phenomena offer three powerful advantages over equation-based modeling in terms of learnability: (1) rules for agents are closer to our intuitive notions of these "objects" as distinct individuals rather than aggregate populations, (2) equational models often require bigger changes or completely new equations even for small adjustments, (3) visualization of individual agents and their dynamics afford greater realism compared to graphs of populations [25]. These advantages make it possible for even high school students to easily learn topics that used to be hard for college graduates in related fields [23].

As Fig. 1 shows, a comparison between the real data, the equation-based model, and the multi-agent-based model shows that real world phenomena produce patterns that are more similar to the outcome of the multi-agent-based model. The outcome of the multi-agent-based model is similar to the equation-based model but with more noisy fluctuations, which the equation-based model shows less, because it is a discrete model. In this paper, we attempt a very similar restructuration of an evolutionary biology topic, which is historically studied through equational models, and re-examine it through multi-agent-based modeling.

3   Developing a Multi-agent-based Thought Experiment on the Evolution of Gamete Dimorphism

There are two main types of reproductive strategies employed by organisms: sexual reproduction and asexual reproduction [6]. The most prevalent sexual reproduction strategy is called gamete dimorphism or anisogamy. Many animal and plant species, including humans, are anisogamous: one mating type (males) provides half the chromosomes by producing small cells in large quantities (sperm) and the other mating type (females) provides half the chromosomes by producing much larger cells in much smaller numbers (egg). When two such cells, called gametes, belonging to opposite sexes fuse, a zygote is formed and this zygote gradually grows into an adult [3,15].

The evolution of anisogamy is a yet to be resolved topic in evolutionary biology and is the foundation of theories on gender differences and relations [4]. This starts with the very question of "why do sexes exist?" [4,17]. Given that asexual production (*parthenogenesis*) actually has some distinct advantages in terms of numerical advantage in progeny, many have wondered why sexual reproduction evolved in the first place [6]. It is also not known why anisogamy prevailed over other sexual reproduction strategies. For instance, there are some fungal species which reproduce through more than two mating types [10] or by producing gametes of equal size (isogamy) [15], but they are exceptions. In this paper, we attempt to address the latter question because the discussion on the evolution of anisogamy mostly revolves around the validity of the assumptions of theoretical models [17]. The equation-based methods used in these models make it harder for beginners to join the conversation and domain experts to manipulate the models for further analysis. We argue that a multi-agent-based thought experiment of anisogamy can afford domain experts the ability to easily plug new assumptions into an existing model while making it significantly easier for non-experts to learn about anisogamy [23]. In this section, we describe the process of developing one such thought experiment through reviewing the literature on anisogamy, determining model assumptions, defining agent rules and designing the user interface.

3.1   Literature Review

Evolutionary theories in general try to show how it is that a trait might be selected when there are many competing treats. In the case of reproductive strategies, there is no clear answer on why anisogamy is a more successful strategy over isogamy or multiple mating types. The most accepted theory on the evolution of gamete dimorphism is called "the Parker-Baker-Smith (PBS) model". It lays out mathematical formulations to determine the conditions for the evolution of anisogamy through a *zygotic fitness function* and a *gametic fitness function*. The PBS model makes three simple but powerful assumptions [5,15]:

1. individuals of a marine ancestor population produce a range of gametes and the fusion between pairs of gametes is at random at sea
2. each adult has only a fixed biomass available for gamete production
3. there is some sort of relationship between zygote fitness and zygote size

It is important to caution that we are far from having a model that offers a universal explanation yet. Many of these theories, including the PBS model, are actively debated [17] and there are still many questions that remain unanswered [4]. The PBS theory of evolution is generally viewed as a foundational model but not the ultimate answer [6]. Both the assumptions and the formulations of the model are challenged by other theorists [4,17]. There are also many theories that build on the PBS model and attempt to offer more explanatory value (e.g., [7]).

3.2   The NetLogo Model of Gamete Dimorphism

We develop our multi-agent-based thought experiment of anisogamy in the NetLogo agent-based modeling environment [21] as it provides powerful tools to model emergent phenomena through a beginner friendly programming environment that allows writing open, easily readable code and a rich set of visualization options [18,22]. In the model[1] [1], adults of two mating types begin with producing middle-sized gametes at approximately the same rate (isogamy). Every time an adult produces new gametes, there is a chance of a small, random mutation in

---

[1] Source code of the NetLogo model of anisogamy is openly available through http://modelingcommons.org/browse/one_model/5007.

the gamete size strategy. These mutations introduce a competition among multiple reproductive strategies. In this section, we describe the model's assumptions, agent rules and interface in detail.

The Assumptions and the Agent Rules. Similar to the existing theories in the literature, our model builds on the following set of basic assumptions that we appropriated from the PBS model and its derivatives [3–5,12,14,15,17,19]:

1. Adults have limited lifetimes.
2. Gamete production budget is fixed and the same for all adults.
3. Gametes have limited lifetimes, too, but much shorter than adults.
4. A zygote has to achieve a minimum mass to survive.
5. There are initially two isogamous mating types in the population.
6. The gamete size and the mating type traits are inherited as a bundle.
7. The chance of a zygote inheriting these traits from either gamete is equal.

Assumptions 2 and 4 directly correspond to the 2nd and 3rd assumptions of the PBS model (Sect. 3.1). We implement the 1st assumption of the PBS model by implementing a random walk algorithm in the model's code. We also implement a lifetime mechanism to simulate successive generations, although there is no mention of this in the PBS model or other equational models. Based on these assumptions, we define three agent types as *adults*, *gametes* and *zygotes* and define simple rules for each agent type.

Rule set for adults *(at each clock-tick)*:
1. turn around randomly and move one step forward.
2. with probability P produce gametes:
   - randomly pick the new gametes' size (m_t) through a normal distribution with *mean = my gamete size strategy (m)* and *standard deviation = σ*.
   - hatch *own mass (M)*/m_t gametes of my mating-type and of the size m_t
3. decrease the remaining lifetime by 1, die if no lifetime left.

Rule set for gametes *(at each clock-tick)*:
1. turn around randomly and move one step forward.
2. fuse (form a zygote) if touching a gamete of the opposite sex:
   - inherit the total mass of myself and my mating partner.
   - randomly inherit the mating type and gamete size strategy as a package
3. decrease the remaining lifetime by 1, die if no lifetime left.

Rule set for zygotes *(at each clock-tick)*:
1. decrease the remaining incubation time by 1. if incubation time is 0:
   - if *own mass (M)* mass is greater than the survival threshold ($M \geq \delta$), turn into an adult.
   - if *own mass (M)* is less than the survival threshold ($M < \delta$), die.

Interface and Parameters. NetLogo's interface affords easy manipulation of the parameters of the model, and we can observe the changes in the system visually through the model's world and plots. The *world* is a graphical window which is not a mere visualization but an actual space where the agents follow the rules and interact with each other [22], seen as the central window shown in Fig. 2. The adults are represented by circles with black dots in them. An adult's color (blue or red) represents its mating type. The tiny arrow shaped agents are the gametes produced by adults. They, too, are either blue or red but vary in size depending on their parents' gamete size strategy. Lastly, the egg-shaped agents with lighter shades of red and blue are the zygotes formed by the fusion of two gametes.

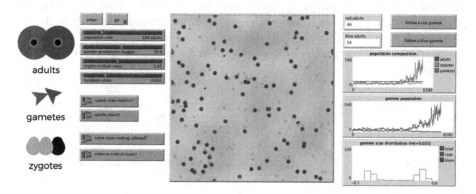

Fig. 2. The interface of the NetLogo Anisogamy model (Color figure online)

The first two plots on the right allow us to see the change in the overall population and the number of gametes of each mating type over time. The histogram on the bottom right shows the distribution of the gamete sizes at the observed clock-tick. The two integer outputs on the top right (blue adults and red adults) allow us to observe if the mating type balance is disrupted or not. The controls on the left allow us to change the parameters of the model so that we can test implicit and explicit assumptions. Each of these controls corresponds to bigger questions that we want to ask through this model. For example, one of the questions we want to ask is *"what, if any, thresholds of zygote critical mass effect the potential evolution of anisogamy"*, so we implement a *ZYGOTE-CRITICAL-MASS* slider that determines the threshold of mass that a zygote needs to achieve to survive. Similarly, we want to investigate whether the assumption of differentiation in mating types is viable, so we place the *SAME-TYPE-MATING-ALLOWED?* switch.

4 Findings and Discussion

A comparison of our multi-agent-based model and equation-based models of anisogamy highlights the advantages of multi-agent-based thought experiments. In this section, we first share the outcomes of our model with the default parameter-set, which corresponds to our basic set of assumptions (see Sect. 3.2). In this condition, we run the model with approximately 100 adults in a confined space. The average lifetime is 500 clock-ticks for adults and 50 clock-ticks for gametes. Because the model's space is 256 square unit-lengths and computing power is limited, we implement a carrying capacity mechanism. Whenever the model's adult population exceeds 100 members, some adults are randomly taken out of the population. This does not apply to gametes or zygotes. All adults are of 1 unit-length, mass of 1 unit-mass, and they move around randomly with the speed of 1 unit-length per clock-tick. Adults can use half of their mass for producing gametes. Initially, all adults have the same reproductive strategy of producing two middle sized gametes. Gametes move around randomly with the same speed, too, and they are only allowed to fuse with gametes of the opposite mating type. Lastly, the critical threshold for a zygote to survive is 0.45 unit-mass.

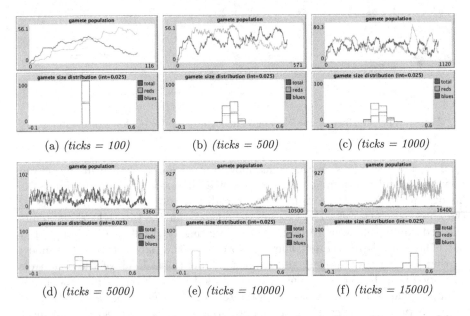

Fig. 3. The emergence of gamete dimorphism over time in the multi-agent model

Figure 3 shows the outcome of a typical run with the default parameters. Each subfigure consists of two plots: a plot showing the change in the number of red versus blue gametes over time and a plot showing the distribution of gamete sizes at the presented clock-tick. Gametes of the two mating-types are represented with red and blue colored lines and bars in the graphs. As our model assumes that the reproduction budget is fixed for all the adults, a large gamete number means smaller gamete size, and vice versa. Figure 3a is a snapshot of the model after 100 clock-ticks and the subsequent subfigures are after 500, 1000,

5000, 10000 and 15000 clock-ticks. In our model, 15000 clock-ticks correspond to approximately 300 generations. This might be extremely small for such an evolutionary process in real life but in the small world of our thought experiment, it is enough to observe meaningful and consistent results.

As the first four subfigures show, the model starts with oscillations between two similar strategies. In this specific run, a stochastic disruptive event happens at about 7000 clock-ticks (Fig. 3e) resulting in one mating type getting committed to producing big gametes and the other to producing small gametes. In other words, anisogamy evolves and is sustained. Figure 4 presents the results of 300 runs with this default parameter-set over 20000 clock-ticks. Each data point presents the average number of red or blue gametes in the last 5000 clock-ticks, which provides more reliable data because the number of gametes in the model oscillates continuously. We clearly observe evolution of two distinct gamete size strategies at the end of each simulation run (Fig. 4). Statistical analysis of this data shows that there was a significant difference between the number of large gametes ($m = 1.735, sd = 0.184$) and the number of small gametes ($m = 437.675, sd = 19.505$); $t(299) = -384.221, p < 0.0005$. These findings provide a theoretical explanation of not only why but also how anisogamy might have evolved, as well as supporting previous theory on the instability of isogamy in the long run [19].

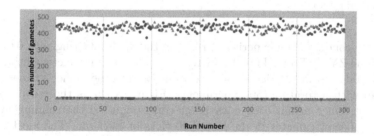

Fig. 4. Testing the model with default parameters (n = 300, ticks = 20000).

The affordances of multi-agent-based thought experiments become even more noticeable when it comes to testing assumptions of a model to answer *"what if?"* questions. In the following sections, we test an explicit and an implicit assumption of the PBS model, as well as another non-PBS assumption that is common in the literature. We not only show the ease of doing this through our model but also demonstrate how powerful the outcomes of such assumption tests can be.

4.1 Zygote Survival as a Function of Zygote Mass

We begin testing assumptions with one of the main assumptions of the PBS model concerning the relationship between viability of a zygote to its size [3, 5, 15]. We call this the ZYGOTE-CRITICAL-MASS assumption, which can be turned on and off easily with a switch on the models interface (see Fig. 2). With the default parameter-set of the model, we observe the emergence of anisogamy after 10000 ticks. We keep all the other parameters the same, but allow zygotes to survive regardless of their mass and run the model again. As seen in Fig. 5b, the gamete sizes and gamete population for both sexes fluctuate over time with the overall direction of reduction in the size. Anisogamy does not evolve when each zygote survives regardless of its mass.

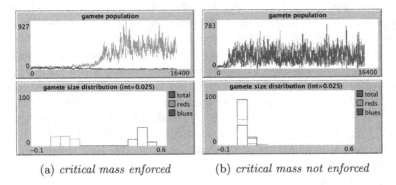

(a) *critical mass enforced*   (b) *critical mass not enforced*

Fig. 5. The comparison of the model outcomes with ENFORCE-CRITICAL-MASS? switch turned on and off.

We also conducted an experiment running the model starting with 0.0 as the value of the ZYGOTE-CRITICAL-MASS variable and then incrementing it by 0.01 until 0.5 over 20000 ticks. For each value, we ran the model 3 times, so we ended up with a total of 150 experiments. Figure 6a shows the results of this experiment. Once again, each data point corresponds to the running average of the number of gametes in the last 5000 ticks of each run. The most important outcome of this test is the fact that anisogamy did not evolve and isogamy was sustained when the value of the ZYGOTE-CRITICAL-MASS parameter was below 0.1, which is consistent with the assumptions of the PBS model [5, 15]. Surprisingly, we also noticed some runs which did not result in anisogamy between the range of 0.3 and 0.45. We hypothesized that anisogamy would still evolve in this parameter space in a longer experiment. Accordingly, we conducted the same experiment but this time over 200000 clock-ticks and the results confirmed our hypothesis (Fig. 6). Once again, these findings align with the PBS model's assumption that *for anisogamy to evolve, some sort of a relationship between the zygote size and zygote survival is necessary* [6, 15].

4.2   Mating Types

Another affordance of multi-agent-based thought experiments is the possibility of testing implicit assumptions. For instance, the existence of two mating types is a common assumption in many models of anisogamy, but it is rarely

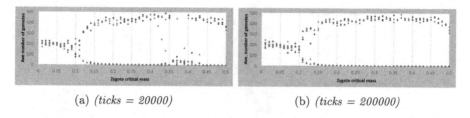

(a) *(ticks = 20000)*   (b) *(ticks = 200000)*

Fig. 6. Testing the model with a range of ZYGOTE-CRITICAL-MASS values between 0 and 0.5 (n = 150).

discussed explicitly (e.g., [5]). Our model assumes two mating types, too, but it is actually possible to test this assumption indirectly by allowing gametes of the same mating type to fuse. When we run the model with this alternative assumption, we observe that anisogamy does not evolve. Instead, there are two possible outcomes. In most of the runs, genetic drift [8] happens and one mating type prevails over the other (Fig. 7a and c). However, in some rare occasions, we observe almost no quantitative change in the population composition (Fig. 7b) because, by random chance, it takes more time for genetic drift to emerge in some runs (as in Sect. 4.1). These results provide support for the implicit assumption that mating types are required for anisogamy to evolve. On the other hand, our model currently does not allow testing the possibility of more than two mating types. This could be an interesting follow up on our test, and it is possible to do it with a few changes in the model's code.

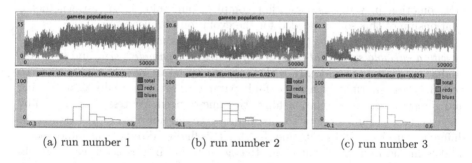

(a) run number 1   (b) run number 2   (c) run number 3

Fig. 7. The outcome of the model when fusion between two gametes of the same mating type is allowed *(ticks = 50000)*

4.3   Adult and Gamete Motility

Another debated topic in models of anisogamy is the role of gamete and/or adult motility in the marine environment [4,17]. Some of the models assume that the speed of a gamete is inversely related to its mass according to Stokes Law [7], while others challenge the validity of this assumption [17]. As the actual physics

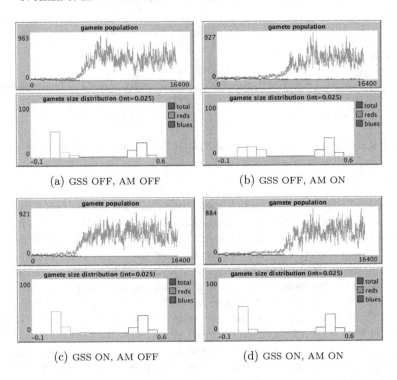

Fig. 8. The outcomes of the model when gamete-speed size relation (GSS) and adult motility (AM) assumptions are tested *(ticks = 15000)*

of locomotion in water is somewhat complex, our point is to test whether a relationship of this sort is needed for the evolution of anisogamy.

Our model allows us to (1) make all the gametes move with the same speed or *with a variable speed that is inversely related to a gamete's size,* and (2) make adults move around randomly with the same speed or *remain stationary* (see Sect. 3.2). In our runs with the default parameter-set, the adults were moving and gamete size had no relationship with gamete speed. We tested the model by varying these parameters but to our surprise, we did not observe any significant differences in the model's outcome (Fig. 8). This finding directly contradicts some studies in the literature that claim that gamete motility is a critical factor in the evolution of anisogamy (e.g., [7,14]).

4.4   A Qualitative Comparison Between the Two Models of Anisogamy

In this section, we present a "relational alignment" [2,24] between our multi-agent-based model and the equational PBS model developed by Bulmer and Parker by qualitatively comparing the relationships between critical parameters of these two models and the evolution of anisogamy as a continuously stable strategy (ESS [12]). These critical parameters are gamete size (m), zygote size

(S), and parameters that determine viability of gametes (α) and zygotes (β). Figure 9 shows two plots from Bulmer and Parker's mathematical formulation of the PBS model. Figure 9a is concerned with the conditions that result with anisogamy as ESS and Fig. 9b is concerned with a critical threshold for zygote survival in an anisogamous ESS [5].

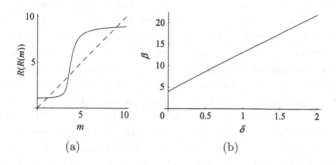

(a)   (b)

Fig. 9. Plots from Bulmer and Parker's equational PBS model of anisogamy: (a) anisogamy as ESS for given m and β values and (b) the critical value of β above which anisogamy evolves as a function of δ [5].

Bulmer and Parker use the PBS model to explore the parameter space for the parameters β and δ to find a parameter range over which anisogamy would evolve as an evolutionary stable strategy (Fig. 9b). β is a parameter that determines the shape of the response strategy function and δ is a parameter related to the gamete critical mass. In our multi-agent model of evolution of anisogamy, we demonstrate that anisogamy evolves as an ESS as reliably over the default parameter range (Fig. 4). We have also demonstrated that our multi-agent-modeling approach to evolution of anisogamy using NetLogo as a modeling environment allows as such comparison where we have investigated the parameter range for zygote-critical-mass (Fig. 6). Hence, these two models are qualitatively similar, or relationally aligned, in terms of inputs (conditions) and outputs (evolution of anisogamy as an ESS).

5   Conclusions

We argued that multi-agent-based models can be used to express scientific domain knowledge in the form of thought experiments. As a case study, we developed a multi-agent-based thought experiment on the evolution of anisogamy, which is the phenomenon of male species producing numerous small sperm cells and female species producing only a handful of large egg cells for reproductive purposes. We noted that anisogamy is a topic in evolutionary biology with direct implications on the evolution of animal and plant species, but it is yet to be resolved. We reviewed the evolutionary biology literature and developed a model in the NetLogo agent-based modeling environment building on a set of assumptions that we adopted from previously research.

Our model provided similar results to the equation-based models of anisogamy but allowed us to easily test explicit and implicit assumptions suggested by previously offered theories. For example, we were able to confirm that the existence of two mating types is a necessary prerequisite for anisogamy to emerge, and we showed why anisogamy does not evolve when any two gametes can fuse with each other [5,15]. On the other hand, we found no evidence of a possible relationship between adult or gamete speeds with the evolution of anisogamy [7,14].

Our study demonstrates that multi-agent-based thought experiments can allow scientists and theorists to explore a wide range of subtle and difficult *"what if"* questions. One can think of a new question and almost immediately manipulate the model to answer it. Even a strong mathematician may not be comfortable changing the equation-based models of anisogamy, but making changes in our multi-agent-based model of anisogamy is almost *mind-to-fingers*. More importantly, our model provides such opportunities not only to scientists but also to informed citizens and younger students without having to master all the formal mathematics. We argue that such multi-agent-based restructurations would make scientific domain knowledge more accessible for a wider population and speed up the progress in currently unresolved topics like the evolution of anisogamy.

5.1   Limitations

It is important to note that the outcomes of our model are by no means definitive as it is the case for all the other theoretical and equational models in the literature [4,6]. Because our goal was to primarily demonstrate the advantages of multi-agent-based thought experiments, we left out some theoretical considerations in this paper such as the possibility of more than two mating types existing in the population or a more comprehensive comparison between our model and the PBS model [5,15]. In future studies, we hope to focus, in greater depth, on the theoretical implications of our model for the field of evolutionary biology. We also hope to conduct research which explores the use of this multi-agent-based thought experiment and similar approaches in educational settings.

Acknowledgments. This work was made possible through generous support from the National Science Foundation (grants CNS-1138461 and CNS 1441041) and the Spencer Foundation (Award #201600069). Any opinions, findings, or recommendations expressed in this material are those of the author(s) and do not necessarily reflect the views of the funding organizations.

References

1. Aslan, U., Dabholkar, S., Wilensky, U.: NetLogo Anisogamy model. http://ccl. northwestern.edu/netlogo/models/Anisogamy. Center for Connected Learning and Computer-Based Modeling, Northwestern University, Evanston, IL (2016)
2. Axtell, R., Axelrod, R., Epstein, J.M., Cohen, M.D.: Aligning simulation models: a case study and results. Comput. Math. Organ. Theo. **1**, 123–141 (1996)

3. Bell, G.: The evolution of anisogamy. J. Theor. Biol. **73**, 247–270 (1978)
4. Blute, M.: The evolution of anisogamy: more questions than answers. Biol. Theo. **7**, 3–9 (2013)
5. Bulmer, M.G., Parker, G.A.: The evolution of anisogamy: a game-theoretic approach. Proc. R. Soc. London B: Biol. Sci. **269**, 2381–2388 (2002)
6. Cox, P.A.: The evolutionary mystery of gamete dimorphism. In: The Evolution of Anisogamy: A Fundamental Phenomenon Underlying Sexual Selection, pp. 1–16 (2011)
7. Cox, P.A., Sethian, J.A.: Gamete motion, search, and the evolution of anisogamy, oogamy, and chemotaxis. Am. Nat. **125**(1), 74–101 (1985)
8. Dennett, D.C.: Darwin's Dangerous Idea: Evolution and the Meanings of Life. Simon and Schuster, New York City (1996)
9. Hastings, A.: Population Biology: Concepts and Models. Springer, New York (2013)
10. Kues, U., Casselton, L.A.: The origin of multiple mating types in mushrooms. J. Cell Sci. **104**(2), 227–230 (1993)
11. Lotka, A.J.: Elements of Physical Biology. Dover, New York (1925)
12. Maynard-Smith, J.: The Evolution of Sex. Cambridge University Press, London (1978)
13. Papert, S.: Mindstorms: Children, Computers, and Powerful Ideas. Basic Books, New York (1980)
14. Parker, G.A.: Selection on non-random fusion of gametes during the evolution of anisogamy. J. Theor. Biol. **73**(1), 1–28 (1978)
15. Parker, G.A., Baker, R.R., Smith, V.G.F.: The origin and evolution of gamete dimorphism and the male-female phenomenon. J. Theor. Biol. **36**(3), 529–553 (1972)
16. Purves, W., Orians, G., Heller, H.: Life: The Science of Biology, 3rd edn. Sinauer Associates, Sunderland (1992)
17. Randerson, J.P., Hurst, L.D.: The uncertain evolution of the sexes. Trends Ecol. Evol. **16**(10), 571–579 (2001)
18. Tisue, S., Wilensky, U.: NetLogo: a simple environment for modeling complexity. Paper presented at the International Conference on Complex Systems, Boston (2004)
19. Togashi, T., Cox, P.A.: The Evolution of Anisogamy: A Fundamental Phenomenon Underlying Sexual Selection. Cambridge University Press, New York (2011)
20. Volterra, V.: Fluctuations in the abundance of a species considered mathematically. Nature **118**, 558–560 (1926)
21. Wilensky, U.: NetLogo (1999). http://ccl.northwestern.edu/netlogo/
22. Wilensky, U.: Modeling nature's emergent patterns with multi-agent languages. In: Proceedings of Eurologo, Linz, Austria (2001)
23. Wilensky, U., Reisman, K.: Thinking like a wolf, a sheep, or a firefly: Learning biology through constructing and testing computational theories - an embodied modeling approach. Cogn. Instr. **24**(2), 171–209 (2006)
24. Wilensky, U., Rand, W.: Making models match: replicating an agent-based model. J. Artif. Soc. Soc. Simul. **10**(4), 2 (2007)
25. Wilensky, U., Papert, S.: Restructurations: reformulations of knowledge disciplines through new representational forms. In: Proceedings of Constructionism, Paris, France (2010)

Norm Identification in Jason Using a Bayesian Approach

Guilherme Krzisch[✉] and Felipe Meneguzzi

School of Computer Science, Pontifical Catholic University of Rio Grande do Sul,
Porto Alegre, Brazil
guilherme.krzisch@acad.pucrs.br, felipe.meneguzzi@pucrs.br

Abstract. Open multi-agent systems consist of a set of heterogeneous autonomous agents that can enter or leave the system at any time. As they are not necessarily from the same organization, they can have conflicting goals, which can lead them to execute conflicting actions. To prevent these conflicts from negatively impacting the system, a set of expected behaviors – which we refer to as *norms* – can desirable; to enforce compliance to such norms, sanctioning of violating agents can be used to deter further violations. As new agents enter the system, they must be able to identify existing norms in order to avoid sanctions. In this context, this paper provides two contributions. First, we propose a normative multi-agent system that can be used to evaluate norm-identification algorithms. Second, we validate an existing bayesian norm-identification approach in this system, confirming its positive result in a set of experiments.

Keywords: Norm identification · Normative system
Multi-agent system

1 Introduction

Multi-agent systems allow the specification, modeling and implementation of complex behaviors generated by multiple autonomous agents interacting in a common environment. If these agents can perform actions that interfere with each other and jeopardize the overall functioning of the system, some kind of coordination mechanism can be employed to prevent this negative impact [5]; this can be achieved using regimentation or enforcement approaches. This first approach restricts the possible actions of the agents by design, completely preventing forbidden actions. While regimentation precludes violations, it also decreases the agent autonomy (e.g. in [6]). The latter, in turn, enforces a set of desirable behaviors (norms) by sanctioning violating agents (e.g. in [3,7,9,20]). This has two main advantages: it allows agents to reason whether to follow a norm-compliant

G. Krzisch—This work is partially supported by grant from CNPq/Brazil (132339/2016-1).

© Springer International Publishing AG, part of Springer Nature 2018
G. P. Dimuro and L. Antunes (Eds.): MABS 2017, LNAI 10798, pp. 62–73, 2018.
https://doi.org/10.1007/978-3-319-91587-6_5

or a norm-violation behavior based on, for example, its resulting expected utility, and it enables an open multi-agent system where agents are not necessarily designed by the same organization [5].

As the expected behavior is not known at design time in enforcement approaches, the participating agents must be able to identify norms currently being enforced in a given system. This can be necessary, for example, in systems in which norms are not explicitly available or if there is no trust between agents. There are many different approaches to norm identification in the literature [1,2,11,12,17,18]. In this paper we leverage an existing Bayesian approach [4] to develop a norm identification procedure within an agent simulation [8]. In order to validate the resulting approach we propose a normative multi-agent system testbed. We perform a set of experiments using this testbed; the results show that the employed approach is able to correctly identify the existing norms in the system, enabling agents to start taking into account these norms in its reasoning process, and thus allowing them to avoid sanctions.

2   Background

In this section we describe the Jason platform which is used to develop the multi-agent system, and its companion CArtAgO to implement artifacts which can be manipulated by agents. Then we describe how we formalize norms and how it relates to the Bayesian norm identification approach.

2.1   Jason with CArtAgO

Jason is based on the AgentSpeak language [13], which in turn implements the BDI architecture (belief, desires and intentions) [14] to simulate agent reasoning. An agent designer provides a set of plan-rules to achieve an implicit goal; these plans are chosen based on the current context of the agent beliefs and the set of available plans for an agent is called the *plan library*.

While Jason provides a framework for the internal reasoning of the agents, CArtAgO (Common ARTifact infrastructure for AGents Open environments) provides the abstraction of a virtual environment [15] in terms of artifacts. Artifacts contain a set of operations available to agents and are a useful abstraction of components used to perform a certain coordinated behavior among agents.

2.2   Norms

Norms exist in a society and are used to define the expected behavior of agents when performing actions in this environment [10]. Their function is to avoid potential harmful behavior that negatively impacts society, e.g. agents driving on the left and on the right side of the road, as this would lead to a high number of car accidents. Norms can be violated by individual agents if they reason that this is the best course of action, i.e. if an agent reasons that the outcome of a norm violating behavior is more desirable than compliance.

This makes norms more flexible than hard-constraint rules specified at design time, and over which agents have no choice, limiting their autonomous behavior. As a norm can be violated, it must be enforced in order to remain active, i.e. agents not following established norms must be sanctioned to deter further violations; this enforcement can be carried out by an authoritative organization or by other agents in the society [16].

According to [16], there are five phases of norm development: creation, identification, spreading, enforcement and emergence. In the current work we focus on the norm identification phase, which refers to the problem of how new agents entering the society can infer the norms created and currently being enforced in the system. We implement and validate a recent approach proposed in the literature, which uses the Bayes Theorem to make this inference, described in the next section.

2.3   Norm Identification Using a Bayesian Approach

In this section we describe a norm identification approach which uses the Bayes Theorem in order to infer a set of norms in a given society [4]; we refer to the original paper to more detailed information. Norm identification approaches usually infer whether a norm exists in the society by looking at the actions performed by existing agents in the system. For this, such approaches assume that they have a model of how the system works and that they can collect a set of observations; the first can be encoded as a state-space graph of the possible transitions in the system, where nodes are states and edges are agent actions, while the second is a list of observations, where each one is a sequence of nodes visited by an existing agent.

In this approach, norms are defined in a subset of linear temporal logic (LTL), which specifies constraints on sequences of states. They can be either obligations (*eventually* or *next*) or prohibitions (*never* or *not next*); having the following six norm interpretations:

1. *eventually*(δ): Constrain a plan execution to include node δ.
2. *never*(δ): Constrain a plan execution to exclude node δ.
3. *next*(γ, δ): Constrain a plan execution to, when agent reaches context node γ, include node δ, where exists an edge from γ to δ in the graph.
4. *not_next*(γ, δ): Constrain a plan execution to, when agent reaches context node γ, exclude node δ, where exists an edge from γ to δ in the graph.
5. *eventually*(γ, δ): Similar to item 3, but it is not necessary to exist an edge from γ to δ. This indicates that node δ will eventually be reached from node γ.
6. *never*(γ, δ): Similar to item 4, but it is not necessary to exist an edge from γ to δ. This indicates that node δ will never be reached from node γ.

Given the above six norm interpretations, there are a number of possible norm hypotheses with respect to a state-space graph; all these possible norm hypotheses are candidates for actual norms in the system. The norm hypotheses

are weighted according to a number of observations given by some new agent
in the system; each observation contains a sequence of states in the state-space
graph, executed by existing agents.

The approach we employ [4] uses an alternative interpretation of the Bayes
Theorem that computes the odds of each possible norm hypotheses against a null
hypothesis (i.e. the hypothesis that there are no norms), given some observed
data D:

$$O(H_1 : H_2 | D) = \frac{p(H_1|D)}{p(H_2|D)} = \frac{p(H_1)p(D|H_1)/p(D)}{p(H_2)p(D|H_2)/p(D)} = O(H_1 : H_2)\frac{p(D|H_1)}{p(D|H_2)},$$

where H are the set of hypotheses and $O(H_1 : H_2)$ is the prior odd of H_1 over H_2.
The prior odds of the null hypothesis is defined as one, while for the other norm
hypotheses is set to an arbitrary value less than one. Note that here, each norm
is considered in isolation against a null hypothesis of there being no norm. The
candidate norms became actual norms when their relative odds is greater than
the odds of other norm hypotheses. We refer to the original paper for further
details, and in the following sections we describe the scenario and experiments
performed.

3 Norm-Detecting System

We developed a multi-agent system testbed in Jason with CArtAgO. The environment is a park (based on [19]), where agents can move in a grid simulating
a park environment. There are bars where agents can buy food or beverages;
after that, they can act in two ways: they can go to a trash can to recycle the
waste or they can discard it somewhere in the park. In the first case they are
non littering agents and in the second they are *littering agents*. Agents perform
these actions and walk randomly in the park until the simulation ends. In this
system, a norm is established when almost every single agent is from the same
type, i.e. *littering* or *non littering*.

Figure 1 shows a park environment example. The trash can is located at the
top left, in gray, and the bar is at the center, in green; yellow diamonds represent
garbage in the environment, and agents are represented by circles (dark and light
blue circles represent *non littering agents* carrying or not litter; gray and black
circles represent *littering* agents carrying or not litter).

All agents start with a score of 100 utility points, being either *littering* or
non littering agents, which we refer to as their *strategy*. The agents change their
strategy once its score reaches a certain threshold; in the current work we set
this threshold to 50 utility points. There are two sources of change in this score:
the first is when they litter or when they recycle; in the first case they have a
gain of utility of 0.5 points, while in the latter case they loss 0.5 points of utility.
These values represent the fact that is easier to litter than it is to find a trash
can and recycle.

The second source of change in the agent scores is when a *non littering
agent* observes another agent littering. This can occur when both agents are

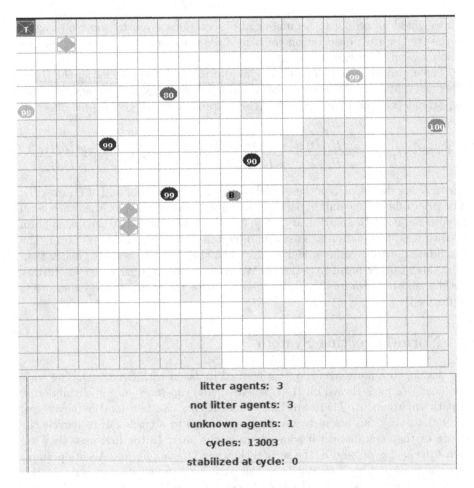

Fig. 1. Example of a park environment with seven agents (Color figure online)

within an observing distance of one another, i.e. agents cannot observe all other agents and their performed actions in the environment. In this situation, the observer agent *yells* at the other agent, losing a very small enforcement cost (0.01 of utility); consequently, the agent that littered loses 10 utility points from its score, representing a reputation loss or some loss derived from a negative emotion (e.g. guilty).

When a new agent enters in the environment, it collects observations to infer the current norms. In order to do this, it first needs a representation of the state-space of the possible states and actions in this system. Figure 2 shows a possible representation, where nodes are states and edges are actions available to the agents. Note that not all actions present in the plan library appear in this graph for readability purposes; we omit irrelevant actions (which will not give us any useful information of the existing norms) in the figure only (but they are

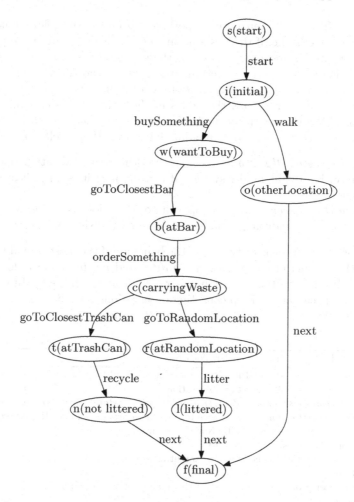

Fig. 2. State-space graph of the plan library for an agent in the park environment

represented internally in the agents), like recursive actions that try to move from one location to another. In the figure, states are labeled as a single character with their corresponding description inside parentheses; as input to the norm identification algorithm we will provide just the single characters.

Having the representation of the state-space graph, we now describe the procedure to infer the established norms, shown in Algorithm 1. It starts with the agent collecting a set of observations, where each observation is a sequence of characters in the graph (Line 2). The algorithm then provides this set of observations as input to the Bayesian norm identification algorithm (Line 3), which in turn calculates the odds of all norm hypotheses; as these odds are not absolute and must be considered as relative to other norm hypotheses, we only retrieve the ten most probable norm hypotheses to infer the current norm

(Line 4). We filter these ten norm hypotheses to detect the relevant norm to our problem (Line 5), i.e. if there is a norm to *litter* or to *not litter*. To perform this filter, we are interested in norm hypotheses where δ is t, n, r or l – i.e. the main nodes in the graph that discriminates between the two behavior we are interested in. For the norm interpretations where there is a node γ, we filter those that are i, w, b or c – i.e. the nodes in the graph which contains a path to nodes in δ. We then perform further processing to check which is the most probable norm based on the corresponding norm hypotheses relation (Line 7):

1. for *next* or *eventually*: if $\delta = (t$ or $n)$, then this is an indication that a *not litter* norm is present in the system; if $\delta = (r$ or $l)$ it is an indication of a *litter* norm.
2. for *not next* or *never*: this is the opposite of the above rule, e.g. if $\delta = (r$ or $l)$, then this is an indication that a *not litter* norm exists in the system.

The new agent in the society adopts the behavior of the most probable norm, based on the number of indications of the *litter* and *not litter* norm; for this, it chooses the norm with the highest number of indications (Line 9). In case of a draw, the agent can either keep collecting observations until it infers a norm or it can arbitrarily adopts a norm (e.g. a *not litter* norm).

Algorithm 1. Norm Inference Procedure

1: **procedure** NormInferenceProcedure(stateSpaceGraph)
2:     *observations* ← collect a set of observations
3:     *normHypotheses* ← *normIdentificationAlgorithm(stateSpaceGraph, observations)*
4:     *topTenNormHypotheses* ← retrieve top ten hypotheses from normHypotheses
5:     *filtered* ← filter relevant topTenNormHypotheses
6:     **for** normHypothesis in filtered **do**
7:         check if normHypothesis indicates a litter or not litter norm
8:     **end for**
9:     return most probable norm based on the number of each norm indications
10: **end procedure**

---

4   Experiments and Results

In order to evaluate the accuracy of correct identification of existing norms, we ran a set of simulations on the environment described in the previous section. More specifically, we added a new agent in the system that collects a set of observations over 10000 execution cycles; this results in an average of two observations for each observable agent in the system.

We designed four different types of experiments: the first one is designed to test the accuracy of new agents detecting a *not litter* norm, while in the second experiment there is a *litter* norm. In the third experiment there is no established norm in the society; finally, in the last experiment we test the accuracy in relation to the number of existing agents in the system.

4.1   Not Litter Norm

For the first experiment we simulate the environment with six existing agents, where all agents are of the *non littering* type, thus this society has an established *not litter* norm. We add a new agent in the system, which collects a set of observations; a sample of a set of observations follows:

1. i, o, f
2. i, w, b, c
3. $i, w, b, c, t, n, f.$

These sequences can be partial in the state-space graph of the scenario, i.e. they do not need to begin in the initial node state and finish in the end node state, because agents have a limited observing time and can only observe a limited set of agents which are at a close distance. From the first observation we cannot infer any norm, because this is a sequence of states of an agent that decided to randomly walk in the park. The second observation represents a partial sequence of states which ends with the state where the agent is "carrying waste"; again, this does not indicate any norm. Finally, the third observation indicates that a *not litter* norm exists, because it is a sequence of states of an agent that has recycled its waste.

An example of the output of the Bayesian norm identification algorithm given this setup is the following top ten norm hypotheses:

1. ('c', 'next', 't')
2. ('c', 'not next', 'r')
3. ('c', 'eventually', 'n')
4. ('l', 'not next', 'f')
5. ('c', 'never', 'r')
6. ('r', 'never', 'l')
7. ('r', 'eventually', 'i')
8. ('l', 'eventually', 's')
9. ('l', 'eventually', 'n')
10. ('r', 'eventually', 'c').

From these hypotheses, we can infer that a *not litter* norm exists. This is supported by: the first norm hypothesis, indicating that after an agent is in node c, it will go to node t (it will recycle); the second norm hypothesis, indicating that agent will not go to a random location to litter; the third norm hypothesis, indicating that agent will eventually recycle; and the fifth norm hypothesis, indicating that agent will never go to a random location to litter. All other hypotheses are irrelevant for the detection of the existing norm. For this experiment, all simulations correctly inferred the *not litter* norm; this enables the new agent to adopt the established norm.

4.2 Litter

This experiment is similar to the previous one, but instead of an existing *not litter* norm, there is a *litter* norm established in the society. An example of the top ten norm hypotheses follows:

1. ('w', 'eventually', 'l')
2. ('n', 'eventually', 'c')
3. ('t', 'not next', 'n')
4. ('n', 'eventually', 'r')
5. ('t', 'eventually', 'o')
6. ('b', 'never', 'n')
7. ('n', 'eventually', 'n')
8. ('i', 'never', 'n')
9. ('never', 'n')
10. ('w', 'never', 't').

Norm hypotheses one, six, eight, nine and ten indicate that there is a *litter* norm, because they lead us to nodes r and l and away from nodes t and n. Running this experiment in a set of simulations resulted in all new agents being able to correctly infer the existing *litter* norm.

4.3 Undefined

While the previous experiments have an established norm, in this experiment we have half *littering* agents and half *non littering* agents; the expected result is that the new agent will not be able to infer any norm. An example of the top norm hypotheses follows:

1. None
2. ('w', 'never', 'w')
3. ('s', 'never', 'n')
4. ('s', 'eventually', 'n')
5. ('l', 'never', 's')
6. ('s', 'never', 'l')
7. ('b', 'never', 's')
8. ('t', 'never', 'l')
9. ('n', 'next', 'f')
10. ('w', 'never', 's')
11. ('f', 'never', 'o').

None of these norm hypotheses indicate that there is an established norm. Accordingly, in the set of simulations the new agents were (correctly) not able to infer any norm.

4.4   Increasing the Number of Agents

For the last experiment we validate the norm identification approach on a society with an increasingly large number of agents. We perform several simulations, and in all cases where all existing agents in the society have a *not litter* norm or where all have a *litter* norm, the new agent was able to correctly infer the established norm.

When the relation between the number of *non littering* and *littering* agents is close to one, and therefore there is no norm currently established, the approach correctly infers so. When this relation is disproportional, i.e. there are many more agents of one type than of the other, the approach is also capable of inferring the norm of the predominant type. For example, with 50 agents, 95% *non littering* agents and the remaining 5% *littering* agents, the approach inferred a *not litter* norm. With 100 agents, 90% *littering* agents, the *litter* norm was inferred.

Table 1 shows results from experiments with an increasingly number of agents, changing the relation between *non littering* and *littering* agents, along with its corresponding inferred norm. When the approach is not able to infer any norm, the new agent being added to the society can either assume an arbitrary norm or can keep collecting observations.

Table 1. Inferred norms for an increasingly number of agents, and the percentage of *littering* and *non littering* agents

Percentage of *littering agents*	# of agents	Inferred norm
100% to 90%	6	Litter
	50	Litter
	100	Litter
85% to 10%	6	None
	50	None
	100	None
5% to 0%	6	Not litter
	50	Not litter
	100	Not litter

5   Conclusion and Future Work

In this paper we described an experiment to validate a norm identification approach in a multi-agent system implemented in Jason with CArtAgO. More specifically, we used a Bayesian norm identification from [4] as a base to get the most probable norm hypotheses, and then process these results to infer if there is a norm established in the society. This paper provides two main contributions. First, we developed a norm inference testbed in a popular agent programming language that can be used for experiments of norm-identification algorithms.

Second, we have conducted further experiments to validate the bayesian norm-identification approach by Cranefield *et al.* [4], confirming their positive result in a multi-agent setting.

In order for the Bayesian norm identification approach classify the norm hypotheses, it needs both the state-space graph of the problem and a set of observations. We manually built the state-space graph of the problem, identifying its key states and actions. For future work we intend to try to automatically generate the state-space graph of the plan library built in Jason; the main challenges would be to identify the key components of the problem and to remove loops which exists inside the plan library. This would allow the Bayesian norm identification approach to be applied to any system built in Jason.

We also intend to run more experiments in different and more complex scenarios, with norms with increasing complexity, to further evaluate the employed approach. We would also like to investigate different ways of combining the top norm hypotheses, maybe introducing weights accordingly to their relative odds.

References

1. Alrawagfeh, W., Brown, E., Mata-Montero, M.: Norms of behaviour and their identification and verification in open multi-agent societies. In: Theoretical and Practical Frameworks for Agent-Based Systems, pp. 129–145. IGI Global (2012)
2. Andrighetto, G., Conte, R., Turrini, P., Paolucci, M.: Emergence in the loop: simulating the two way dynamics of norm innovation. In: Dagstuhl Seminar Proceedings. Schloss Dagstuhl-Leibniz-Zentrum für Informatik (2007)
3. Boella, G., Van Der Torre, L., Verhagen, H.: Introduction to normative multiagent systems. Comput. Math. Org. Theory **12**(2–3), 71–79 (2006)
4. Cranefield, S., Savarimuthu, T., Meneguzzi, F., Oren, N.: A Bayesian approach to norm identification. In: Proceedings of the 2015 International Conference on Autonomous Agents and Multiagent Systems, pp. 1743–1744. International Foundation for Autonomous Agents and Multiagent Systems (2015)
5. Dignum, F.: Autonomous agents with norms. Artif. Intell. Law **7**(1), 69–79 (1999)
6. Esteva, M., Rosell, B., Rodriguez-Aguilar, J.A., Arcos, J.L.: AMELI: an agent-based middleware for electronic institutions. In: Proceedings of the Third International Joint Conference on Autonomous Agents and Multiagent Systems, vol. 1, pp. 236–243. IEEE Computer Society (2004)
7. García-Camino, A., Rodríguez-Aguilar, J.A., Sierra, C., Vasconcelos, W.: Constraint rule-based programming of norms for electronic institutions. Auton. Agents Multiagent Syst. **18**(1), 186–217 (2009)
8. Krzisch, G., Meneguzzi, F.: Norm identification in Jason using a Bayesian approach, March 2017. https://doi.org/10.5281/zenodo.438046. Accessed 24 Mar 2017
9. Luck, M., d'Inverno, M., et al.: Constraining autonomy through norms. In: Proceedings of the First International Joint Conference on Autonomous Agents and Multiagent Systems, pp. 674–681. (2002)
10. Luck, M., Mahmoud, S., Meneguzzi, F., Kollingbaum, M., Norman, T.J., Criado, N., Fagundes, M.S.: Normative agents. In: Ossowski, S. (ed.) Agreement Technologies. LGTS, vol. 8, pp. 209–220. Springer, Dordrecht (2013). https://doi.org/10.1007/978-94-007-5583-3_14

11. Mahmoud, M.A., Ahmad, M.S., Ahmad, A., Yusoff, M.Z.M., Mustapha, A.: The semantics of norms mining in multi-agent systems. In: Nguyen, N.-T., Hoang, K., Jędrzejowicz, P. (eds.) ICCCI 2012. LNCS, vol. 7653, pp. 425–435. Springer, Heidelberg (2012). https://doi.org/10.1007/978-3-642-34630-9_44

12. Oren, N., Meneguzzi, F.: Norm identification through plan recognition. In: Proceedings of the workshop on Coordination, Organization, Institutions and Norms in Agent Systems, COIN 2013@ AAMAS (2013)

13. Rao, A.S.: AgentSpeak(L): BDI agents speak out in a logical computable language. In: Van de Velde, W., Perram, J.W. (eds.) MAAMAW 1996. LNCS, vol. 1038, pp. 42–55. Springer, Heidelberg (1996). https://doi.org/10.1007/BFb0031845

14. Rao, A.S., Georgeff, M.P., et al.: BDI agents: from theory to practice. In: ICMAS, vol. 95, pp. 312–319 (1995)

15. Ricci, A., Viroli, M., Omicini, A.: CArtAgO: a framework for prototyping artifact-based environments in MAS. In: Weyns, D., Parunak, H.V.D., Michel, F. (eds.) E4MAS 2006. LNCS, vol. 4389, pp. 67–86. Springer, Heidelberg (2007). https://doi.org/10.1007/978-3-540-71103-2_4

16. Savarimuthu, B.T.R., Cranefield, S.: Norm creation, spreading and emergence: a survey of simulation models of norms in multi-agent systems. Multiagent Grid Syst. 7(1), 21–54 (2011)

17. Savarimuthu, B.T.R., Cranefield, S., Purvis, M.A., Purvis, M.K.: Obligation norm identification in agent societies. J. Artif. Soc. Soc. Simul. 13(4), 3 (2010)

18. Savarimuthu, B.T.R., Cranefield, S., Purvis, M.A., Purvis, M.K.: Identifying prohibition norms in agent societies. Artif. Intell. Law 21(1), 1–46 (2013)

19. Savarimuthu, B.T.R., Purvis, M., Purvis, M., Cranefield, S.: Social norm emergence in virtual agent societies. In: Baldoni, M., Son, T.C., van Riemsdijk, M.B., Winikoff, M. (eds.) DALT 2008. LNCS, vol. 5397, pp. 18–28. Springer, Heidelberg (2009). https://doi.org/10.1007/978-3-540-93920-7_2

20. de Pinninck, A.P., Sierra, C., Schorlemmer, M.: Friends no more: norm enforcement in multi-agent systems (2007)

Uncertainty Assessment in Agent-Based Simulation: An Exploratory Study

Carolina G. Abreu$^{(\boxtimes)}$ and Célia G. Ralha

Department of Computer Science, University of Brasília (UnB),
Brasília, DF, Brazil
{carolabreu,ghedini}@unb.br

Abstract. This paper presents an overview of uncertainty assessment in agent-based simulations, mainly related to land use and cover change. Almost every multiagent-based simulation review has expressed the need for statistical methods to evaluate the certainty of the results. Yet these problems continue to be underestimated and often neglected. This work aims to review how uncertainty is being portrayed in agent-based simulation and to perform an exploratory study to use statistical methods to estimate uncertainty. MASE, a Multi-Agent System for Environmental simulation, is the system under study. We first identified the most sensitive parameters using Morris One-at-a-Time sensitivity analysis. The efforts to assess agent-based simulation through statistical methods are paramount to corroborate and improve the level of confidence of the research that has been made in land use simulation.

1 Introduction

Land use and cover change (LUCC) investigation are of importance to promote insightful management of Earth's land use to refrain environmental damage. Moreover, LUCC is a complex process that relates the interaction between environmental, economic and social systems at different temporal and spatial scales. Computational frameworks are the most used technique to simulate LUCC models for its ability to cope with its complexity.

Agent-based model (ABM) has been incorporated into LUCC models, and many other real-world problems, to explicitly simulate the effects of human decisions in complex situations. They are based on the multi-agent system paradigm that features autonomous entities that interact and communicate in a shared environment. These entities perceive the environment, reason about it and act on it to achieve an internal objective. Therefore, ABM can capture emergent phenomena and provide an original description of the modeled system.

The Multi-Agent System for Environmental simulation (MASE) is a freeware software developed at the University of Brasilia. MASE is a tool for exploring

This papers has already been published in: © Springer International Publishing AG 2017 G. Sukthankar and J. A. Rodriguez-Aguilar (Eds.): AAMAS 2017 Best Papers, LNCS 10642, pp. 36–50, 2017. https://doi.org/10.1007/978-3-319-71682-4_3

© Springer International Publishing AG, part of Springer Nature 2018
G. P. Dimuro and L. Antunes (Eds.): MABS 2017, LNAI 10798, pp. 74–88, 2018.
https://doi.org/10.1007/978-3-319-91587-6_6

potential impacts of land use policies that implement a land use agent-based model [28]. Considering the purpose and reliance upon external data, MASE may be characterized as a predictor-type agent-based simulation (ABS) model [12]: a data-driven model with the overall goal of performing medium to long term predictions. MASE simulations were calibrated to match available GIS data [4]. Simulation results were validated according to a standard methodology for spatially explicit simulations [27] and then compared to similar frameworks [29]. MASE performance was found to be higher than other 13 LUCC modeling applications with nine different traditional peer-reviewed LUCC models according to [27]. Despite this fact, the lack of uncertainty assessment and sound experimentation is the main reason for criticism and questioning about the real contribution of frameworks to decision support for LUCC.

According to [3], any ABS has levels of uncertainty and errors associated with it. ABS continues to harbor subjectivity and hence degrees of freedom in the structure and intensity of agent's interactions, learning, and adaptation [18]. There are significant chances of finding results which may be the consequence of biases. Furthermore, almost every ABS review have expressed the need for statistical methods to validate models and evaluate the results to improve the transparency, replicability and general confidence in results derived from ABS. These problems continue to be underestimated and often neglected. Some authors [12], likewise, argued that validation is one of the most important aspects of a model building because it is the only means that provides some evidence that a model can be used for a particular purpose. However, at least 65% of the models in their survey were incompletely validated. Of the models validated in some way, surprisingly less than 5% used statistical validation techniques. Traditionally, ABS types of systems are difficult to analyze given their non-linear behavior and size [6].

Treatment of uncertainty is particularly important and usually difficult to deal with in the case of ABM's stochastic models. While acknowledging the differences in data sources and the causes of inconsistencies, there is still need to develop methods to optimally extract information from the data, to document the uncertainties and to assess common methodological challenges. To look away could reinforce inconsistent results and damage the integrity and quality of simulation results.

This work aims to briefly discuss how uncertainty is being portrayed in ABS and to perform an exploratory study to use statistical methods to estimate uncertainty in a LUCC agent-based prediction simulation tool. The MASE system will be the simulator under study. The Cerrado case study simulations [29] will be the basis for the analysis. As a first investigation step, we assessed the uncertainty within the inputs and configuration parameters of the simulation. Our final goal would be to document, quantification and to foresee its propagation impacts in the results. A particular challenge in performing measurements is coming up with appropriate metrics. The thorough experimentation and repeatability would, therefore, improve our understanding of the uncertainty and relations among the variables that characterize a simulation. The remainder of the paper is structured as follows. In Sect. 2, we present some background on uncertainty and in Sect. 3 some related work. In Sect. 4, we summarize the MASE characteristics and case study. We also present the methodology for the exploratory study. In Sect. 5 we show results together with discussions. In Sect. 6 we conclude with a summary.

2   Overview of Uncertainty in ABS

The relevance of the treatment of uncertainty is dependent of the modeling objective. Requirements regarding model uncertainty may be less critical for social learning models, where communication and interaction among stakeholders would be of more significance. Conversely, parameters, measurements, and conditions used for model runs influence much more data-based predictions of future states. Projection, forecasting and prediction models are usually very affected by the variation of a system output from observed models.

Also, there are different sources of uncertainty that can influence the prediction of a simulation model. It can arise from simulation variability in stochastic simulation models or from structural uncertainty within assumptions of a model. We will emphasize input uncertainty, what McKay [24] defined as incomplete knowledge of 'correct' values of model inputs, including model parameters. If the inputs of a model are uncertain, there is an inherent variability associated with the output of that model. Therefore it is crucial to communicate it effectively to stakeholders and technical audiences when outputting model predictions.

Uncertainty in environmental prediction simulations may limit the reliability of predicted changes. This issue is one of the recurrent conclusions of the Intergovernmental Panel on Climate Change (IPCC). Back at 1995, IPCC stated that "uncertainties in the simulation of changes in the physical properties have a major impact on confidence in projections of future regional climate change" [13] and that was necessary to reduce uncertainties to increase future model capabilities and improve climate change estimates. Since 2010, IPCC dedicates an integral feature of its reports to the communication of the degree of certainty within IPCC assessment findings [23]. In the most recent report, IPCC assesses a substantially larger knowledge base of scientific, technical and socio-economic literature to reduce uncertainty and uses a large number of methods and formalization [7]. Especially for future predictions, validating a model's predictive accuracy is not straightforward due to a lack of appropriate data and methods for 'validation' [15]. That is another reason why applications, frameworks, and methods of formalization in this research area are relevant and should be promoted.

Regarding the type of modeling, there are approaches such as Bayesian networks, able to explicitly deal with uncertainty in the interpretation of data, measurements or conditions. In contrast, other approaches such as ABMs require the development of comprehensive or compelling analysis of output data and a lot of resource-intensive attention [18]. The level of testing required to develop this understanding is rarely carried out, mainly due to time and other resource constraints [15].

Indeed, uncertainty assessment in ABM can be a hard task for even relatively small models. Due to their inherent complexity, ABS are often seen as black boxes, where there is no purpose in explaining why the agents acted as they did, as long as the modeler presents some form of validation (i.e., shows a good fit). According to Marks [22], ABMs simulations can prove existence, but not in general necessity. Despite that, there is a research effort to make ABS more transparent and to demonstrate that the simulations behave as intended through efforts in standardization in simulation model analysis and result sharing [21]. Besides from verification, uncertainty assessment aims to increase understanding, to improve the reliability of the predicted changes and to inform the degree of certainty of key findings. To achieve this effort, some techniques and methods such as uncertainty and sensitivity analysis should be part of the modeling process.

Uncertainty Quantification is defined as the identification, characterization, propagation, analysis and reduction of uncertainties. Sensitivity analysis (SA) is defined as the study of how uncertainty in the output of a model can be apportioned to different sources of uncertainty in the model input [30] and is a method to assess propagation of uncertainties. SA responds the question of which inputs are responsible for the variability of outputs. Local SA explores the output changes by varying one parameter at a time, keeping all the others constant. Although it is a useful and straightforward approach, it may be location dependent. Global SA gives a better estimate of uncertainty by varying all parameters at the same time by using probability density functions to express the uncertainty of model parameters. Uncertainty analysis is a related broader uncertainty propagation practice to SA. It focuses rather on quantifying uncertainty in model output, addressing the variability of results. Ideally, uncertainty and SA should be run in tandem.

3   Related Work

There are a growing number of attempts to assess uncertainty in ABS. However, there is a lack of specific guidance on effective presentation and analysis of the simulation output data. There is a variety of approaches to quantifying or reduce uncertainty. The work of [18] offers an overview of the state-of-the-art methods on the social simulation area, in particular examining the issues around variance stability, SA and spatiotemporal analysis. Because of our interest in LUCC simulations, we choose to review how those approaches are being applied and communicated on spatially-explicit simulations.

In [1], the authors propose an algorithm as an alternative to goodness-of-fit traditional validation to answer if the agents in a simulation are behaving as expected. To them, the key for effective interaction in multi-agent applications is to reason explicitly about the behavior of other agents, in the form of a hypothesized behavior. This approach would allow an agent to contemplate the correctness of a hypothesis. In the form of a frequentist hypothesis test, the algorithm allows for multiple metrics in the construction of the test statistic and learns its distribution during the interaction process. It is an interesting approach to addressing the uncertainties within the model and agents behavior. We believe it would be even more effective if coupled with an uncertainty quantification technique.

The work of [26] assesses uncertainty that is characteristic of spatially explicit models and simulations. The authors propose a benchmarking scheme of LUCC modeling tools by various validation techniques and error analysis. The authors investigate LUCC tools that are based on map comparisons to analyze the accuracy of LUCC models in terms of quantity, pixel by pixel correctness and LUCC components such as persistence and change. Also, they investigated the map outputs of these simulations to test the fidelity of spatial patterns and the congruency of the simulation maps from different modeling tools. Although the variability of LUCC models does not allow strict comparisons, there is still room for improvements in methodologies, validation and uncertainty quantification.

The work of [8] assesses model output analysis through a global SA, a commonly used approach for identifying critical parameters that dominate model behaviors. They use the Problem Solving environment for Uncertainty Analysis and Design Exploration (PSUADE) software, to evaluate the effectiveness and efficiency of widely used qualitative and quantitative SA methods. Each method is tested using a variety of sampling techniques to screen out the most relevant parameters from the insensitive ones. The Sacramento Soil Moisture Accounting (SAC-SMA) model, which has thirteen tunable parameters, is used for illustration. The South Branch Potomac River basin near Springfield, West Virginia in the U.S. is chosen as the study area. The authors show how different sampling methods and SA measurements can indicate different sensitive and insensitive parameters and that a comprehensive SA is paramount to avoid misleading results.

The work of [20] also performed a global SA to show which model parameters are critical to the performance of land surface models. The authors considered 40 adjustable parameters in The Common Land Model and therefore compare different SA methods and sampling. The size of each sample would vary as well. The sampling techniques and SA measures that were considered optimal were distinct from the results found by [8], meaning that not all LUCC ABS propagate uncertainty the same way.

Another approach was performed by [17], also in a LUCC model. They use the method of independent replication. In the case study, the authors replicated the simulation 12 times for each mechanism and computed the mean values of the impact indicators and their confidence intervals (CI) at a reliability of 95%. They used uncertainty quantification to define a minimum certainty threshold in the simulation outputs.

All these authors used several indicators to measure the variability of model results based on changing input parameters. Table 1 illustrates a brief comparison among those works. MASE exploratory uncertainty assessment will be described in the next sections. A large panel of statistical tools exist to help with the accuracy of the predictions such as Dakota[1], PSUADE [32], UQ-PyL[2], MEME Suite[3] and MC2MABS [2]. There are initiatives to apply the potential of classic Design of Experiments (DOE) for ABS [16,21]. ABS field of research would benefit from a systematic empirical research with standardized procedures, but

---

[1] https://dakota.sandia.gov/.

[2] http://www.uq-pyl.com/.

[3] http://meme-suite.org/.

ABS idiosyncrasies in model output turn the task even harder. Researchers so far failed to reach consensus and to determine sound methodological guidelines. Hence the studies are still mostly investigative and exploratory.

Table 1. Overview of the general characteristics of each related work

Reference	Model	Uncertainty methods
[1]	Generic ABS	Correctness Hypothesis test and run-time statistical verification in the agent's behavior
[26]	Land use models	Image statistical comparison of pixel/maps and error analysis to find uncertainty drivers
[8]	SAC-SMA hydrological model	Global SA with 15 sampling techniques, 9 different sample sizes and 12 SA methods
[20]	Land surface model	Local SA and 4 Global SA methods with 3 sampling techniques, and 6 sample sizes
[17]	LUDAS: land use ABS	Independent Replications and Confidence Intervals to assess output variation
MASE	MASE: land use ABS	Global SA with different sample configurations, independent replications, and Confidence Intervals

4 MASE Exploratory Study

The MASE Project[4] objective is to define and implement a multi-agent tool for simulating environmental change. MASE enables modeling and simulations of LUCC dynamics using a configurable user model. The multi-agent architecture is composed of three hierarchical layers (from top to bottom) [29]: a User Interface (UI), a Pre-processing and an Agent layer. In the agent layer, there are cell agents representing land units hosting natural processes, such as crop/forest grow, and there are transformation agents, representing human agents and their behavior as farmers or cattle rancher.

The Cerrado-LUCC model of MASE is used as a test problem. The simulations depict the land use and cover changes of the most endangered biome in Brazil. The Cerrado is the second largest biome in South America and harbors significant endemism and biodiversity. The landscape has been undergoing severe transformation due to the advance of cattle ranching and soy production. To promote transparency and replicability, the Cerrado-LUCC simulation

---

[4] Software Availability: http://mase.cic.unb.br/.

model was documented and described employing the standard ODD-protocol (Overview, Design concepts, and Details) [10,11]. We also applied empirically grounding ABM mechanisms for the characterization of agent behaviors and attributes in socio-ecological systems [31]. In this article, we provide some core information of MASE and the Cerrado-LUCC Model, mainly about the parameters and outputs. Readers who are interested in the details of this model and the implementation of MASE multi-agent system should refer to [28,29], respectively.

The input of the simulation is a couple of grid raster maps consisting of the land cover of the region, from two different time periods (an initial and a final map). Also, each simulation carries a set of maps to describe the physical characteristics of the environment, such as water courses, water bodies, slope, buildings, highways, environmental protected areas, and territorial zoning maps.

The simulations are calibrated from the two time-steps and project the land use and cover change for future steps. The result of a MASE simulation is a couple of predicted maps (Fig. 1), with the allocation of change and a set of metrics calculated during runtime. The resulting image is submitted to a goodness-of-fit measurement and the quality and errors of the quantity of change and allocation of land use change are calculated.

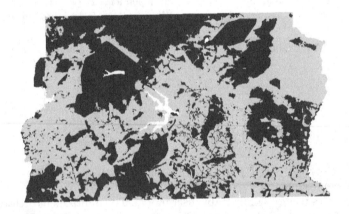

Fig. 1. A land cover predicted map of the Cerrado in Federal District, Brazil

Methodology

The objective is to perform an exploratory analysis, based on classical statistics, to reduce uncertainty and to understand how the model behave. MASE LUCC model is under input uncertainty investigation, to calculate their influence in the simulation output. For exploratory purposes, we want insight on the parameters that affects the multi-agent system implementation, so we selected a subset of Cerrado-LUCC model inputs for this demonstration. The subset of input parameters of the multi-agent system are displayed in Table 2: TA-Number of Transformation Agents, *TG*- Number of Group Transformation Agents, *IE*-Potential of Individual Exploration and *GE*- Potential of Group Exploration. These parameters characterize the instantiation of MASE agents and therefore, should be analyzed regarding uncertainty.

Table 2. MASE multi-agent input configuration parameters

ID	Parameter	Description	Range
I1	TA	Number of transformation agents	[1, 100]
I2	TG	Number of group transformation agents	[10, 100]
I3	IE	Potential of individual exploration	[1, 500]
I4	GE	Potential of group exploration	[1, 1500]

The number of transformation agents is a parameter that reflects the number of computational agents (in the multi-agent system paradigm) instantiated in a simulation run. In this study case, one agent does not represent one single individual. The Cerrado-LUCC model was formulated based on an empirical characterisation of agent behaviors, proposed by [31], with two basic steps: the development of behavioral categories and the scaling to the whole population of agents. TA was derived from the Brazilian Agricultural Census of 2006 and comprises a set of Producer legal status. The range of 1 to 100 is an abstraction to the 3407 register producers in the region that may be active or inactive in a given period. The details of this agent characterization are thoroughly illustrated in [29]. Likewise, a particular type of agent is GT, which represent not an individual but an organization, cooperative, business or so. The range is an abstraction of the 548 group producers, 10 of which have permanent exploration licenses.

The potential of exploration, individual or of a group, represent the impact an agent can produce in the natural vegetation cover of a cell during a step. In the Cerrado LUCC Model, considering the deforestation process, the potential of exploration is again an abstraction for the amount of m^3 of wood that can be obtained from a particular grid cell, until a nominal limit that represents resource depletion.

In addition to the final LUCC maps, the simulation generates a set of metrics as results, mainly spatial analysis measurements, which includes pixel by pixel comparison, a quantitative and an allocation agreement. Those measurements are certain statistical LUCC indices to determine the produced map accuracy, proposed by [27]. It includes an objective function called the figure of merit (FoM), a ratio between correct predicted changes and the sum of observed and predicted changes. To evaluate the response of the model to the different parameters, the experiments considered the outputs described in Table 3 and tried to identify and quantify the influence of the simulation input configurations on the model outputs. The identification (ID) of each of the outputs follows the numbering of its generation in the file *.csv* produced by MASE at the end of each simulation.

Table 3. MASE output parameters

ID	Output	Description
O1	TM	Total time of the simulation
O4	FoM	Figure of merit
O5	PA	Image producer's accuracy
O6	UA	Image user's accuracy
O7	WC	*Pixel's Wrong Change*: observed change predicted as persistence
O8	RC	*Pixel's Right Change*: observed change predicted as change
O9	WP	*Pixel's Wrong Persistence*: observed change predicted as persistence

To identify and analyze these uncertainties we performed a method of elementary effects (EE) of global SA on the MASE LUCC model. For this calculation, we used the software package developed by Tong [32] called PSUADE, containing various methods for parameter study, numerical optimization, uncertainty analysis and SA.

Screening methods are based on a discretization of the inputs in levels, allowing a fast exploration of the system behavior [14]. The aim of this type of method is to identify the non-influential inputs with a small number of model calls. The most used screening method is based on the one-parameter-at-a-time (OAT) design, where each input is varied while fixing the others. The simplicity is one of OAT's advantages, but there are drawbacks when applying to ABM. For one, it does not consider parameter interactions and may cover a slight fraction of the input space.

The EE method we chose to apply is the Morris method (MOAT) proposed by [25] and refined by [5], an expansion of the OAT approach that forsakes the strict OAT baseline. It means that a change in one input is maintained when examing a switch to the next input and the parameter set is multiply repeated while randomly selecting the initial parameters settings. EE is suited for spatially explicit simulations, usually computationally expensive models with large input sets.

MOAT allows classifying the inputs into three groups: inputs having a negligible effect, inputs having large linear effects without interactions and inputs having significant non-linear and interaction effects. In overall effect and interaction effect of each parameter can be approximated by the mean μ and standard deviation σ of the gradients of each parameter sampled from r.

The MOAT sampling technique was designed for the particular MOAT method. The work of [8] details how the MOAT sampling works: the range of each parameter is partitioned into $p - 1$ equal intervals. Thus the parameter space is an n-dimension p-level orthogonal grid, where each parameter can take on values from these p determined values.

First, r points are randomly generated from the orthogonal grid; and then, for each of the r points, other sample points are generated by perturbing one dimension at a time. Therefore, sample size will be $(n + 1) \cdot r$. For the sampling size, [19] report that one needs at least $10 \cdot n$ samples to identify key factors among the parameters.

To avoid the effect size on the sample, we determining a minimum sample size of $800(= 20 \cdot 4)$, for four inputs. For MOAT sampling we used 160 replications, resulting in sample size of $800(= (4 + 1) \cdot 160)$.

Moreover, as in other stochastic models, it is not advisable to draw conclusions from a single MASE simulation run. For an initial uncertainty assessment, we applied the method of independent replications proposed by [9]. We run the model approximately eighty-five thousand times (an arbitrary choice to explore all the input parameter space) and randomly clustered the results into five independent replication groups. We computed the mean values of the outputs and their confidence intervals (CI) at a reliability of 95%. Another approach to estimating the uncertainty of the model output is to study the variance in the model outputs by using the Coefficient of Variation (CV) (the ratio of the standard deviation σ of a sample to its mean μ), to compare the variance of different frequency distributions.

5 Results

In the current work, we analyzed four input parameters, displayed in Table 2, regarding the multi-agent configuration of MASE LUCC model. First, we present the results of the SA. Figure 2 presents the EE of CERRADO-LUCC model parameters. Figure 2 (left) illustrates the modified means of MOAT gradients and also their spreads based on bootstrapping. The results show that GE and TA are the most sensitive parameters in term of having the largest average median (26.466 and 25.205, respectively). The other two parameters have median sensitivities close to zero, denoting the impact of these parameters on the simulation output is minimal.

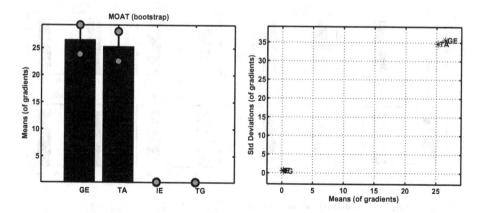

Fig. 2. Parameter sensitivity rankings of MOAT method

Figure 2 (right) is a MOAT diagram that shows a consensus view among mean μ and standard deviation σ of the gradients of each parameter sampled from r. The more sensitive the parameter, the closer it is to the upper right corner of the graph. These results show a positive correlation between input and output uncertainties. Since GE and TA describe the amount of land transformation in a simulation, high values of these parameters will increase the model output. GE is the most sensitive parameter, followed by TA. To understand and to reduce uncertainty within this two variables will, therefore, reduce the uncertainty of the simulation as a whole.

GE represents the amount of land cover that is transformed by a group of human agents in a cell of the map. GE is a sensitive value for it indicates the voracity and velocity of the current land exploitation, what will directly affect the result of the simulation. GE is probably sensitive because the socio-economic groups responsible for large-scale cattle ranching and permanent agriculture are the principal driver of deforestation in Cerrado. Their rates of land change are more significance than the number of groups, what explain TG as an insensitive parameter to the output. As for TA, the more agents one instantiates in a simulation, more land cover will be affected, higher will be the land use transformation rates. Conversely, the potential of exploration of a single individual is less determinant than the number of single individuals acting on the land, with SA indicating TA a sensitive and IE as an insensitive parameter.

To investigate MOAT sensitivity results, we used different replications times r and different levels p to know for sure the relevance of the parameters as displayed in Fig. 3. It is possible to see that even within the same method, results may vary. The results for four replications are not very consistent with the other replication results, mainly with the mean. The results with $r = 56$, $r = 108$ and $r = 160$ present minor variations. We can infer that four replications are not enough to identify the parameters sensitivity in the MASE model successfully and therefore the number of replications should be higher to be effective.

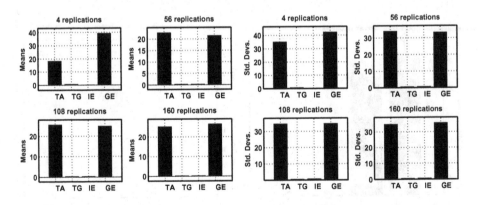

Fig. 3. Sensitivity of parameters at different replication times r

Table 4 is a summary of the Basic Output Statistics of the MASE LUCC model. Each replication is assigned by $i = [1 \ldots 5]$, the sample mean from the coefficient variation by CV_i, and the mean of all replications by $\bar{Z}$. We performed independent replications to verify the variation of the indicators, and for an initial analysis, we consider this variation as noise (uncertainty). Any impact conclusions in predictions can only be drawn if the changes in standards are greater than the uncertainty rate. Therefore, we have a first threshold to define if some result is valid, compared to the simulations behavior.

We also estimated the expected average FoM for simulations, using the five replication grouped results ($b = 5$). Considering the $\bar{Z}_{FoM} = 43.87$ and the estimated Variance $\hat{V}_R = 100.99$, we have an approximately $100(1 - \alpha)\%$ two-sided CI for θ, according to the formalization proposed by [9]. For level $\alpha = 0.05$, we have $t_{0.025,4} = 2.78$, and gives $[31.39, 56.34]$ as a 95% CI for the expected FoM for MASE simulations.

Table 4. Coefficient of variation for MASE outputs

Output	CV_1	CV_2	CV_3	CV_4	CV_5	$\bar{Z}$
Time	0.300	0.130	0.250	0.260	0.200	**0.230**
Figure of merit	0.015	0.011	0.008	0.007	0.090	**0.100**
Producer's accuracy	0.015	0.011	0.008	0.007	0.009	**0.010**
User's accuracy	0.006	0.005	0.004	0.004	0.003	**0.004**
Wrong change	0.030	0.030	0.030	0.030	0.020	**0.030**
Wrong persistence	0.007	0.007	0.008	0.008	0.013	**0.009**
Right change	0.015	0.011	0.008	0.008	0.009	**0.010**

6 Conclusions

In this study, we first identified the most sensitive parameters for the MASE LUCC model using MOAT SA. We investigated some proper sampling design and sample size needed for MOAT screening the parameters effectively. Although these conclusions are model-specific, it corroborates possible variation among sampling techniques and SA methods.

This paper is the first exploratory study towards quantifying uncertainty within MASE simulations. Following experiments must be done to promote more standardization to this effort through the application of Design of Experiments. We look forward to investigating further on the model parameters, analyzing the remaining inputs besides the agent's quantities and their impacts.

This paper is the first exploratory study towards quantifying uncertainty within MASE simulations. The presented results allow us to understand the uncertainty when defining the parameters of the simulation of the LUCC model under study. Our feeling is that the uncertainty is very high which means that either model need to dramatically improve or LUCC policy need to be reevaluated. Most simulation tools fail to validate models and to state the uncertainty in simulation results. Consequently, policymakers and the general public develop opinions based on misleading research that fails to give them the appropriate interpretations required to make informed decisions. The efforts to assess ABMs through statistical methods are paramount to corroborate and improve the level of confidence of the research that has been made in LUCC simulation.

References

1. Albrecht, S.V., Ramamoorthy, S.: Are you doing what I think you are doing? Criticising uncertain agent models. In: Proceedings of the 31st Conference on Uncertainty in Artificial Intelligence, Amsterdam, Netherlands, p. 10 (2015)
2. Herd, B., Miles, S., McBurney, P., Luck, M.: MC²MABS: a Monte Carlo model checker for multiagent-based simulations. In: Gaudou, B., Sichman, J.S. (eds.) MABS 2015. LNCS (LNAI), vol. 9568, pp. 37–54. Springer, Cham (2016). https://doi.org/10. 1007/978-3-319-31447-1_3
3. Bommel, P.: Foreword. In: Adamatti, D.F. (ed.) Multi-Agent Based Simulations Applied to Biological and Environmental Systems, pp. xv–xviii. IGI Global, Hershey (2017)
4. Coelho, C.G., Abreu, C.G., Ramos, R.M., Mendes, A.H., Teodoro, G., Ralha, C.G.: MASE-BDI: agent-based simulator for environmental land change with efficient and parallel auto-tuning. Appl. Intell. 45(3), 904–922 (2016)
5. Campolongo, F., Braddock, R.: The use of graph theory in the sensitivity analysis of the model output: a second order screening method. Reliab. Eng. Syst. Saf. 64(1), 1–12 (1999). https://doi.org/10.1016/S0951-8320(98)00008-8
6. Casti, J.L.: Complexification: Explaining a Paradoxical World through the Science of Surprise. HarperCollins, New York (1995). (Reprint edn.)
7. Intergovernmental Panel on Climate Change: Climate Change 2013 The Physical Science Basis: Working Group I Contribution to the Fifth Assessment Report of the Intergovernmental Panel on Climate Change. Cambridge University Press (2014)
8. Gan, Y., Duan, Q., Gong, W., Tong, C., Sun, Y., Chu, W., Ye, A., Miao, C., Di, Z.: A comprehensive evaluation of various sensitivity analysis methods: a case study with a hydrological model. Environ. Model. Softw. 51, 269–285 (2014)
9. Goldsman, D., Tokol, G.: Output analysis procedures for computer simulations. In: Joines, J., Barton, R.R., Kang, K., Fishwick, P. (eds.) Proceedings of the 2000 Winter Simulation Conference, pp. 39–45 (2000)
10. Grimm, V., Berger, U., Bastiansen, F., Eliassen, S., Ginot, V., Giske, J., Goss-Custard, J., Grand, T., Heinz, S.K., Huse, G.: A standard protocol for describing individual-based and agent-based models. Ecol. Model. 198(1–2), 115–126 (2006). http://linkinghub.elsevier.com/retrieve/pii/S0304380006002043
11. Grimm, V., Berger, U., DeAngelis, D.L., Polhill, J.G., Giske, J., Railsback, S.F.: The ODD protocol: a review and first update. Ecol. Model. 221(23), 2760–2768 (2010). http://linkinghub.elsevier.com/retrieve/pii/S030438001000414X
12. Heath, B., Hill, R., Ciarallo, F.: A survey of agent-based modeling practices (January 1998 to July 2008). JASSS 12(4), 1–49 (2009)
13. Houghton, J., Filho, L.M., Callander, B., Harris, N., Kattenberg, A., Maskell, K. (eds.): Climate Change 1995 The Science of Climate Change. The Intergovernmental Panel on Climate Change (1996)

14. Iooss, B., Lemaître, P.: A review on global sensitivity analysis methods. In: Dellino, G., Meloni, C. (eds.) Uncertainty Management in Simulation-Optimization of Complex Systems. ORSIS, vol. 59, pp. 101–122. Springer, Boston (2015). https://doi.org/10.1007/978-1-4899-7547-8_5

15. Kelly (Letcher), R.A., Jakeman, A.J., Barreteau, O., Borsuk, M.E., ElSawah, S., Hamilton, S.H., Henriksen Jr., H., Kuikka, S., Maier, H.R., Rizzoli, A.E., van Delden, H., Voinov, A.A.: Selecting among five common modelling approaches for integrated environmental assessment and management. Environ. Model. Softw. **47**, 159–181 (2013)

16. Kleijnen, J.P., Sanchez, S.M., Lucas, T.W., Cioppa, T.M.: A user's guide to the brave new world of designing simulation experiments. INFORMS J. Comput. **17**(3), 263–289 (2005). https://harvest.nps.edu/papers/UserGuideSimExpts.pdf

17. Le, Q.B., Seidl, R., Scholz, R.W.: Feedback loops and types of adaptation in the modelling of land-use decisions in an agent-based simulation. Environ. Model. Softw. **27–28**, 83–96 (2012)

18. Lee, J.S., Filatova, T., Ligmann-Zielinska, A., Hassani-Mahmooei, B., Stonedahl, F., Lorscheid, I., Voinov, A., Polhill, G., Sun, Z., Parker, D.C.: The complexities of agent-based modeling output analysis. JASSS **18**(4), 1–25 (2015)

19. Levy, S., Steinberg, D.M.: Computer experiments: a review. AStA Adv. Stat. Anal. **94**(4), 311–324 (2010)

20. Li, J.D., Duan, Q.Y., Gong, W., Ye, A.Z., Dai, Y.J., Miao, C.Y., Di, Z.H., Tong, C., Sun, Y.W.: Assessing parameter importance of the Common Land Model based on qualitative and quantitative sensitivity analysis. Hydrol. Earth Syst. Sci. Discuss. **10**(2), 2243–2286 (2013)

21. Lorscheid, I., Heine, B.O., Meyer, M.: Opening the 'Black Box' of simulations: increased transparency and effective communication through the systematic design of experiments. Comput. Math. Organ. Theory **18**(1), 22–62 (2012)

22. Marks, R.E.: Validating simulation models: a general framework and four applied examples. Comput. Econ. **30**(3), 265–290 (2007)

23. Mastrandrea, M.D., Field, C.B., Stocker, T.F., Edenhofer, O., Ebi, K.L., Frame, D.J., Held, H., Kriegler, E., Mach, K.J., Matschoss, P.R., Plattner, G.K., Yohe, G.W., Zwiers, F.W.: Guidance note for lead authors of the IPCC fifth assessment report on consistent treatment of uncertainties. In: Intergovernmental Panel on Climate Change (IPCC), pp. 1–7 (2010)

24. McKay, M.D., Morrison, J.D., Upton, S.C.: Evaluating prediction uncertainty in simulation models. Comput. Phys. Commun. **117**(1–2), 44–51 (1999)

25. Morris, M.D.: Factorial sampling plans for preliminary computational experiments. Technometrics **33**(2), 161–174 (1991)

26. Paegelow, M., Camacho Olmedo, M.T., Mas, J.F., Houet, T.: Benchmarking of LUCC modelling tools by various validation techniques and error analysis. Cybergeo **701**(online), 29 (2014)

27. Pontius, R.G., Boersma, W., Castella, J.C., Clarke, K., Nijs, T., Dietzel, C., Duan, Z., Fotsing, E., Goldstein, N., Kok, K., Koomen, E., Lippitt, C.D., McConnell, W., Mohd Sood, A., Pijanowski, B., Pithadia, S., Sweeney, S., Trung, T.N., Veldkamp, A.T., Verburg, P.H.: Comparing the input, output, and validation maps for several models of land change. Ann. Reg. Sci. **42**(1), 11–37 (2008)

28. Ralha, C.G., Abreu, C.G.: A multi-agent-based environmental simulator. In: Adamatti, D.F. (ed.) Multi-Agent Based Simulations Applied to Biological and Environmental Systems, Chap. 5, pp. 106–127. IGI Global, Hershey (2017)

29. Ralha, C.G., Abreu, C.G., Coelho, C.G., Zaghetto, A., Macchiavello, B., Machado, R.B.: A multi-agent model system for land-use change simulation. Environ. Model. Softw. **42**, 30–46 (2013)
30. Saltelli, A., Ratto, M., Andres, T., Campolongo, F., Cariboni, J., Gatelli, D., Saisana, M., Tarantola, S.: Global Sensitivity Analysis: The Primer. Wiley, Hoboken (2008)
31. Smajgl, A., Brown, D.G., Valbuena, D., Huigen, M.G.A.: Empirical characterisation of agent behaviours in socio-ecological systems. Environ. Model. Softw. **26**(7), 837–844 (2011). https://doi.org/10.1016/j.envsoft.2011.02.011
32. Tong, C.: PSUADE Short Manual (Version 1.7). Lawrence Livermore National Laboratory (LLNL), Livermore (2015)

Enhancing the Behavior of Agents in Social Simulations with Emotions and Social Relations

Mathieu Bourgais[1]([✉]), Patrick Taillandier[2], and Laurent Vercouter[1]

[1] Normandie Univ, INSA Rouen, UNIHAVRE, UNIROUEN, LITIS,
76000 Rouen, France
`mathieu.bourgais@insa-rouen.fr`
[2] MIAT, INRA, 31000 Toulouse, France

Abstract. Social Simulations need agents with a realistic behavior to be used as a scientific tool by social scientists. When simulating a human society, a realistic behavior implies the use of cognition, social relations between people but also to take into account emotions and the dynamic between these features. However, developing such a behavior is often too complex for people with little knowledge in programming. In this paper, we present a formalism to represent cognition, social relations and emotions, which is integrated in an agent architecture to give a dynamic emotional behavior to social agents. This architecture is implemented in the open-source multi-agent platform GAMA. A use case about evacuation during bush fires in Australia is used to show the possibilities of our work.

Keywords: Social simulation · Emotions · Cognition
Agent architecture

1 Introduction

Multi-agent simulation has become an important tool, especially in social sciences where it is used to study complex systems composed of hundreds or thousands of simulated humans. In this particular case, we now speak of social simulation [17] which means simulation featuring social agents.

A social agent can be described as a simulated human. In other words, a social agent is an agent with a cognitive behavior able to interact with its environment and with other agents through a social behavior. This social behavior can feature an emotional engine, a personality, an engine to cope with social norms or social relations.

In order to increase the accuracy of social simulations, these ones have to be as close as possible to real cases studied. This goal for realism leads to the use of believable social agents, i.e. agents with more and more of social features [43].

Let's take the example of bush fires in Australia studied with multi-agent simulation [2]. In this study, the goal was to simulate the evacuation of an area

© Springer International Publishing AG, part of Springer Nature 2018
G. P. Dimuro and L. Antunes (Eds.): MABS 2017, LNAI 10798, pp. 89–104, 2018.
https://doi.org/10.1007/978-3-319-91587-6_7

in the context of bush fires in Australia. The authors used a BDI architecture [11] for the modeling of their agent's cognition but in this situation, a person also reacts to his/her emotions and his/her social relations.

In this paper, we tackle this issue by adding dynamic emotions and social relations into an existing cognitive architecture. The main goal is to provide a formalism for the creation of emotions through cognition and for the evolution of social relations according to an agent's mental state and to integrate it in an agent architecture. However, modeling and simulating such behavior requires high level skills in computer programming and in artificial intelligence, so it is out of reach of most modelers coming from social sciences. Our work was implemented in the open-source simulation platform GAMA [20]. The main benefit of integrating our agent architecture inside this platform is to take advantages of the modeling language offered by GAMA that eases its use for modelers who are not expert in programming.

This paper is structured as follows: in Sect. 2, we show existing works to create social agents with a cognitive behavior, an emotional engine or social relations. In Sect. 3, we propose a formalism used to deal with the mental state of the agent in terms of cognition, emotion and social relations. In Sect. 4, we describe the integration of this formalism into a cognitive agent architecture. In Sect. 5, we present an example to illustrate how our social architecture can be used on a model of evacuation in the context of bush fires in Australia. Finally, Sect. 6 serves as a conclusion.

2   Related Works

Creating believable agents is a key point in social simulations. In this section, we present various works dealing with the integration of cognition, emotions or social relations in agents to improve the realism of social simulations.

2.1   Cognition in Social Agents

Adding cognition is a first step in order to increase the realism of social simulations [3,5]. To give a cognitive behavior to agents, some cognitive architectures have been proposed such as SOAR [26], ACT-R [13] or BDI [11], which is the most adapted to simulation context [3]. The BDI paradigm uses modal logic [14] to define the concepts of beliefs, desires and intentions that compose the mental state of the agent. It then provides logical links between these concepts and a collection of action plans to give a cognitive behavior to agents.

To ease its use, the BDI architecture has been implemented in different frameworks. A classic one is the Procedural Reasoning Systems (PRS) [28] which is based on three steps: firstly, a perception of the environment to update the belief base, then a deliberation between desires and the state of the world and finally the selection of an action to execute. PRS serves as a base for many other frameworks such as JACK [21], JADE [8] or Jadex [33].

Some researchers have tried to integrate the BDI architecture in modeling and simulation platforms. An extension to NetLogo [47] implements a simplified BDI architecture for educational purposes [38]. Sing and Padgham [40] decided to connect a multi-agent platform with an existing BDI framework (JACK or Jadex for example) and, in the same spirit, an application connecting the Matsim platform [6] with the GORITE BDI framework [36] has been proposed.

2.2   Emotional Architectures

Various works have shown that adding emotions to agents increases the believability of their behavior [7,29]. This improvement of credibility is useful in social simulations as the main goal of these simulations is to be as realistic as possible.

In psychology, there is no consensus about a unique emotional theory. The most used theory in AI is the cognitive appraisal theory of emotion [4,41] and more particularly the OCC theory [32] that is specifically developed to integrate emotions in artificial intelligence.

The OCC model of emotions defines twenty-two emotions distributed in eleven pairs according to the cognitive appraisal of a situation by an agent. This cognitive appraisal is made according to three aspects: the consequences of events, the actions of other agents and the aspect of objects.

Different implementations of emotional systems for multi-agent simulations have been proposed. For example, DETT (Disposition, Emotion, Trigger, Tendency) [46] considers the perception of a situation as the triggering condition to the creation of emotions based on the OCC model. Gratch and Marsella proposed a different approach with their EMA model [19] that not only creates emotions based on the appraisal of a situation thanks to appraisal variables, but which also study the coping behavior created by emotions. Finally, eBDI [23] proposes to integrate directly the OCC model into a BDI architecture.

2.3   Social Relation in Multi-agent Simulations

As people create social relations when living with other people, it seems logical to model social relations between agents that simulate humans. In [37], the agent's behavior is computed with a social-psychological model featuring personality, emotions and attitude of the agent against its environment. Gratch [18] adds a social level to modify the behavior of an agent according to the social state of the world.

In those models of social agents, social relations are represented with a finite number of variables, each one of them defining a precise dimension of the relation. As it is pointed out by Ochs [30], there is actually no consensus on the type and number of variables required to correctly model a social relation but four variables seem to be used more frequently than other ones. These variables correspond to the ones present in the dimensional model of interpersonal relation of Svennevig [44]:

- The degree of **liking** for another agent [22,34].
- The degree of **dominance** one agent has over another one [34,37]. It represents the degree of power an agent thinks having over another one.
- The degree of **solidarity** also known as the social distance [9,12]. It indicates the similarity in terms of desires, beliefs and values between two agents.
- The degree of **familiarity** that characterizes the number and the type (private/public) of information that can be transmitted to another agent [9].

In works cited above, social relations are studied as behavioral change factors, so they are only used as static variables. But obviously, a social relation between two people can evolve in time. To tackle this issue, Ochs [30] has proposed an agent architecture incorporating personality and using emotions to add dynamism to social relations to non playable characters of video games.

2.4 Synthesis

These three notions, cognition, emotions and social relations, have never been combined in simulation to provide a realistic behavior to social agents. Moreover, each of them has never been implemented to be easy to use for social scientists who do not have high level skills in computer science.

This paper aims at proposing an architecture for social simulation that deals with cognition, emotions and social relations and that can be used by modelers with low level skills in programming. To do so, we use the principles of the multi-agent simulation platform GAMA [20] that has proved its ease of use [27,35] thanks to its modeling language GAML that we extended to use our architecture.

3 Creating Emotions and Social Relations with Cognition

The main contribution of this article consists in defining a formalism to represent and to articulate mental states of a social agent. This mental state is composed of a cognitive state, an emotional state and social relations with other agents.

3.1 Representing Mental States of Agents

Representing the Cognition with Predicates. The cognitive part of our architecture is based on the BDI paradigm [11], in which agents have a belief base, a desire base and an intention base to store the cognitive states about the world. We also use a base for uncertain beliefs that are expected, called the uncertainty base, and used to create emotions about expected facts.

To represent this knowledge, we use predicates. A predicate unifies the representation of the information about the world so it can represent a situation, an event or an action. As the goal of this work is to create emotions from cognition about events and values of actions from other agents, we represent an information P caused by an agent j with a praiseworthiness value of pr by

$\mathbf{P}_{j,pr}$. The praiseworthiness value can be positive (in this case, the information P is praiseworthy) or negative (in this case, the information P is blameworthy). A predicate $\mathbf{P}_j$ represents an information caused by an agent j with any praiseworthiness value and a predicate $\mathbf{P}$ represents an information caused by any agent with any praiseworthiness value. We represent the opposite of a predicate P by **not P**.

Depending on the storage base, a predicate can be considered as a belief, an uncertain belief or a desire and it is represented as follows:

- **Belief$_i$(P):** indicates that the predicate P belongs to the belief base of the agent i.
- **Expect$_i$(P):** indicates that the predicate P belongs to the uncertainty base of the agent i.
- **Desire$_i$(P):** indicates that the predicate P belongs to the desire base of the agent i.

Formal Representation of Emotions. For the definition of emotion, we base our work on the OCC theory of emotions [32]. According to this theory, an emotion is a valued answer to the appraisal of a situation. As we use emotions to update dynamically social relations, our definition of an emotion also needs to contain the agent causing the emotion. With this definition, we represent an emotion by $\mathbf{E}_i(\mathbf{P}, \mathbf{A}, \mathbf{I}, \mathbf{D})$ with the following elements:

- **$\mathbf{E}_i$:** the name of the emotion felt by agent i.
- **P:** the predicate that represents the fact about which the emotion is expressed.
- **A:** the agent causing the emotion.
- **I:** the intensity of the emotion.
- **D:** the decay of the emotion's intensity.

For example, if an agent Alice feels fear about an action P caused by agent Bob with an intensity of 4.5 and a decay value of 0.6, this will be represented by the emotion Fear$_{Alice}(\mathrm{P}_{Bob}, \mathrm{Bob}, 4.5, 0.6)$. An emotion with no specific intensity nor decay is represented by $\mathbf{E}_i(\mathbf{P}, \mathbf{A})$ and an emotion with no specific agent causing it is represented by $\mathbf{E}_i(\mathbf{P})$.

Formalization of Social Relations. Based on the work of Svennevig [44] exposed in Sect. 2, we define a social link with another agent as a tuple <agent, liking, dominance, solidarity, familiarity> with the following elements:

- **Agent:** the agent concerned by the link, identified by its name.
- **Liking:** a real value between -1 and 1 representing the degree of liking with the agent concerned by the link. A value of -1 indicates that the concerned agent is hated, a value of 1 indicates that the concerned agent is liked.
- **Dominance:** a real value between -1 and 1 representing the degree of power exerted on the agent concerned by the link. A value of -1 indicates that the concerned agent is dominating, a value of 1 indicates that the concerned agent is dominated.

- **Solidarity:** a real value between 0 and 1 representing the degree of solidarity with the agent concerned by the link. A value of 0 indicates no solidarity with the concerned agent, a value of 1 indicates a complete solidarity with the concerned agent.
- **Familiarity:** a real value between 0 and 1 representing the degree of familiarity with the agent concerned by the link. A value of 0 indicates no familiarity with the concerned agent, a value of 1 indicates a complete familiarity with the concerned agent.

With this definition, a social relation is not necessarily symmetric. For example, let's take two agents, Alice and Bob, with a social link towards each other. The agent Bob may have a social link <Alice, 1, −0.5, 0.6, 0.8> (Bob likes Alice with a value of 1, he thinks he is dominated by Alice, he is solidary with Alice with a value of 0.6 and is familiar with Alice with a value of 0.8) and Alice may have a social link <Bob, −0.2, 0.2, 0.4, 0.5> (Alice dislikes Bob with a value of 0.2, she thinks she is dominating Bob, she is solidary with Bob with a value of 0.4 and she is familiar with Bob with a value of 0.5).

3.2   Creating Dynamics in Emotions and Social Relations

Dynamic Creation of Emotions. We base the automatic creation of emotions according to the mental states of the agent on the OCC model [32] and its logical formalism [1], which has been proposed to integrate the OCC model in a BDI architecture.

According to the OCC theory, emotions can be split into three groups: emotions linked to events, emotions linked to people and actions performed by people and emotions linked to objects In this work, as we focus on relations between social agents, we only work on the first two groups of emotions (emotions linked to events and people), so we do not deal with emotions related to objects.

The twenty emotions defined in this paper can be divided into three parts: eight emotions related to events, four emotions related to other agents and eight emotions related to actions. These twenty emotions are defined according to the logical formalism previously done [1]. Moreover, all the emotions are created without intensity nor decay value as there is no generic way to define them.

The eight emotions related to events have the following definition:

- $\mathbf{Joy}_i(\mathbf{P}_j, \mathbf{j}) = \mathrm{Belief}_i(P_j) \,\&\, \mathrm{Desire}_i(P)$
- $\mathbf{Sadness}_i(\mathbf{P}_j, \mathbf{j}) = \mathrm{Belief}_i(P_j) \,\&\, \mathrm{Desire}_i(\mathrm{not}\ P)$
- $\mathbf{Hope}_i(\mathbf{P}_j, \mathbf{j}) = \mathrm{Expect}_i(P_j) \,\&\, \mathrm{Desire}_i(P)$
- $\mathbf{Fear}_i(\mathbf{P}_j, \mathbf{j}) = \mathrm{Expect}_i(P_j) \,\&\, \mathrm{Desire}_i(\mathrm{not}\ P)$
- $\mathbf{Satisfaction}_i(\mathbf{P}_j, \mathbf{j}) = \mathrm{Hope}_i(P_j, \mathrm{j}) \,\&\, \mathrm{Belief}_i(P_j)$
- $\mathbf{Disappointment}_i(\mathbf{P}_j, \mathbf{j}) = \mathrm{Hope}_i(P_j, \mathrm{j}) \,\&\, \mathrm{Belief}_i(\mathrm{not}\ P_j)$
- $\mathbf{Relief}_i(\mathbf{P}_j, \mathbf{j}) = \mathrm{Fear}_i(P_j, \mathrm{j}) \,\&\, \mathrm{Belief}_i(\mathrm{not}\ P_j)$
- $\mathbf{Fearconfirmed}_i(\mathbf{P}_j, \mathbf{j}) = \mathrm{Fear}_i(P_j, \mathrm{j}) \,\&\, \mathrm{Belief}_i(P_j)$

On top of that, according to the logical formalism [1], four rules can be defined:

- The creation of **fear confirmed** or the creation of **relief** will replace the emotion of **fear**.
- The creation of **satisfaction** or the creation of **disappointment** will replace a **hope** emotion.
- The creation of **satisfaction** or **relief** leads to the creation of **joy**.
- The creation of **disappointment** or **fear confirmed** leads to the creation of **sadness**.

The four emotions linked to other agents have the following definition:

- $\mathbf{Happyfor}_i(\mathbf{P}, \mathbf{j}) =$ i likes j & $Joy_j(P)$
- $\mathbf{Sorryfor}_i(\mathbf{P}, \mathbf{j}) =$ i likes j & $Sadness_j(P)$
- $\mathbf{Resentment}_i(\mathbf{P}, \mathbf{j}) =$ i hates j & $Joy_j(P)$
- $\mathbf{Gloating}_i(\mathbf{P}, \mathbf{j}) =$ i hates j & $Sadness_j(P)$

The terms "i likes j" and "i hates j" have the following definitions:

- **i likes j:** agent i has a social relation with agent j with a positive liking value.
- **i hates j:** agent i has a social relation with agent j with a negative liking value.

Finally, the eight emotions linked to actions performed by agents have the following definition:

- $\mathbf{Pride}_i(\mathbf{P}_j, \mathbf{i}) = Belief_i(P_j)$ & P_i praiseworthy
- $\mathbf{Shame}_i(\mathbf{P}_j, \mathbf{i}) = Belief_i(P_j)$ & P_i blameworthy
- $\mathbf{Admiration}_i(\mathbf{P}_j, \mathbf{j}) = Belief_i(P_j)$ & P_j praiseworthy
- $\mathbf{Reproach}_i(\mathbf{P}_j, \mathbf{j}) = Belief_i(P_j)$ & P_j blameworthy
- $\mathbf{Gratification}_i(\mathbf{P}_j, \mathbf{i}) = Pride_i(P_j, i)$ & $Joy_i(P_i)$
- $\mathbf{Remorse}_i(\mathbf{P}_j, \mathbf{i}) = Shame_i(P_j, i)$ & $Sadness_i(P_i)$
- $\mathbf{Gratitude}_i(\mathbf{P}_j, \mathbf{j}) = Admiration_i(P_j, j)$ & $Joy_i(P_j)$
- $\mathbf{Anger}_i(\mathbf{P}_j, \mathbf{j}) = Reproach_i(P_j, j)$ & $Sadness_i(P_i)$

The terms "praiseworthy" and "blameworthy" have the following definitions:

- **praiseworthy:** indicates that the fact P has a positive praiseworthiness value.
- **blameworthy:** indicates that the fact P has a negative praiseworthiness value.

Updating Automatically Social Relations. As explained in Sect. 2, some works have shown that social relations are meant to be dynamic. Based on the previous work of Ochs [30], we integrate in our architecture a social engine that updates the social links of an agent according to its cognitive and emotive states.

In the following, we study the update of the social link <j, Liking, Dominance, Solidarity, Familiarity> possessed by agent i. Each variable of this social link evolves according to its own rule.

- **Liking:** according to Ortony [31], the degree of liking between two agents depends on the valence (positive or negative) of the emotions induced by the corresponding agent. In our model, *joy* and *hope* are considered as positive emotions (*satisfaction* and *relief* automatically raise *joy* in our engine) while *sadness* and *fear* are considered as negative emotions (*fear confirmed* and *disappointment* automatically raise *sadness* in our engine). This evolution is made by a fixed level α for each positive or negative emotion involved. Thus, the evolution is not related to the intensity of the concerned emotions as our engine creates emotions without intensities.

  Moreover, some works have shown that the degree of liking is influenced by the solidarity value [42]. The computation formulation can be formalized as follows with $nbPE(t)$ the number of positive emotions caused by agent j to agent i at time t, $nbNE(t)$ the number of negative emotions caused by agent j to agent i at time t and α the evolution coefficient between 0 and 1:

$$liking(t+1) = liking(t) * (1 + solidarity(t))$$
$$+ \alpha * (nbPE(t+1) - nbNE(t+1))$$

- **Dominance:** Keltner and Haid [24] and Shiota *et al.* [39] explain that an emotion of fear or sadness caused by another agent represents an inferior status. But Knutson [25] explains that perceiving fear and sadness in others increases the sensation of power over those persons. The computation formulation can be formalized as follows with $nbONE(t)$ the number of negative emotions caused by agent i to agent j at time t and $nbSNE(t)$ the number of negative emotions caused by agent j to agent i at time t and α the evolution coefficient between 0 and 1:

$$dominance(t+1) = dominance(t)$$
$$+ \alpha * (nbONE(t+1) - nbSNE(t+1))$$

- **Solidarity:** As explained in Sect. 2, the solidarity represents the degree of similarity of desires, beliefs and expectations between two agents. In our work, the evolution of the solidarity value depends on the ratio of similarity between the desires, beliefs and uncertainties between agent i and agent j. We compare the desire, belief and uncertainty bases of the two agents and look for similarities and differences. If the predicates are equal and have the same truth value, it is a similarity, otherwise, if the predicates are equal but with a different truth value, it is a difference. For each similarity (resp. difference), the solidarity value increases (resp. decreases) of one α level. On top of that, according to de Rivera and Grinkis [16], negative emotions tend to decrease the value of solidarity between two people. The computation formulation can be formalized as follows with $nbS(t)$ the number of similarities at time t and $nbD(t)$ the number of differences at time t, $nbNE(t)$ the number of negative emotions caused by agent j to agent i at time t and α the evolution coefficient between 0 and 1:

$$solidarity(t+1) = solidarity(t)$$
$$+ \alpha(nbS(t+1) - nbD(t+1) - nbNE(t+1))$$

- **Familiarity:** In psychology, emotions and cognition do not seem to impact the familiarity. However, Collins and Miller [15] explain that people tend to be more familiar with other people they appreciate. We model this notion by basing the evolution of the familiarity value on the liking value between two agents. The computation formulation can be formalized as follow:

$$familiarity(t+1) = familiarity(t) * (1 + liking(t+1))$$

4   An Agent Architecture Mixing Cognition, Emotions and Social Relations

The formalism proposed in this article has been used to enhance an existing agent architecture in order to ease the definition of social agents with a behavior combining cognition, emotions and social relations. The developed architecture has been implemented in GAMA, a modeling and multi-agent simulation platform [20].

4.1   Presentation of the Architecture

We integrate our work as an extension of the architecture presented in Fig. 1 which has been defined in [10].

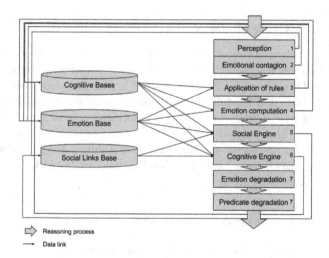

Fig. 1. Schema of our cognitive, emotional and social architecture

In this architecture, a predicate (see Sect. 3.1) is implemented with a tuple <Name, Values, Priority, Truth, Lifetime, Praiseworthiness, Cause_Agent> with the following elements:

- **Name** (mandatory): the name of the predicate.
- **Values** (optional): a map containing the values stored by the predicate.
- **Priority** (optional): a real positive priority value to compare two predicates.
- **Truth** (optional): a boolean value that indicates if the predicate is true or false.
- **Lifetime** (optional): an integer value that indicates the number of steps the predicate will exist.
- **Praiseworthiness** (optional): a real value between -1.0 and 1.0 that indicates if the predicate is praiseworthy (a positive value) or blameworthy (a negative value).
- **Cause_Agent** (optional): the agent causing the predicate.

We implement emotions defined in Sect. 3.1 as a tuple <Name, Predicate, Cause_Agent, Intensity, Decay> with the following elements:

- **Name** (mandatory): the name of the emotion.
- **Predicate** (optional): the predicate, identified by its name, that represents the fact about which the emotion is expressed.
- **Cause_Agent** (optional): the agent causing the emotion.
- **Intensity** (optional): a real positive value of the intensity of the emotion.
- **Decay** (optional): a real positive value which will be subtracted from the intensity value at the end of each time step.

We implement social relations with the tuple <agent, liking, dominance, solidarity, familiarity> as exposed in Sect. 3.1.

4.2 Reasoning Cycle of the Agent

The first step in the reasoning cycle of the agent with our architecture is the perception of the environment (step 1 in Fig. 1). Perception updates the beliefs of the agent and creates social links with other agents met. On the same model, the emotional contagion module (step 2) serves as an emotional perception of the environment as it updates the agent's emotions according to the emotions of agents nearby. This step of perception can be parametrized with different variables such as a distance value for example. Figure 2 shows a definition of a perception in GAML, the programming language of GAMA. This example enables to perceive "people" agents at a distance of 10 m.

```
perceive target:people in:10
```

Fig. 2. Definition of a perception in GAML

Then, the agent applies inference rules (step 3), defined by the modeler, to manage the belief base and the desire base according to its previous perceptions. This step gives a dynamic to the overall behavior as the agent can act according to a change in the environment. These inference rules can also be influenced by

```
rule belief:belief1 new_desire:desire1;
```

Fig. 3. Definition of an inference rule in GAML

emotions or social relations. Figure 3 shows the definition of an inference rule in GAML to create the desire "desire1" if the agent possesses the belief "belief1".

The emotion computation module (step 4) is the engine that creates automatically, with no intervention from the modeler, emotions. The emotions are created according to the rules defined in Sect. 3.2.

The social engine (step 5) is used to dynamically update the social relations of the agent. This evolution of social relations is based on the rules exposed in Sect. 3.2 and is done only with the other agents perceived. The idea is that a person updates its social relation with someone else only if they both are in contact. The same process is applied through our architecture.

The cognitive engine (step 6) is based on the BDI paradigm [11] and selects a desire to create a current intention. Then it selects a plan described by the modeler to answer the current intention. This whole process is influenced by the cognitive bases but also by the emotions and the social relations of the agent and, through the execution of plans, can influence back these bases. This cognitive engine is described in details in [45].

The final step of the reasoning cycle is the degradation of the agent's knowledge (step 7). The predicates stored in the cognitive bases are reduced in lifetime and the intensity of emotions are reduced by their decay value. This mechanism gives a temporal dynamic to the agent's behavior.

This architecture (with its new extension) is already available within the GAMA platform. Modelers can easily use it - with just few lines of codes - through the GAMA dedicated modeling language.

5   Example Case

The architecture defined in Sect. 4 has been used on the example case of an evacuation of a large open area during a bushfire in Australia.

5.1   Presentation of the Example

Bushfires in Australia. Bushfires are a true concern in Australia as they kill people and destroy properties each year. A study has been carried out to simulate the evacuation of an area during a bushfire using a BDI architecture to create the agent's behavior [2]. If the BDI model proposed in the cited paper shows interesting results in terms of replication of the real situation, it has some limitations.

The goal of this example, in our work, is not to provide a realistic model to simulate the evacuation of an area during a bushfire, but to show how to use emotions and social relations provided by our architecture. We take as a basis the model developed by [2] and we explain how to add emotions and social relations and how these new features can change the agents' behavior. Note that the proposed model of bushfires evacuation was implemented using the BDI architecture of GAMA platform [45], so adding new social and emotional properties to the agents only required to write few lines of code that we present here.

Description of the Basic Model. The basic model is made of an environment composed of buildings, shelters and fires and defines civil agents that will try to survive to fires. Shelters are safe places that can not be damaged by fire while buildings can burn. Fires are placed randomly in the environment and along the simulation, they can grow, propagate, burn buildings and people, and finally disappear.

The civil agents have two main behaviors: either they stay in their house and fight the fire or they escape to the nearest known shelter. In details, civil agents have a probability to be aware of the danger, a motivation value to escape and a motivation value to fight the fire that is different for each agent. When an agent perceives a fire within a certain distance, if this agent is aware of the danger, it will add desires both to stay and to escape. Depending on their motivation, they will chose the intention to fight or to flee. If the motivation to escape becomes bigger than the motivation to stay, the agent can decide to give up its fight and try to flee to a shelter.

5.2 Implementation of the Example Using the Developed Architecture

Adding Social Links Between Agents. We propose to improve the agent's behavior in terms of realism by giving them social relations. Social links between agents can be included at the start of the simulation or can dynamically appear during the simulation.

An example of social relation that can exist at the start of the simulation is a family relation. In the context of bushfires, we can easily imagine that two members of a family will try to help each other surviving the catastrophe.

From the point of view of the implementation, the modeler only need to add the family link in the initialization phase of the agent. This relationship will be represented by a social link with the family member with a familiarity value of 1.0 as shown in Fig. 4.

```
do add_social_link(
    new_social_link(familyMember) set_familiarity 1.0
);
```

Fig. 4. Definition of a family link

Social relations can also be used dynamically when agents are escaping to a shelter but do not know the shelter's location. When meeting another escaping agent, a social link is created. If the solidarity value of the link is high enough, the two agents will help each other going to a shelter.

After dynamically creating a social relation as shown in Fig. 5, the modeler only needs to change the plan to escape to make an agent follow another agent if there is a social link between them with a particular solidarity value.

```
perceive target: pedestrianBDI{
            socialize;
    }
```

Fig. 5. Definition of dynamic creation of social links

Creating Emotions to Change the Agents' Behavior. To add emotions to civil agents, we use the emotional module of our architecture that automatically creates emotions depending on the mental states of the agent.

The simulation runs a first time with no emotions as a training session. An agent that decided to escape after fighting the fire is proud to have fled if it is alive and its house is destroyed. This pride emotion increases its motivation to escape for a future fire. If it is alive and its house is not destroyed, it is ashamed to have fled and this emotion decreases the motivation to escape for a future fire.

The implementation consists in adding the belief that the agent is alive or dead, has tried to flee or not and its house is destroyed or not at the end of the training run of the simulation as shown by Fig. 6. Eventually, the modeler defines rules to change the internal motivations of the agent depending on its emotions as explained in Fig. 7.

```
do add_belief(flee with_praiseworthiness -1.0);
```

Fig. 6. Adding a belief corresponding to the state of the agent at the end of the training run

```
if(has_emotion(shameFlee)){
    if(escape_motivation>0.0){
        escape_motivation <-
        escape_motivation*(1.0-0.2);
    }
}
```

Fig. 7. Using a shame emotion to update the escape motivation

The complete model can be found at the following site: https://github.com/mathieuBourgais/ExampleModels.

5.3   Discussion

As shown by the implementation of the example, a modeler can easily enhance the behavior of his/her agents by just writing few lines of GAML code, the programming language of the GAMA platform. As shown by [27,35], this programming language is quite easy to learn and to use by social scientists who are not expert in computer science.

On top of that, modelers with more knowledge in programming and in AI can use our architecture deeper to create complex behaviors. For example, an expert user in emotions can easily manually redefine emotions thanks to the definition of inference rules or use multiple emotions with different intensities and different social links to create believable agents for social simulations.

6   Conclusion

In this paper, we have presented a formalism to use emotions and social relations in the modeling of cognitive social agents. This formalism has been integrated in an agent architecture and implemented in a multi-agent simulation platform to show its ease of use from the point of view of people not expert in programming. The example of bushfires in Australia indicates a way to use our work on the simulation of an evacuation in an open and large area.

In the future, we want to carry out experiments with modelers to test the ease of use of our architecture. We also plan to improve our work by adding a personality to create social agents more and more realistic while keeping in mind the constraint of easiness for modelers who are not expert in programming.

Acknowledgment. This work is partially supported by two public grants overseen by the French National Research Agency (ANR) as part of the program PRC (reference: ESCAPE ANR-16-CE39-0011-01 and ACTEUR ANR-14-CE22-0002).

References

1. Adam, C.: Emotions: from psychological theories to logical formalization and implementation in a BDI agent (2007)
2. Adam, C., Dugdale, J.: Comparing agent architectures in social simulation: BDI agents versus finite-state machines. In: HICSS (2016)
3. Adam, C., Gaudou, B.: BDI agents in social simulations: a survey. Knowl. Eng. Rev. **31**, 207–238 (2016)
4. Arnold, M.B.: Emotion and Personality. Columbia University Press (1960)
5. Balke, T., Gilbert, N.: How do agents make decisions? A survey. J. Artif. Soc. Soc. Simul. **17**(4), 1–3 (2014)
6. Balmer, M., Rieser, M., Meister, K., Charypar, D., Lefebvre, N., Nagel, K., Axhausen, K.: MATSim-T: architecture and simulation times. In: Multi-agent Systems for Traffic and Transportation Engineering (2009)
7. Bates, J.: The role of emotion in believable agents. Commun. ACM **37**, 122–125 (1994)

8. Bellifemine, F., Poggi, A., Rimassa, G.: JADE-A FIPA-compliant agent framework. In: Proceedings of PAAM, London (1999)
9. Bickmore, T., Cassell, J.: Relational agents: a model and implementation of building user trust. In: Proceedings of the SIGCHI Conference on Human Factors in Computing Systems. ACM (2001)
10. Bourgais, M., Taillandier, P., Vercouter, L.: An agent architecture coupling cognition and emotions for simulation of complex systems. In: SSC (2016)
11. Bratman, M.: Intentions, Plans, and Practical Reason. Harvard University Press (1987)
12. Brown, P., Levinson, S.C.: Politeness: Some Universals in Language Usage, vol. 4. Cambridge University Press, Cambridge (1987)
13. Byrne, M.D., Anderson, J.R.: Perception and action. In: The Atomic Components of Thought (1998)
14. Cohen, P.R., Levesque, H.J.: Intention is choice with commitment. Artif. Intell. **42**, 213–261 (1990)
15. Collins, N.L., Miller, L.C.: Self-disclosure and liking: a meta-analytic review. Psychol. Bull. **116**, 457–475 (1994)
16. de Rivera, J., Grinkis, C.: Emotions as social relationships. Motiv. Emot. **10**, 351–369 (1986)
17. Gilbert, N., Troitzsch, K.: Simulation for the Social Scientist. McGraw-Hill Education, London (2005)
18. Gratch, J.: Socially situated planning. In: Dautenhahn, K., Bond, A., Cañamero, L., Edmonds, B. (eds.) Socially Intelligent Agents. Springer, Boston (2002). https://doi.org/10.1007/0-306-47373-9_22
19. Gratch, J., Marsella, S.: A domain-independent framework for modeling emotion. Cogn. Syst. Res. **5**, 269–306 (2004)
20. Grignard, A., Taillandier, P., Gaudou, B., Vo, D.A., Huynh, N.Q., Drogoul, A.: GAMA 1.6: advancing the art of complex agent-based modeling and simulation. In: Boella, G., Elkind, E., Savarimuthu, B.T.R., Dignum, F., Purvis, M.K. (eds.) PRIMA 2013. LNCS (LNAI), vol. 8291, pp. 117–131. Springer, Heidelberg (2013). https://doi.org/10.1007/978-3-642-44927-7_9
21. Howden, N., Rönnquist, R., Hodgson, A., Lucas, A.: Jack intelligent agents-summary of an agent infrastructure. In: 5th International Conference on Autonomous Agents (2001)
22. Isbister, K.: Better Game Characters by Design: A Psychological Approach. Elsevier, San Francisco (2006)
23. Jiang, H., Vidal, J.M., Huhns, M.N.: EBDI: an architecture for emotional agents. In: Proceedings of the 6th International Joint Conference on Autonomous Agents and Multiagent Systems. ACM (2007)
24. Keltner, D., Haidt, J.: Social functions of emotions (2001)
25. Knutson, B.: Facial expressions of emotion influence interpersonal trait inferences. J. Nonverbal Behav. **20**, 165–182 (1996)
26. Laird, J.E., Newell, A., Rosenbloom, P.S.: SOAR: an architecture for general intelligence. Artif. Intell. **33**, 1–64 (1987)
27. Macatulad, E.G., Blanco, A.C.: 3DGIS-based multi-agent geosimulation and visualization of building evacuation using GAMA platform. In: The International Archives of Photogrammetry, Remote Sensing and Spatial Information Sciences (2014)
28. Myers, K.L.: User guide for the procedural reasoning system. Technical report, SRI International AI Center (1997)

29. Nair, R., Tambe, M., Marsella, S.: The role of emotions in multiagent teamwork. In: Who Needs Emotions (2005)

30. Ochs, M., Sabouret, N., Corruble, V.: Simulation of the dynamics of nonplayer characters' emotions and social relations in games. IEEE Trans. Comput. Intell. AI Games **1**, 281–297 (2009)

31. Ortony, A.: Value and emotion. In: Memories, Thoughts, and Emotions: Essays in Honor of George Mandler (1991)

32. Ortony, A., Clore, G.L., Collins, A.: The Cognitive Structure of Emotions. Cambridge University Press, Cambridge (1990)

33. Pokahr, A., Braubach, L., Lamersdorf, W.: Jadex: a BDI reasoning engine. In: Bordini, R.H., Dastani, M., Dix, J., El Fallah Seghrouchni, A. (eds.) Multi-Agent Programming. Springer, Boston (2005). https://doi.org/10.1007/0-387-26350-0_6

34. Prendinger, H., Ishizuka, M.: Social role awareness in animated agents. In: Proceedings of the Fifth International Conference on Autonomous Agents. ACM (2001)

35. Ramli, N.R., Razali, S., Osman, M.: An overview of simulation software for non-experts to perform multi-robot experiments. In: ISAMSR. IEEE (2015)

36. Rönnquist, R.: The goal oriented teams (GORITE) framework. In: Dastani, M., El Fallah Seghrouchni, A., Ricci, A., Winikoff, M. (eds.) ProMAS 2007. LNCS (LNAI), vol. 4908, pp. 27–41. Springer, Heidelberg (2008). https://doi.org/10.1007/978-3-540-79043-3_2

37. Rousseau, D., Hayes-Roth, B.: A social-psychological model for synthetic actors. In: Proceedings of the Second International Conference on Autonomous Agents. ACM (1998)

38. Sakellariou, I., Kefalas, P., Stamatopoulou, I.: Enhancing NetLogo to simulate BDI communicating agents. In: Darzentas, J., Vouros, G.A., Vosinakis, S., Arnellos, A. (eds.) SETN 2008. LNCS (LNAI), vol. 5138, pp. 263–275. Springer, Heidelberg (2008). https://doi.org/10.1007/978-3-540-87881-0_24

39. Shiota, M.N., Campos, B., Keltner, D., Hertenstein, M.J.: Positive emotion and the regulation of interpersonal relationships. In: The Regulation of Emotion (2004)

40. Singh, D., Padgham, L.: OpenSim: a framework for integrating agent-based models and simulation components. In: Frontiers in Artificial Intelligence and Applications, ECAI 2014, vol. 263. IOS Press (2014)

41. Smith, C.A., Lazarus, R.S.: Emotion and Adaptation. Psychology Press (1990)

42. Smith, E.R., Mackie, D.M., Claypool, H.M.: Social Psychology. Psychology Press, Hove (2014)

43. Sun, R.: Cognition and Multi-agent Interaction: From Cognitive Modeling to Social Simulation. Cambridge University Press, Cambridge (2006)

44. Svennevig, J.: Getting Acquainted in Conversation: A Study of Initial Interactions. John Benjamins Publishing, Amsterdam (2000)

45. Taillandier, P., Bourgais, M., Caillou, P., Adam, C., Gaudou, B.: A BDI agent architecture for the GAMA modeling and simulation platform. In: MABS (2016)

46. Van Dyke Parunak, H., Bisson, R., Brueckner, S., Matthews, R., Sauter, J.: A model of emotions for situated agents. In: Proceedings of the Fifth International Joint Conference on Autonomous Agents And Multiagent Systems. ACM (2006)

47. Wilensky, U., Evanston, I.: NetLogo: Center for Connected Learning and Computer-Based Modeling. Northwestern University, Evanston (1999)

An Initial Study of Agent Interconnectedness and In-Group Behaviour

F. Jordan Srour[1] and Neil Yorke-Smith[2,3(✉)]

[1] Adnan Kassar School of Business, Lebanese American University,
Beirut, Lebanon
`Jordan.Srour@lau.edu.lb`
[2] Delft University of Technology, Delft, The Netherlands
`n.yorke-smith@tudelft.nl`
[3] Olayan School of Business, American University of Beirut, Beirut, Lebanon

Abstract. This paper asks whether agent-based simulation can give insight into social factors surrounding corrupt behaviour in a technical process. The specific case study adopted, for studying the effects of social interconnectedness on corrupt behaviours, is the domain of maritime customs. Taking our previously-developed agent-based simulation, we add to the simulation a nuanced model of actor relatedness, consisting of clan, in-group (sect), and town of origin, and encode selected behavioural norms associated with these factors. Using the simulation, we examine the effects of social interconnectedness on domain performance metrics such as container outcomes, time, revenue, coercive demands, and collusion. Initial results confirm that as actor interconnectedness increases, established policies to combat corruption, such as process re-engineering, become less effective.

1 Introduction

This paper demonstrates that agent-based simulation offers a lens into otherwise obtuse and difficult-to-study behaviours: the effects of social interconnectedness on corruption. The World Bank offers a definition of corruption as "the misuse of public office for private gain" [25]. In socio-technical systems, whenever a process has the opportunity or obligation for actors to negotiate, then there is a possibility of corruption.

The negative repercussions of corruption upon institutions, societies, and nations include poverty, tax evasion, political instability, weakened democracy and rule of law, and reduced national competitiveness. Furthermore, corruption—whether *collusive* or *coercive*—reinforces disenfranchisement and hinders development, being "one of the most serious barriers to overcoming poverty" with a strong correlation between perceived corruption and income per capita [26].

It is known that the interconnectedness of actors is an antecedent for collective corruption, which in turn can lead to endemic corruption [14,17] and its

© Springer International Publishing AG, part of Springer Nature 2018
G. P. Dimuro and L. Antunes (Eds.): MABS 2017, LNAI 10798, pp. 105–120, 2018.
https://doi.org/10.1007/978-3-319-91587-6_8

many repercussions. For example, studies in Eastern Europe noted how government structures can allow for the formation of elite cliques which can design and coordinate entire networks of corruption [12]. Studies in China explored the influence of corrupt in-group networks which, in situations of collective corruption, tend towards rewriting norms and thus legitimizing further corruption [6].

Previous work on social interconnectedness and corruption falls into two broad categories. The first—exemplified by the studies in cited above—examines observed in-practice behaviours, usually in a particular societal context. The second category of work uses mathematical modelling or simulation—sometimes agent-based simulation [22]—to examine in-theory behaviours in a synthetic or stylized setting.

Our work initially reported in this paper provides a blend of these two approaches. We adopt agent-based simulation as a tool to study corrupt behaviours, but in a validated simulation of an actual case study domain: maritime customs, namely the import of sea-based containers. The domain is in itself important, because customs revenue contributes can comprise a notable component of public finances, particularly in developing countries, and the Organization for Economic Co-operation and Development (OECD) finds that widespread corruption often hampers customs efficiency [10].

The paper is structured as follows. After providing background (Sect. 2) and a brief review of related work (Sect. 3), we build on our extant agent-based simulation of maritime customs imports [24]. The goal of the simulation model is not to simulate precise behaviours or to make quantitative forecasts, but to simulate archetypal process deviations and suggest possible qualitative outcomes of policy and reform measures.

To the extant simulation we add a nuanced model of actor relatedness, consisting of clan, in-group (sect), and town of origin, and encode associated behavioural norms (Sect. 4).

We examine the effects of social interconnectedness on domain performance metrics, such as revenue collected and revenue diverted, container outcomes, time, and instances and type of corrupt practices (Sect. 5). Initial results reported in this paper confirm that, when corruption is widespread, localized punitive- or incentive-based policies are further weakened, and that the effect of process re-engineering, which has been found to offer more promise, is frustrated as interconnectedness increases beyond a critical point.

We conclude the paper by noting future work from the starting point we report here (Sect. 6).

2   Background

A port, including its customs import and export processes, can be seen as an instance of a complex socio-technical system with multiple stakeholders. The literature concludes that customs corruption not only has serious implications, but that it is not easily combated by policy changes, that reform policies can have unexpected side-effects, and that a broadly-based, systemic approach is required [13, 16, 19].

It is argued that in order to counter established, widespread corrupt practices, a deeper understanding is required of the processes in which corruption features, together with a deeper understanding of the corrupt practices that occur, within the broader socio-political, socio-economic, governmental and cultural situation [1,10,13,17].

A crucial role in the process of moving a container through customs is played by the *freight forwarder* (FF), a company that manages and organizes shipments for others. The process is based on a match between shipping documents and customs documents. If this match is made and the involved actors are considered trustworthy, then the container may proceed following payment of standard duties. Otherwise, or if it should be randomly selected, the container then is subject to search and may see additional duties or fines. The import of each container can be seen as one round in a repeated game between a mostly fixed set of agents, who have specified and fixed roles.

Possible *deviations* from an archetypal customs import process (see Fig. 1) include incomplete, inaccurate, or fictitious documentation; waived or additional inspection; inaccurate value estimation; waiving true fines or imposing additional fines; and delaying or expediting certain containers. Although outside our scope, in some situations a whole grey 'parallel customs' system evolves [11,17].

Policy efforts led by the International Monetary Fund, OECD, World Customs Organization, World Bank, and other organizations have focused on reducing trade barriers, reforming trade procedures, and building 'cultures of integrity'. As the contemporary political economy literature concludes, such policy engineering has, more than not, proved ineffective [13,16,19,20].

3   Related Work

Agent-based models and multi-agent-based simulation (MABS) have been successful in maritime container logistics, port management, and transport policy analysis. Agent-based simulation has also been used to study corruption. Hammond [7] develops an agent-based population model in an effort to explain shifts in corruption levels. Corruption is modelled as a simple, game-theoretic repeated interaction on the micro level. In a tax-evasion domain, endogenous shifts in global corruption levels are observed as emerging from the micro-behaviour.

Situngkir [22] is interested in the link between corrupt behaviours in individual agents and the normative societal and cultural environment in which they interact. He builds a MABS inspired by corrupt bureaucrats in Indonesia and obtains system-wide results. However the model is highly stylized and does not capture a real process in any detail.

Our previous work adopted MABS to study customs process and corruption of a Mediterranean container port [23,24]. Although the model featured a simple construct of agent interconnectedness, we did not study the effects of this aspect of the organization on the performance metrics.

From an anthropological perspective, Makhoul [15] study interconnectedness and in-group effects in a Mediterranean Arab context, while Sidani and Gardner

[21] study work practices, including corruption. Roman and Miller [18] find that status in social hierarchy and familial connections are "precursors" for corruption. Ferreira et al. [5] show the importance of in/out-group agent behaviour.

Abdallah et al. [1], among studies of social behaviour, demonstrate that peer-punishment is more effective than an overly strong centralized punishment in promoting cooperation, if actors are able to bribe centralized authorities.

Bloomquist and Koehler [2] simulate individuals' compliance to tax regulations. Elsenbroicha and Badham [4] develop a simulation of extortion, noting the importance of social factors beyond game-theoretic models. Lauchs et al. [14] apply social network simulation for the case of a real corrupt police network.

Besides MABS focused on illicit or corrupt behaviour, the literature is extensive on simulation studies of norms, social networks, and organizational effects. We mention just Villatoro et al. [27], who highlight how agents' norm internalization can provide an alternative regulation mechanism when external regulation is difficult, such as when the regulative agents are themselves corrupt.

Generalizing from the literature, empirical study of corruption by means of simulation—and, we argue, MABS in particular—offers a lens into otherwise obtuse and difficult-to-study behaviours.

4   Simulation Model

Our work focuses on ports in high-corruption Mediterranean countries. In this section we outline the simulation model with emphasis on the developments in the model in the present work, which concern agent interconnectedness. For background on the domain and a full description of the basic model, we refer to our earlier papers [8, 23, 24].

The simulation models collusive and coercive corruption, in-group relationships, and agents' adaptive behaviours in negotiation. At the heart of the MABS are the actors' progression through the documented processes for each shipment, the points of possible deviation, the decisions whether to engage in—or how to respond to—non-standard practices, and the negotiation that may ensue.

Basic Model [24]. We describe the role of the main agents, and then describe the process in which they interact.

Owner's Agent (OA). Decides what to declare based on the tariff for the actual container contents, and estimates of the cost of bribes necessary and probability of inspection.

Freight Forwarder (FF). Offers bribe to the Customs Officer (CO), part of which will be passed on to other actors in customs, to expedite container if its due date is close. Offer a bribe to the Head Customs Officer (HCO) to obtain assignment to a preferred CO, i.e., a CO to whom the FF has a relationship. Offers bribe to CO obtain a GREEN decision if the expected cost of doing so is less than the cost of fines and fees; assumes that all COs will accept a bribe of sufficient amount (a warranted assumption when corruption is endemic). If the CO demands, will increase bribe amount up to the maximum amount where expected cost would

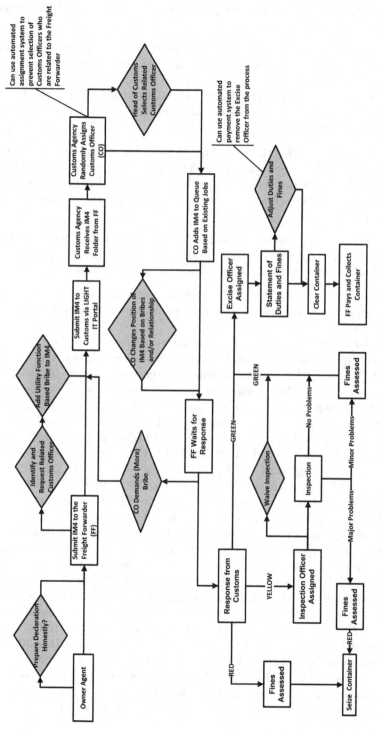

Fig. 1. Flowchart of archetypal import process as implemented in the MABS [24].

exceed expected value. Routinely offers tips. We include the role of the customs broker [11] into the FF.

Customs Officer (CO). Unless opposed to bribes in principle, accepts any bribe of sufficient amount, to either expedite the container, waive inspection, or change decision outcome. May demand a bribe if none offered or if its amount is too low. May impose an unnecessary inspection unless bribed. Works slowly on a container unless given a tip. Always declares GREEN a container whose owner or consignee is related closely enough.

Head Customs Officer (HCO). Supportive of the COs, turns blind eye to non-standard practices [11]. Does not overrule a CO's decision, except for RED decisions for a sufficient bribe. Will override the departmental IT system's assignment of container to a CO, for a sufficient bribe. HIO and HEO behave similarly to the HCO.

Inspection Officer (IO). Unless opposed to bribes in principle, accepts any bribe of sufficient amount, to waive or expedite the inspection, to or report a different contents than the actual found. Works slowly unless given a tip.

Excise Officer (EO). Unless opposed to bribes in principle, accepts any bribe of sufficient amount, to set lower duty than the published tariff rules. Works slowly unless given a tip.

We model the documented customs **process** as follows (Fig. 1): (1) owner's agent submits documents ('IM4') to the freight forwarder company, which assigns a specific FF agent; (2) FF submits documents to customs agency via the *LIGHT* electronic portal; (3) *LIGHT* assigns the case to a specific customs officer (CO); (4) the CO sees output of the *STAR* computer system and can override: the decision is RED (fines imposed, seize container), YELLOW (inspect container), or GREEN (approve container, duty imposed); (5) if inspection is required, *LIGHT* assigns a specific inspection officer (IO); (6) the IO inspects the container and sends the report to the CO via *STAR*; (7) the CO revises a YELLOW decision to RED or GREEN and informs the FF; (8) approved GREEN containers proceed to the Excise Department and are assigned by *LIGHT* to a specific excise officer (EO); (9) the EO computes the final duty, fines (if any), and other costs (handling, storage, etc.) and informs the FF; (10) the FF pays the due amount (plus applicable interest); and (11) the CO approves the release of the container. The heads of the respective departments can override both the assignment of officers (by *LIGHT*) and the decisions of officers (in *STAR*).

Indicated in grey in Fig. 1, **deviations** can occur from the documented process as follows. First, the FF can offer bribes (to the HCO) to attempt to obtain its preferred CO, (to the HCO or CO) to expedite the container, (to the CO) to have duties reduced, or (to the CO) to have a *deviant* container (i.e., illegal or misdeclared) pass through as GREEN. Second, the HCO can accept a bribe and assign the preferred CO. Third, the CO can accept a bribe (collusive), or it can demand (more) bribe (coercive). Fourth, the IO can waive, expedite, or report differently the inspection. Fifth, the EO can change the amount due.

Lastly, **audits** occur randomly at two points in the process. We assume in this paper that audits are effective, and will find the actual container contents and value. The first audit point is after IO's inspection. The second audit point is after the CO's decision. The audits constitute a learning opportunity: the deviational behaviour of all customs actors are reinforced if they are not caught by audit, but the behaviour is reduced if caught. For example, a CO that accepted a bribe and was not caught is more likely to accept bribes in future, but one that was caught is less likely. For the FF, whether a deviant container made it through as GREEN or was stopped as RED (whether by a customs employee or by audit) is a learning opportunity about bribe success and amounts, and CO characteristics.

In-Group Relationships. The degree to which two agents share an affinity, and the obligations that come from such an in-group relationship, is a cornerstone of business and society in all Arab and many other Mediterranean countries [9,13,21]. As we noted earlier, interconnectedness of actors is an antecedent for various forms of corruption.

We capture such relationships by a three-part profile of each agent's clan (family relationship), in-group (e.g., sect), and ancestral place of origin (village, town, or city quarter). The form of relationship modelled is the same as our previous work, but the instantiation of the profiles is richer and the behavioural accommodation of agents in the simulation according to their relationship with other agents is now implemented, rather than comprising a token effect. In fact, although we previously identified their potential relevance, the effect of interconnectedness on the simulation results was unexplored in our previous work.

An agent's profile is instantiated as follows. First, the clan is chosen randomly among the set of clans, labelled $1, \ldots, C$. Second, the agent's origin ('town') is set based on the clan. Towns are divided logarithmically from largest clan (1) to smallest (C): clan 1, the largest clan, has approximately $\frac{1}{2}$ of the towns; clan 2 has approximately $\frac{1}{2}$ of the remainder, and so on, with the constraint that every clan has at least one town. If the agent is to live in one of its clan's towns (based on chance), the town is assigned randomly among them; otherwise the town is assigned randomly from all the other clans' towns. Third, the agent's sect is set based on the town. Note that this means that not every agent from a given clan will have the same sect. Let s_t be the sect of the majority clan of town t. If the agent is to have the sect of the town it is living in, it is assigned sect s_t; otherwise it is assigned a sect randomly from all the other sects.

Based on the relationship between two agents, the propensity to offer, accept, and demand bribes, the bribe amounts, and customs actor behaviours (e.g., cooperation with requests, speed of work, inspection decisions, assessed tariff levels, fines raised/waived), may all change. An agent quantifies its relationship with another agent as two parts: static relationship (closeness between profiles) and dynamic trustworthiness (based on interactions to date with the other agent). These two parts capture respectively pedigree and performance. They are combined linearly, with equal weight.

Static relationship is defined as the weighted mean of three factors:

$$\frac{1}{6}(3 * sameClan? + 2 * sameSect? + sameOrigin?)$$

Exploration of different weights is left for future work.

Dynamic relationship depends on the agent type (CO, IO, etc) and the agent's remembered history of interactions with the other agent. For example, for a FF agent assessing its relationship with a CO agent, factors include: % of bribes accepted, % of containers approved, % of favours done, and number of interactions. This can be seen a computation of one agent's emergent trust in another; social trust in illicit networks is necessary for their function [14]. The FF considers all the COs it knows about, and—assuming the net expected utility is favourable, after accounting for expected cost including fines if caught—offers a bribe to the HCO to have its preferred CO selected.

Notwithstanding the computed interconnectedness, the strongest component of relationship in Arab culture is familial. If two agents hail from the same clan, then cultural norms require that they act selflessly for the welfare of the other [15]. Hence, a CO will accept a bribe from a family member even if the expected value of the bribe is negative. The Head Customs Officer will, for a family member in the customs department, assign more lucrative work, and for a related FF, readily assign a container to the FF's preferred CO.

The final major development in the model is the role of the assigned Customs Officer as what we might call the 'corrupt ambassador' of the containers assigned to him by the HCO, should the CO accept a bribe. In effect, having accepted a bribe for a container, it is in the CO's interest to ensure that the container receives favourable treatment from the subsequent customs actors; it is the CO who decides how much of the bribe to allocate to the latter agents. Here, we model behaviour in the studied port customs system, but also effectively encode a norm that might emerge in a repeated game setting: COs who accept a bribe, but fail to deliver on their side of the implied bargain, will in the long term be 'punished' by the FFs who learn that the CO is not trustworthy.

5   Experiments on Agent Interconnectedness

We implemented the simulation using the Java-based agent toolkit Jadex [3]. Compared with dedicated MABS environments (e.g., MASON, NetLogo, Repast), Jadex readily allows BDI-style agents, i.e., agents with explicit representations of beliefs, goals, and plans; and it also provides simulation support. The development, calibration, and validation and verification of the MABS are treated in our earlier paper [24]. Results reported here cannot be compared directly with those of our earlier model [24], however, due to the developments in the model outlined in the previous section, and to minor changes in how the Key Performance Indicator (KPI) metrics are computed.

Table 1. Main simulation parameters [24].

Parameter	Baseline value
Illicit container %	10%
Standard tariff rate	5–10%
VAT rate	10%
Fine penalty	10x tariff
Chance of inspection	25%
Inspection success	80%
Chance of audit	2%
Audit penalty	6x salary
Work-slow ratio	3 times
CO collusive propensity	75%
CO coercive propensity	60%
Number of clans	50
Number of in-groups (sects)	16
Number of towns of origin	6

Baseline Results. Table 1 gives the baseline parameter values extrapolated from the modelled system [24]. Note that the baseline number of clans yields a 2% chance of the FF and CO being related. The baseline value of the number of places of origin ('towns') is small, reflecting the six main regions of the country of the modelled port.

The baseline parameters produced the KPIs reported in Table 2. Results reported are averaged over 100 runs of 1,600 containers each. Metrics are reported as the average per container, with the exception of the percentage columns, which reflect the total proportion of all containers. Note that column Time is total elapsed time between submission of a container to the customs department and its release (or seizure) from customs; it does not include the time that the container waits with the FF prior to its submission.

In the second section of rows of Table 2, we report the effects of a range of localized policy measures; and in the third section, characteristic process re-engineering measures identified in the literature as promising. The former localized measures are: moral reform campaigns (leading to greater honesty by the owner (50% less willing to permit bribe), or less (by 50%) collusive or coercive behaviour by customs staff), higher tariffs (x4), punitive fines on owners (x4), more inspection (x2), perfect inspection (a deviant container will always be revealed, if inspected), more customs staff (x2), higher customs salaries (x5), more audits (x3, x10, or 100%), and higher penalties on caught customs staff (x10).

The latter process re-engineering measures are respectively (1) strengthening the *LIGHT* IT system, so that allocations of containers to Customs Officers

Table 2. Snapshot KPI results for baseline scenario, localized policy changes, and process re-engineering.

Experiment	Time (hrs)	Delay (hrs)	Cost ($)	Deviations	Iterations	% Illicit	% Not caught deviant	Revenue ($)	Bribe ($)
Baseline	2703	14345	34191	48.20	6.38	10.08	97.04	22286	3282
Owner honesty	2470	13439	35266	47.28	6.24	9.88	96.88	24179	3052
Lower collusion	715	270	28782	14.79	1.57	9.91	97.82	20767	756
Lower coercion	1498	5390	35843	34.80	4.42	10.06	96.69	25743	2128
Higher tariff	2935	15513	93666	49.36	6.55	9.98	96.77	80312	3376
Punitive fines	2958	15864	71506	49.35	6.55	9.99	96.81	59158	3371
More inspection	3713	37286	34277	83.02	11.43	9.93	97.10	18180	6168
Perfect inspection	2928	20712	36462	57.71	7.78	9.92	96.73	23502	4025
More staff	601	853	32674	41.95	5.46	9.98	97.35	21147	2931
Higher salary	2565	14625	49330	49.89	6.63	10.03	97.28	21822	15656
More audits	1885	5367	31990	34.17	4.33	9.89	96.95	21040	2469
Many more audits	433	147	36817	15.92	2.31	10.13	94.10	25075	1311
100% audits	386	67	44841	9.01	1.11	10.06	82.02	33757	1708
Higher penalties	2096	10385	47189	35.70	6.23	10.17	96.49	33467	848
Empowered IT system	2153	11724	31965	37.52	6.52	10.14	96.61	23360	803
Electronic payment	2646	16338	34510	49.76	6.89	10.06	97.14	22260	3520
IT & electronic	1935	9787	31374	33.91	6.20	9.87	96.71	22846	786
Static relationships	2409	21014	33156	57.40	7.73	10.10	97.55	20340	3962

Table 3. Correlation between independent variables (rows) and dependent variables (columns). Significance codes: *** < 0.001, ** < 0.01, * < 0.05, · < 0.1

input	% Not caught: Illicit	% Not caught: All deviant	Cost	Fee	Tariff + Fine	Bribe Revenue	% Diverted	Time Delay	Iterations	CO–FF linkage: Static	CO–FF linkage: Total	% Deviations Audited	Cost of Enforcement
clans	***		***	*	*	***	*	***	***	***	***	***	
ingroups	·	*	*		·	*		·	*	**	***	*	
hometowns	***	*	***	*	*	*		*	*	**	***	*	
adaptive	*		***	·	***	*		**	***			***	
process		***	·		***	*		**	***			·	
illicit	**	***					***						
tariff			*	***	**	***	***		*			*	
fine			***	***	***	***	***				*		
staff		*	***	***						·			***
audit	***			***	**	***	***					***	***
penalty			***	***	***	***	***		·				

cannot be overridden by the HCO, (2) streamlining payment sub-process so that the EOs no longer have an intermediary role, and (3) both measures combined together.

In the final row of Table 2, we report the effect of regressing the model to purely static (profile-based) relationship computation. The most interesting observation is that the number of CO–FF iterations and the number of deviations both increase, along with the average bribe value. We attribute this to the FF not taking into account dynamically which COs are more conducive and which will accept lower bribes for the same action. A similar effect occurs if agents' adaptive (learning) behaviour is disabled.

Effect of Interconnectedness. We systematically explored the parameter space of clans ($C = [2, 100]$), in-groups ($S = [2, 128]$), and places of origin ($T = [2, 48]$). We performed pairwise type-2 ANOVA tests between the independent variables (*clans, sects, towns, process, illicit%, tariff, fine, staff, audit, audit-penalty*) and the dependent variables (all the metrics of Table 2, together with additional variables, including internal variables such as the relationship between CO and FF). Variable *process* takes discrete levels $\{0, \ldots, 3\}$, corresponding respectively to the regular process, empowered IT, electronic payment, or both. Table 3 reports the significance levels of the ANOVA p-values. The initial results reported here have the limitation that we did not condition on *process*.

Clans appears to be the most significant relatedness variable. As the number of clans decrease, the chance of any two agents being 'statically' related, i.e., through the familial linkage, increases. There is a significant effect on the percentage illicit containers not caught (higher), on the FF's fee (lower), on the bribe amount (lower), on delay (lower), and on the number of FF-CO iterations (fewer); and some effect on other output variables. The number of process deviations increases, because of the increased interconnectedness and with it the reduced risk of the FF's bribe being rejected.

Second, as with clans, when the number of **sects** decrease, the chance of agents' static linkage increases. The effect is weaker than that of clans, but still with some significant effect on fee, number of iterations, and number of deviations. Third, as the number of **towns** decrease, again the chance of agents' static linkage increases. There is a significant effect on percentage deviant not caught and on fee, and some effect on bribe, delay, number of iterations, and number of deviations.

Effect of Process *on* Clans. In order to begin to examine the effect of interconnectedness on process re-engineering, we plot *bribe, delay, revenue,* and *iterations* versus *clans*, for each of the four values of *process*.

Because the data points correspond to simulation scenarios with many values of other input variables (e.g., *tariff*), Fig. 2 plots locally weighted regressions to smooth misleading variation. Note that we conducted more exploration of the parameter space for values of clans in [10, 25], meaning more data points in this region coming from more values of other variables, and hence more variation.

Neither the trends in figure nor the variation should not be attributed excessive significance. Rather, the point indicated is that greater interconnectedness, i.e., fewer clans, beyond a critical point (around $C = 10$) tends to lead to greater corruption, whatever the process variation.

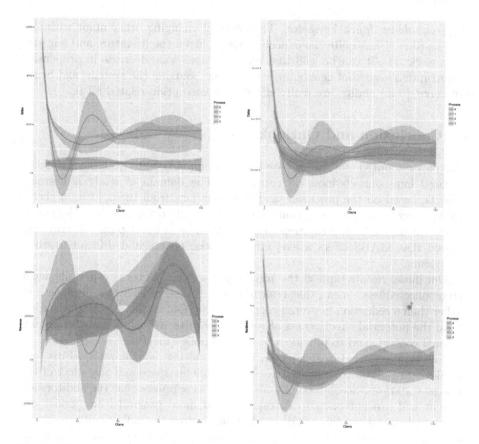

Fig. 2. Effect of *clans* on four KPIs (*bribe, delay, revenue, iterations*), factored by *process*. Shaded areas depict errors of the fitted lines.

Effect of Other Variables. To conclude the analysis, we briefly note the observed effects of other parameters.

Process Input Variables. Whether the agents are adaptive or not has little effect on bribe levels, but significant effect on the percentage of uncaught deviant containers, fee, number of iterations, and number of deviations. It has some effect on most other KPI variables, notably delay. The process variations through re-engineering have significant impact on bribe level, because the empowered

IT system reduces the incidence of preferred COs. However, the effect on CO–FF linkage overall is not significant. We attribute this to the static agent linkages (which process changes do not directly address) and to the continuation of dynamic linkages between those agents who interact in non-automated steps of the customs process.

Non-relatedness Input Variables. The effect of changing other input variables such as *illicit%* has quite the expected effects, given the literature and our previous work [24]. It can be said that only a system-wide decrease in propensity to corruption across all agents, or external (i.e., outside the system, and hence not corruptible) audits, are really effective on corruption-related KPIs.

6   Conclusion and Outlook

This paper adopted multiagent-based simulation (MABS) to examine the effects of social interconnectedness on corruption. The domain of study is customs imports, based on the processes, and the deviations from them, at an archetypal Mediterranean port in a context of widespread corruption. The domain is important due to its contribution to public finances in developing countries. We showed that MABS offers a lens into otherwise obtuse and difficult-to-study behaviours.

Our initial results support the argument that social factors—especially agent interconnectedness—mean that reform measures tend to lead to a displacement rather than a reduction in overall corruption [20]. Our ultimate goal is to understand the potential effectiveness of reform measures in their social and organizational context, and to provide a tool to aid policy makers.

The work reported in this paper, while promising, is exploratory. First, our simulation results incompletely treat the parameter space and the effect of the process variations. Second, our simulation model supposes that the auditors are diligent and are not open to corruption; and more generally, our model can be expanded in scope by including additional actors (including auditor agents) and enhancing individual agent negotiation behaviours. Third, while we examine the effect of agent interconnectedness on policy efficacy, we have not examined specific social network structures. Fourth, in view of the existing case studies on tackling endemic corruption, interesting connections with several MABS topics are norm change mechanisms, norm internalization [27], and evolution of norms in a social network.

Acknowledgements. We thank the MABS'17 anonymous reviewers and the workshop participants in São Paulo. Thanks to A. Komashie and B. Reinsberg. This work was supported in part by University Research Board grant numbers A88813 and 288810 from the American University of Beirut. Author NYS also gives thanks to the fellowship at St Edmund's College, Cambridge.

References

1. Abdallah, S., Sayed, R., Rahwan, I., LeVeck, B.L., Cebrian, M., Rutherford, A., Fowler, J.H.: Corruption drives the emergence of civil society. J. Roy. Soc. Interface **11**(93), 20131044 (2014)
2. Bloomquist, K.M., Koehler, M.: A large-scale agent-based model of taxpayer reporting compliance. J. Artif. Soc. Soc. Simul. **18**(2), 20 (2015)
3. Braubach, L., Pokahr, A.: The jadex project: simulation. In: Ganzha, M., Jain, L. (eds.) Multiagent Systems and Applications. ISRL, vol. 45, pp. 107–128. Springer, Heidelberg (2013). https://doi.org/10.1007/978-3-642-33323-1_5
4. Elsenbroich, C., Badham, J.: The extortion relationship: a computational analysis. J. Artif. Soc. Soc. Simul. **19**(4), 8 (2016)
5. Ferreira, N., Mascarenhas, S., Paiva, A., di Tosto, G., Dignum, F., McBreen, J., Degens, N., Hofstede, G.J., Andrighetto, G., Conte, R.: An agent model for the appraisal of normative events based in in-group and out-group relations. In: Proceedings of AAAI 2013, pp. 1220–1226 (2013)
6. Gong, T.: Dangerous collusion: corruption as a collective venture in contemporary China. Communist Post-Communist Stud. **35**(1), 85–103 (2002)
7. Hammond, R.: Endogenous transition dynamics in corruption: an agent-based computer model. Working Paper 19. Brookings Institution (2000)
8. Harb, H., Srour, F.J., Yorke-Smith, N.: A case study in model selection for policy engineering: simulating maritime customs. In: Dechesne, F., Hattori, H., ter Mors, A., Such, J.M., Weyns, D., Dignum, F. (eds.) AAMAS 2011. LNCS (LNAI), vol. 7068, pp. 3–18. Springer, Heidelberg (2012). https://doi.org/10.1007/978-3-642-27216-5_2
9. Horden, P., Purcell, N.: The Corrupting Sea: A Study of Mediterranean History. Blackwell, Oxford (2000)
10. Hors, I.: Fighting corruption in customs administration: what can we learn from recent experiences? OECD Development Centre Working Paper 175, OECD (2001)
11. Illeik, H.: Port of Beirut: a sea of corruption. Al Akhbar, 11 January 2012. https://english.al-akhbar.com/node/3261/
12. Jancsics, D., Jávor, I.: Corrupt governmental networks. Int. Public Manag. J. **15**, 62–99 (2012)
13. Johnston, M.: Syndroms of Corruption: Wealth, Power, and Democracy. Cambridge University Press, New York (2005)
14. Lauchs, M., Keast, R., Yousefpour, N.: Corrupt police networks: uncovering hidden relationship patterns, functions and roles. Polic. Soc. **21**(1), 110–127 (2011)
15. Makhoul, J., Harrison, L.: Intercessory wasta and village development in Lebanon. Arab Stud. Q. **26**(3), 25–41 (2004)
16. Mungiu-Pippidi, A.: The Quest for Good Governance: How Societies Develop Control of Corruption. Cambridge University Press, Cambridge (2015)
17. Nardin, L.G., Andrighetto, G., Conte, R., Székely, Á., Anzola, D., Elsenbroich, C., Lotzmann, U., Neumann, M., Punzo, V., Troitzsch, K.G.: Simulating protection rackets: a case study of the Sicilian Mafia. Auton. Agent. Multi-agent Syst. **30**(6), 1117–1147 (2016)
18. Roman, A.V., Miller, H.T.: Building social cohesion: family, friends, and corruption. Adm. Soc. **46**(7), 775–795 (2014)
19. Rose-Ackerman, S.: Corruption and government. Int. Peacekeeping **15**(3), 328–343 (2008)

20. Sequeira, S.: Displacing corruption: evidence from a tariff liberalization program (2013). http://personal.lse.ac.uk/sequeira/Displacing_Corruption_Sequeira. pdf. Accessed 28 Sept 2015
21. Sidani, Y., Gardner, W.L.: Work values in the Arab culture: the case of Lebanese workers. J. Soc. Psychol. **140**(5), 597–607 (2000)
22. Situngkir, H.: Money-scape: a generic agent-based model of corruption. Computational Economics Archive 0405008. EconWP (2004)
23. Srour, F.J., Yorke-Smith, N.: Towards agent-based simulation of maritime customs. In: Proceedings of AAMAS 2015, pp. 1637–1638 (2015)
24. Srour, F.J., Yorke-Smith, N.: Assessing maritime customs process re-engineering using agent-based simulation. In: Proceedings of AAMAS 2016, pp. 786–795 (2016)
25. The World Bank. Helping countries combat corruption: The role of the World Bank (1997). www1.worldbank.org/publicsector/anticorrupt/corruptn/ coridx.htm. Accessed 16 Dec 2016
26. Transparency International. The Global Corruption Report 2004: Political corruption (2004). www.transparency.org/whatwedo/publication/global_corruption_ report_2004_political_corruption. Accessed 16 Dec 2016
27. Villatoro, D., Andrighetto, G., Conte, R., Sabater-Mir, J.: Self-policing through norm internalization: a cognitive solution to the tragedy of the digital commons in social networks. J. Artif. Soc. Soc. Simul. **18**(2), 2 (2015)

A Stylized Model of Individual-Society Interaction Based on Luhmann's Theory

Marcos Aurélio Santos da Silva[1,2]([✉])(iD) and Christophe Sibertin-Blanc[2]

[1] Embrapa Tabuleiros Costeiros, Brazilian Agricultural Research Corporation,
Av. Beira Mar, 3250, Aracaju, SE 49040-025, Brazil
marcos.santos-silva@embrapa.br
[2] Institut de Recherche en Informatique de Toulouse,
Université de Toulouse 1 - Capitole, UMR IRIT,
2 Rue du Doyen-Gabriel-Marty, 31042 Toulouse, France
sibertin@ut-capitole.fr

Abstract. The computational modeling and simulation of social phenomena based on social theory as a theoretical framework is a challenging endeavor. Mainly, due to the difficulties to translate abstract conceptualizations of the social sciences into formal languages. The main goal of this paper is the translation of some Luhmann's concepts such as perturbation, dissipation, social communication and power, into a model using a spatial social subsystem as a metaphor, to make more concrete these very abstract concepts. The model has been used to improve the social theory understanding and to evaluate the effect of different parameterization in the global stabilization and authorities' distribution. It has been designed to comply with the Luhmann's social theory, and to be scalable and simple to understand. The experiment implemented one instantiation of the proposed model and showed how it can be used to evaluate a micro-macro interaction based on a simple mechanism of Luhmannian social communication.

Keywords: Social theory · Social communication
Evolutionary power

1 Introduction

According to [43], to model a social phenomena it is necessary to define an *object of research* that precises what should be modeled, a *reference framework* that will guide the mental model construction, a *social theory* that will instruct what aspects of the society will be modeled, and a *generic formal model* based on this theory which formalizes computationally or mathematically the abstractions and conceptualizations of the theoretical framework. Hence, the *model* will be one instance of the object of research using this generic model as reference, and it could be used to simulate the social dynamics to foresee different scenarios.

The *social phenomenon* that inspired this study is the collective action and power relations in the councils of Rural Territories in Brazil [39, 41, 42]. Rural

© Springer International Publishing AG, part of Springer Nature 2018
G. P. Dimuro and L. Antunes (Eds.): MABS 2017, LNAI 10798, pp. 121–140, 2018.
https://doi.org/10.1007/978-3-319-91587-6_9

Territories are new institutions for regional sustainable management at the landscape level. They had being created by two federal territorial public policies, the National Program for Sustainable Development of Rural Territories (PRONAT) [27] and the Program Territories of Citizenship (PTC) [5]. To formally study this social phenomenon, da Silva [39] conceptualized each Rural Territory as a complex socioterritorial system (CSTeS) based on the works of Moine [28, 29].

As the conceptualized CSTeS suggests, one *referential framework* is the Complexity Science. In fact, the studied social phenomenon is considered to show the properties of a complex social system as stated by [7]. Another referential framework is the systemic approach which aims to describe the social phenomenon by identifying the key components and relations between them [20].

Also considering the referential framework, there are, at least, two epistemological alternatives to model a social phenomenon, the critical-realism and the constructivism [7]. According to Castellani and Hafferty [7], the former is more connected to the theories and methods of the natural sciences, and the other more attached to the historical and qualitative analysis from the social sciences. This division becomes more clear when you observe the differences between behaviorist approaches at the micro social scale [34] and sociological approaches at the macro scale [6, 17]. In fact, in this work it is used these two epistemological currents in a constructive way.

Considering the object of research, the CSTeS, and the complex systems as referential framework, the choice for the *social theory* should be compliant to the systemic approach and the complexity paradigm. So, despite the myriad of theoretical sociological systemic propositions it is worth to realize the relevance and completeness of the Luhmann's Social System proposition [11, 23–25]. The Luhmann constructivism work reinterprets the concepts of complexity and systems theory, adapting it to his sociological studies, and sheds light on important aspects of our society as the social evolution by recursive mechanisms of self-differentiation by social communication.

Despite the compliance of the Social Systems with the complexity and systemic approach, the high level of Luhmann's abstraction makes the proposition of a *generic formal model* a very challenge task. In general, the models based on Luhmann's theory focus on specific aspects of the theory as observed in [3, 10, 12, 13, 15, 21, 38].

This research proposes a translation of some Luhmann's concepts (social subsystem, perturbation, dissipation, social communication and power) into a generic model using a stylized spatial society as a metaphor of a Luhmann's social subsystem. The model has been used to improve the social theory understanding and to evaluate the effect of different parameterization in the global stabilization and power distribution.

The model has been based on an existing experience [38] and is focused on the implementation of the mechanisms of perturbation/dissipation between the social subsystem and psychic system, and the translation into computational language of the Luhmann's societal power and communication process based on three selections (information, utterance and meaning).

This paper is organized as follows. Section 2 presents the concepts and definitions of the Luhmann's Social Systems. The Sect. 3 shows a brief review of some models designed from Luhmann's propositions. The Sect. 4 unveils the proposed generic formal model and the stylized spatial-social subsystem. The Sect. 5 shows the results and discussion of a simple simulation experiment. Finally, the Sect. 6 presents the conclusions.

2   Luhmann's Social Systems

2.1   General Description

According to Luhmann [23,25], Social Systems can be interpreted as a type of *autopoietic system* (self-reproductive system) and are divided into three classes (society, organizations, and face-to-face interactions) (Fig. 1). *Society* is unique and composed of interrelated subsystems (e.g., economy and politics) that are intertwined in a complementary way. *Organizations* are formalized systems for decision making, guided by goals and operational capabilities. The third component is the personal, *face-to-face*, interactions between individuals, represented in the Luhmann's formulation as *psychic systems*, separated from the society.

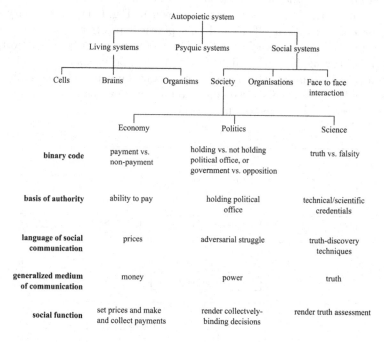

Fig. 1. General organization of the Luhmann Social Systems [23].

The societal subsystems interact with each other according to internal and external processes of social communications. The existence of each subsystem is due to a mechanism of differentiation, which is responsible to reduce the inherited complexity of the human society. The scientific subsystem, for example, emerged from the society need for falsifiable scientific statements that will be used by scientists and appropriate by organizations at some point in a recursive way [32].

2.2   Rempel's Terminology

Rempel [32] organized the Luhmannian subsystems according to its five components, namely: the binary code, the basis of authority, the language of social communication, the generalized medium of communication and the social function (Fig. 2). According to Rempel, the *binary code* is a linguistic construction that establishes how dichotomized a social subsystem will behave vis-à-vis the environmental disturbances. The *basis of authority* refers to the effective capacity of negotiation, communication and action of the subsystem to be legitimized by the possession of a jurisdiction in a specific area. In the *language of social communication* we will find the rules and conditions for the operation of the subsystem. The *generalized medium of communication* is what is exchanged, communicated, and must be recognized by all members in a subsystem. Finally, the *social function* is the purpose of the subsystem.

For instance, the political subsystem shown in Fig. 1 has as a binary code holding or not a political office, and this political position will be the basis of authority. The language of social communication in the political world is the adversarial struggle, so they fight for strategical positions trying to increase their power, which is interpreted here as a generalized medium of communication. Every side of this political scenario must interact to allow the political subsystem to render collective decisions for the society.

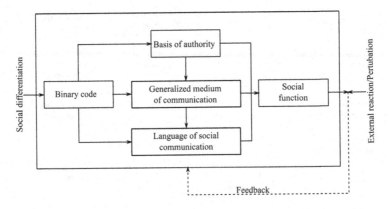

Fig. 2. The five components of each subsystem as defined by Rempel [32].

2.3   Social Communication

The Luhmannian work opposes the methodological individualism, but without eliminating the subject, the individual [1,30,36]. In Social Systems, the society is not anthropogenic, because the social processes are very far from the individual. However, for Luhmann, the actions of individuals are necessary for the social dynamic and they make it happen by a coupling mechanism between the social and psychic systems (individuals). So, a intervention mechanism of *perturbation/dissipation* is responsible for the connection between the psychic system and social systems, and this ignites the social communication process (a micro-macro linking process).

In fact, *social communication* in Social Systems is a mechanism for reducing the complexity (choose one, among an infinite set of options) by three types of selections: *information selection* (choice of content), *utterance selection* (choice of how that content will be communicated) and *meaning selection* (choice of meaning) (Fig. 3). For example, if the government chooses the content of supporting family farming (information), this can be implemented by special public funding or developing a new research project (utterance). The utterance process results in one or more contracts between small farmers and banks or research agencies (meaning).

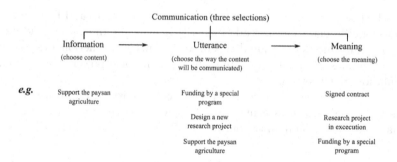

Fig. 3. Social System's communication according to Luhmann's theory.

In the Luhmannian social communication, there is not a clear message sent by a transmitter that passes through a transmission medium to reach a receiver within a period of time. In his formulation, Luhmann states that the social communication is not deterministic, neither synchronized, suffer from lack of accuracy and there is no general persistence in the selections of information, utterance and meaning. This definition of social communication is important to understand the reinterpretation of Luhmann's theory by Borch [4] and Rempel [32] in order to define *power*.

2.4   Social and Individual Power

Power can be interpreted in the Luhmann's work in three ways. As the mean of generalized medium of communication of the political social subsystem [22,24], as the basis of authority of all social subsystems [32] and as a capacity to generate meaning through time by the social communication process [4,18,32].

The power as the mean of generalized medium of communication of the political social subsystem can be interpreted as a capacity to influence someone as proposed by Castelfranchi [8].

The power as the basis of authority can be viewed as a capacity to act by means of internal (e.g., cognition) or external (e.g., resources) abilities also as exposed in [8].

The power as a capacity to generate meaning can be interpreted as an efficient and evolutionary production of meaning by psychic systems (individual) actions as exposed by [4,18] and in the same direction as proposed by Foucault [14]. In fact, Borch [4] established a bridge between the Foucault's notion of power and its relation with the knowledge production/location and the theoretical formulation of meaning generation in the Luhmannian social communication. According to Borch [4, p. 159]:

> *This definition of power, as a relation between action and action, is equivalent to the Foucauldian definition of power (in the form of government) as conduct - with the application that Luhmann is explicitly concerned with the regulations of selections, of selected action up selected action.*

Borch [4] presents some convergences between Luhmann and Foucault, such as: focus on differentiation instead of identity; social communication and its evolution through time as the main driver of society, instead of action and structure; power exercise as a cooperative game, not zero-sum one; power as a mechanism of regulation, not coercion.

So, individual power can be interpreted as the basis of authority (power-of [8]) as the social power as a measure of capacity to generate meaning by the Luhmannian social communication.

3   Related Work

The initiatives to design models inspired by the Luhmann's social theory can be divided into three groups: emergence of social order according to agents' expectations [3,10,15,16,21,26]; social subsystem implementation [13,18]; and micro-macro link [38].

3.1   Emergence of Social Order

The models focused on social order start from the Luhmann's idea that it emerges as a result of mutual expectations (double contingency) among the social agents during a social communication process [10]. Dittrich et al. [10, p. 2] stated that "... every entity expects that the other entity has expectations about its next activity". In fact, the authors explored the interpretation of the double-contingency concept to design a mechanism of information proliferation using the expectations as the main social process between agents. Barber et al. [3] and Fullsack [15,16] used the same idea to design their model of expectations. The main characteristic of this approach is that the communication between agents is implemented as a face-to-face interaction using the Shannon paradigm [35]. Analogously, Leydesdorff [21] proposed a system of anticipation [33] based on iterative expectations in an information flow based on face-to-face interactions.

The solutions proposed by these authors present some similarities, such as: there is no need to have an observer to send messages across the agents; each agent has all knowledge about his own actions in the system, for instance, they know how the others reacted from his own action; the social relations are dyadic and explicit; and all agents have memory to be able to perform anticipatory actions.

3.2 Social Subsystem

One of the first initiative to model a social subsystem can be found in Grant et al. [18]. The authors interpreted the Luhmannian society as a dynamic system where the six main subsystems coexist and communicates with each other by means of state variables and information (inactive and active) transfers according to the Ashby Cybernetics [2]. They proposed a model which represents different reaction times for each social subsystem, the rate of the social randomness, the power of each social subsystem to transform one inactive information into active and the amount of information inside each social subsystem. The authors coupled a socio-ecological system (collective livestock) with a stylized law social subsystem to emulate a coercitive effect on the natural resource use. So, without coercion this social system falls into the Hardin's Commons Tragedy [19], and with coercion the socio-ecological system reaches a sustainable state.

Fleischmann [13] implemented a simple Luhmann economy model based on scarcity and on the ownership code (the first economic level in the Luhmann's formulation of the economic evolution [13]). The main assumptions in this model are: (a) the social structure is based on expectations; (b) the communication is a matter of rejecting or not utterances; (c) and the systems are defined by its own operators; and (d) psychic and social systems co-evolve. The goal of this simple economic system is the accumulation of wealth and the result is inequality. This model confirmed the Luhamnn's hypotheses where he stated that the economic subsystem starts from inequality and reproduces it indefinitely to maintain its own existence.

In these models there is no reference to perturbation, the social communication is very simple and the mechanism of co-evolution is not clear.

3.3 Micro-macro Link

da Silva et al. [38] proposed a quite complete model to investigate the micro-macro link, or the interaction between the social system (macro) and the psychic system (micro). This model mapped many Luhmann's concepts like expectation, perturbation, dissipation and social and psychic communication. Despite the usefulness of the model as shown in [38] it is important to note that there are so many modules and connections between them that limits the results interpretation. Another remark is that it uses the same mechanism of communication for both micro (Agent-P) and macro (Agent-S) agents.

The Fig. 4 shows a simplified diagram of the model proposed by [38] and used as the basic framework of the proposed model. Both the social systems (Agent-S) and the psychic system (Agent-P) are composed of a dissipation module dedicated to send information to the environment (other systems) motivated by internal deliberation or external stimulus, a perturbation module which is responsible for the interpretation of dissipation actions by other systems, and a memory module where the experiences, knowledge, and rules of the system are stored. The Agent-S has a social system module which implements the social dynamic strategies. The Agent-P has a psychic system module which is responsible for the implementation of the behavioral aspects of the micro (individual) level.

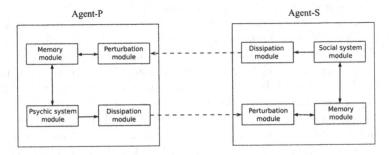

Fig. 4. Simplified diagram of the model proposed by [38].

In the original proposition [38], these modules were implemented in a very detailed way in an attempt to implement a generic model for any social subsystem. For instance, the psychic system module was composed of four submodules: central analyzer, contingency analyzer, dissipation manager and expectation manager [38]. In fact, the excess of inputs-outputs makes the general simulation output interpretation a very difficult task. Besides, the communication mechanism in both agents, Psychic and Social, is implemented in the same way and is not entirely compliant with the original Luhmannian formulation of social communication based on the three selections (information, utterance and meaning) as stated in Sect. 2.

3.4   Comparison Between These Three Groups

In summary, Luhmann's Social Systems are not fully represented by these models. In general, it is necessary to oversimplify the model as in [10] to make possible the formalization of some Luhmann's abstractions like the double contingency and expectations. On the other hand, da Silva et al. [38] proposed a very comprehensive formalization of the Social Systems which makes the interpretation of the simulation outcomes a challenge task or even meaningless.

One of the drawbacks of the analyzed models is the implementation of the social communication process. In all propositions it is treated as a simple traditional message transfer among agents.

Therefore, the proposition of [38] appeared to be the most complete computational formalization of the Luhmann's theoretical abstraction and was used as reference in this paper. Table 1 summarizes the comparison between these three groups of models based on Luhmann's theory.

It is also worth noting that none of the analyzed models interpreted the Luhmann' social subsystems as proposed by Rempel [32], and did not explored any interpretations of the power concepts.

Table 1. Comparison between the three groups of models based on Luhmann's social theory

	Emergence of social order	Social subsystems	Micro-macro link
Goal	Formalization of the core concepts of the Luhmann's theory	Model and simulation of a particular social system [13, 18]	Model of macro behavior of the social system
Technology	Multi-agent systems [3, 16]; social network [10]; and anticipatory systems [21]	Dynamic systems [18] and multi-agent systems [13]	Multi-agent system
Implemented Luhmann's concepts	Double-contingency, anticipation, expectation and social communication	Social communication, the binary code and the interface between social subsystems	Double-contingency, anticipation, expectation and social communication
Other theories used	General System Theory, Shannon's Information Theory and Anticipatory Theory [21, 33]	Ashby's Cybernetics [18]	Lewin's Field theory

4   Proposed Model Using a Spatial Social Subsystem as a Metaphor

4.1   A Stylized Spatial Social Subsystem

To overcome the problems shown in Subsect. 3.3, it is proposed in this work a simple mechanism for each module for Agent-P and Agent-S, based on a stylized spatial social subsystem as a metaphor of the Luhmann' social subsystem. The goal is to make a parallel between a well-known field of research, Spatial Analysis, and its problems (e.g., spatial dependence) and methods (e.g., spatial autocorrelation measure) with a formalization of the Luhmann's theory using multi-agent paradigm. So, our generic formal model subsystem will be composed of a set of neighbors cells, where each one can be associated to an Agent-P (Agent-P has authority over this cell). These agents will have stakes at disposal to change cell's values (Agents-P actions). The main goal of each Agent-P is to increase their authorities (number of cells under their control), and the main goal of the Agent-S is to increase the overall positive autocorrelation measure.

The rest of the section will describe the S4Luhamnn model according to the Rempel's terminology, the proposed Luhmannian social communication process, a new power definition based on propositions of Rempel [32], Borch [4] and Luhmann [22,24] and, finally, the details about Agent-S and Agent-P.

The Proposed Stylized Spatial Social Subsystem According to the Rempel's Terminology. Using the terminology of Rempel [32] to describe this stylized spatial-social subsystem we have as **binary code**, holding or not holding cells values; the **basis of authority** is the capacity to change spatial cells; the **language of social communication** is the struggle for cells authority; the **generalized medium of communication** is the artificial stake at disposal of each Agent-P; and the **social function** is the increasing of the positive spatial autocorrelation.

The Luhmannian Social Communication. The proposed social communication process for the S4Luhamnn model is resumed in Table 2 and consists of an information selection based on the reinforcement of positive autocorrelation, the utterance selection that will allow positive or negative incremental changes in cells at each time step, initiated by the Agent's-P and approved by the Agent-S, and a meaning selection where Agent-S changes the status of neighbor cells according their values, affecting the power share.

Table 2. The Luhmannian social communication in the spatial subsystem

Selection mechanism	Description
Information	Reinforcement of positive autocorrelation
Utterance	Positive or negative incremental changes in cells at each time step
Meaning	Agent-S changes the status of neighbor cells according their values, affecting the power share

The Rempel-Borch-Luhmann Power Definition. The power of each Agent-P can be interpreted as the number of cells under his authority. And the power of the Agent-S as a measure of positive spatial autocorrelation. Both powers may be originated from the Luhmannian communication process of perturbation/dissipation between Agents-P and Agent-S. It is important to note that there is no face-to-face communication among Agents-P.

4.2 Proposed Model

Agent-S - Social Subsystem. Agent-S is unique and composed of one spatial rectangular board divided in regular cells. Each cell of the Agent-S may be active (admit changes) or inactive (do not admit changes) and assume a value in $[0, 100]$. The main goal of the Agent-S is to increase his Moran's I spatial autocorrelation [9], expressed by the equation

$$I = \frac{N}{\sum\sum w_{ij}} \frac{\sum\sum w_{ij}(X_i - \bar{X})(X_j - \bar{X})}{\sum(X_i - \bar{X})^2}$$

where N is the number of cells, w_{ij} is an element of the spatial neighborhood (rook type) matrix $\mathbf{W}$ and assumes the value 1 if i and j are neighbors or 0 otherwise, X is the variable of interest (value of each cell) and $\bar{X}$ the mean of the X. The Agent-S admits internal perturbation by Agent-P and irritates Agent-P at a probability p. At each time step the social subsystem evaluates their Moran's I index and change the authority of each cell (capacity to change the cell values by Agent-P) if there is a local spatial correlation (see dissipation module description in Table 3). Table 3 summarizes the mechanisms of the four modules for the proposed Agent-S.

Table 3. Description of the elements of the proposed Agent-S

Agent-S module	Description
Perturbation	Admit internal perturbation (changes in X by Agent-P) at a probability p
Dissipation	If a cell and his neighbors (rook type) have similar values in some of two extremes, according to some thresholds, then put them as inactive. Thresholds: for Agent-P Alter $[0, 30)$; for Agent-P Ego $(70, 100]$
Memory	Spatial rectangular board divided in regular cells. For each cell is associated a real value in $[0, 100]$
Social	Evaluate the Moran's I statistics

To clarify this mechanism, let's use a hypothetical example of a spatial-social subsystem (Agent-S) composed of a 4×4 spatial board following the mechanism described above, with two Agents-P (Alter and Ego). In fact, Agents-P are struggling to increase their power on the spatial board without a direct communication between them. The Fig. 5 shows three hypothetical final spatial board configurations after a number of social simulation steps where empty squares represent cells with values near zero (under Alter's authority), and gray squares represent cells with values near 100 (under Ego's authority).

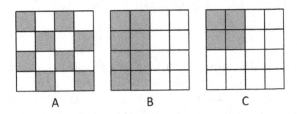

A   B   C

Fig. 5. Hypothetical final spatial board configurations after a number of social simulation steps. (A) negative spatial autocorrelation; (B) positive spatial autocorrelation with the same authorities for each Agent-P; (C) negative spatial autocorrelation; (B) positive spatial autocorrelation with different authorities for each Agent-P

In the Fig. 5-A each Agent-P has the same amount of power (8 cells for each) but the general goal of the social subsystem was not achieved because with this configuration the Moran's I will be equal to minus one (strong negative spatial autocorrelation). The Fig. 5-B shows a similar situation where each Agent-P shares the same amount of power (8 cells for each) but with a strong positive spatial autocorrelation. The Fig. 5-C shows also a strong positive spatial autocorrelation, but with an imbalance of power between Agents-P. The final configuration of the spatial board will depend on the social communication mechanism.

Agent-P - Psychic System. The goal of each Agent-P is to approximate the values of cells in the social board memory toward his own target. In this proposition there are two types of Agent-P, Alter and Ego. So, at each time step Alter act in order to change one cell value, at random, of the space board, toward zeros, and Ego do the same but the cell's values are pushed toward the value 100 by adding negative and positive increments, respectively, by the dissipation mechanism.

The amount of the increment and the localization of the cell is defined at random in the entire board or in a defined area of it. So, each Agent-P changes the value of one cell at a time using one of two strategies: (1) choosing one cell completely at random; (2) choosing one cell in a small area of the board, also chosen randomly, depending on the increase of the level of authority of the agent, that will be checked periodically. Table 4 summarizes the mechanisms of the four modules for the proposed Agent-P.

Table 4. Description of the elements of the proposed Agent-P

Agent-P module	Description
Perturbation	Admit internal perturbation by Agent-S at a probability q
Dissipation	Propose changes in cell's values of the spatial board by adding or subtracting a ΔX value
Memory	Information about the past levels of power on board cells
Psychic	Each Agent-P has a *capacity of action* and they use part of this "energy" to act. There are two possible strategies: (1) tries do change a cell chosen at random considering all possible cells in the spatial board; (2) tries do change a cell chosen at random considering a small portion of cells in the spatial board. The Agent-P can use only the first strategy or switch between these two options according to the level of Agent-P's power (authority over cells), checked in a defined time delay

4.3   Implementation

The model, called Stylized Spatial-Social Subsystem based on Luhmann's theory (S4Luhmann), had been implemented using Netlogo platform and it can be retrieved at [40]. Figure 5 shows a snapshot of the Netlogo implementation of the proposed model. Following it is described the variables, the social dynamic, and the model's observable results.

Variables. In this implementation, there are ten variables:

1. *rate*, which is the amount of rate of energy used by agents to change the cell's values by small positive and negative increments;
2. *BoardSize*, the side length of the squared regular spatial board;
3. *num-agents-Alter*, number of agents which aim to approximate the cells' values toward zero;
4. *num-agents-Ego*, number of agents which aim to approximate the cells' values toward one-hundred;
5. *init-capacity-Alter*, the amount of stakes available for Alters to change the values of the cells;
6. *init-capacity-Ego*, the amount of stakes available for Egos to change the values of the cells;
7. *change-strategy?*, if true the Agents-P use two strategies, otherwise they will use only one strategy;
8. *time-analyze-behavior*, interval of times that the Agents-P will check if they need to change behavior;
9. *delay-observation*, the length of the memory of each Agent-P;
10. *radius-searching*, the radius of searching for the second strategy.

The Model Dynamic. The spatial board is initialized with random values between [0, 100] and every cell is active. The two types of Agents-P (Alter and Ego) are instantiated. At each discrete time t the Agents-P sends messages to change spatial board cells. Agent-S accept or not these changes. After the cells update, the Agent-S act making groups of neighbors cells inactive according to its internal rules. At each time step the Agents-P evaluates if it is necessary to change the strategy used to change cells according to their level of authority. The simulation stops when all cells are inactive.

Observable Results. The graphics on the right of the Fig. 6 show the Moran's I, the total of energy of the board, and the capacity of action and authority of each type of Agent-P. The spatial board shows the final spatial pattern of distributed authority between Alters (gray) and Egos (dark gray).

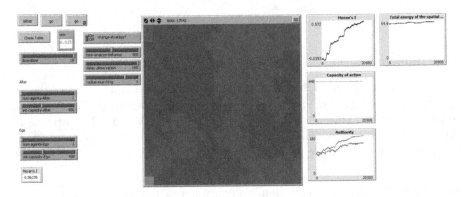

Fig. 6. Snapshot of the Netlogo implementation of the proposed model.

4.4 Sociological Interpretation

There is a direct relationship between the proposed model and the Rempel's decomposition of the Luhmann's social subsystems [32]. Then, the model's outputs can be interpreted as stylized outputs of real social subsystems such as the economic or politic social subsystems presented in Fig. 1. For instance, the model can represents a political subsystem composed of two political parties struggling for power (*authority over each cell*) and the final configuration of the spatial board of the Agent-S may represents the general distribution of power (very *fragmented* if low Moran's I or *cohesive* for high I).

The *spatial distribution* of authorities in the Agent-S's spacial board may also be a representation of a persistent pattern originated from the Luhmannian social communication. As explained in Sect. 2, the result of a social communication is originated from the meaning selection process output, and this can be a signed contract, a research project in execution, a funding by a special governmental program or something else (see Fig. 3). Using the model in this way, the model could be used to verify if there is any correlation between the pattern observed in the real world (spatial or not) and the spatial pattern of the model's output.

Power is a important concept in many fields of research as in sociology, social psychology, political science, behavior science, etc. As stated by Rempel [32] and Borch [4], the Luhmann's theoretical framework can be extended to embraced the Foucault's evolutionary definition of power [14]. Therefore, the model can be used to observe different mechanisms of *power evolution* according to different parametrization or agent's strategies.

Observe power relations dynamics in complex socioterritorial systems (CSTeS) can follow these approaches. Thereby, the CSTeS can be viewed as a political social subsystem and the Agents-P implemented as political groups. Another way is to implement how the CSTeS council's members communicate and observe the emergent power's pattern, such as persistent arguments, decisions, relations, etc.

In fact, at this moment, the model may be used as a tool to test theoretical speculations about Luhmannian social communication, power (individual and social) evolution and individual-society interaction.

5   A Simple Simulation Experiment

Let's consider a model of a stylized political subsystem where Alter and Ego represents two political parties and the Agent-S the society and its political preference distribution. The experiment using the proposed model should evaluate the effect of the two Agents-P strategies (see Table 4 in Sect. 4) on the general power distribution (share of authority), the spatial distribution of each party influence and the cohesiveness of the spatial aggregation by means of the Moran's I statistics.

The experiments were conducted considering some variables as constants ($rate = 0.0125$; $BoardSize = 18$; $num-agents-Alter = num-agents-Ego = 1$; $init-capacity-Alter = init-capacity-ego = 400$; $p = q = 100$) and the others varying according to some subset of values ($change-strategy?$ $\{true, false\}$; $time-analyze-behavior$ $\{500, 1000\}$ time steps; $delay-observation$ $\{50, 100\}$; $radius-searching$ $\{3, 4, 5\}$. The time limit steps for each run was set to 20000, for 10 runs.

Analyzing the mean of the Moran's I of the spatial board and of the authority's share for each type of Agent-P, Figs. 7 and 8, it is easy to identify a huge change when comparing these two strategies. The experiments 04, 05, 07 and 10, which the Agent-P uses two strategies, showed a very sharp increase in the Moran's I when compared with the only random strategy. The same difference is observed when looking at the shares of authority. In the experiments 04 and 05 the level of global positive spatial autocorrelation is greater than the other experiments due to the combination of a short time-analyze-behavior (500) and a greater memory delay-observation (100). In the graphic of authority it is observed that the Agent-P Ego end with more authority in both cases, but this is not true all the time, and the authority tends to be similar due to the fact that the Agents-P share the same strategies.

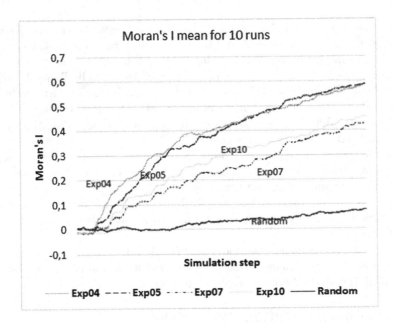

Fig. 7. Moran's I mean for 10 runs, 20000 time steps each.

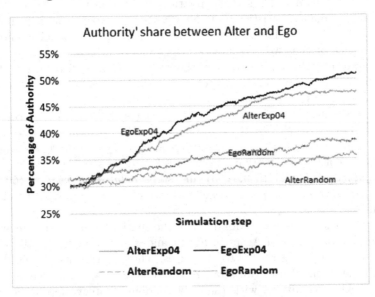

Fig. 8. The share of authority for some experiments.

The Fig. 9 shows the Moran's I curve for two types of simulation. The first one (left) represents the result of a simulation where Agents-P choose spatial board cells always randomly. The other uses the strategy to switch from completely

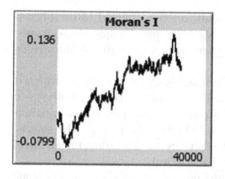 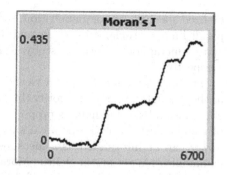

Fig. 9. Moran's I curve for one simulation run considering *change-strategy? = False* reaching a modest I less than 0.136 after 30000 simulation steps (left) and considering *change-strategy? = True, time-analyze-behavior = 500, delay-observation = 50,* and *radius-searching = 3* reaching a Moran's I greater than 0.4 after only 6000 simulation steps (right).

at random in all spatial board and in a small location of it. It is worth noting that the second strategy (right) converges very quickly and follows a particular pattern between a long time of stability and a sharp increase in I in a short period of time.

Comparing the two strategies of the Agents-P's according to the share of authority (Agent-P's power), spatial distribution, cohesiveness and Agent-S's power evolution it is possible to elaborate some sociological speculations to be confirmed empirically, if possible.

Share of authority. It is observed a increasing of general share's authority for the second strategy, but in all strategies Alter and Ego have the same amount of power due to the fact that there is no different in terms of strategies between them.

Spatial distribution. In this case the spatial authority distribution does not allow any conclusion because it was not established a correlation between each cell and a geographical space with a political meaning. Besides, the second strategy generated a more cohesive and segregated political system.

Agent-S's power evolution. The positive autocorrelation increasing curve for the second strategy of Agents-P (see Fig. 7) shows a clear pattern for the social power evolution.

6   Conclusions

The S4Luhmann model represents one step toward a more comprehensive formalization of the Luhmann's social theory. The metaphor strategy showed to be useful to make the theoretical concepts more concrete for implementation and interpretation.

The Rempel [32] decomposition of the Luhmann's subsystems in five components (binary code, basis of authority, language of social communication, generalized medium of communication and social function) helped to establish a parallel among social subsystems and facilitated the use of a spatial-social subsystem metaphor as a way to study social phenomenon through the Luhmann's perspective.

From the individual point of view the Luhmannian power can be interpreted as the amount of basis of authority (in our model the amount cell's authority), so, going beyond the Luhmann's proposition of power as only generalized medium of communication of the political subsystem. On the other hand, the society power can be interpreted as a measure of efficiency of the Luhmannian social communication (in our model the Moran's I statistics).

A sociological interpretation of the model outputs demands a parsimonious analysis due to the fact that the use of the spatial metaphor may not appropriate to represent all social phenomena.

The simple experiment showed that even a simple change in the way the psychic system and social system interact can generate very different patterns shares and spatial distribution of authority, social cohesiveness and societal power evolution.

Future work may address the implementation of other key Luhmann's concepts such as anticipation/expectation mechanisms as proposed by [3,10,15,21]. Another focus may be the confrontation of this evolutionary definition of power with other formal propositions as stated by Castelfranchi [8], Sibertin-Blanc et al. [37] and Pereira et al. [31].

References

1. Arnoldi, J.: Niklas Luhmann: an introduction. Theory Cult. Soc. **18**(1), 1–13 (2001)
2. Ashby, W.R.: An Introduction to Cybernetics. Methuen & Co. Limited, London (1956)
3. Barber, M., Blanchard, P., Buchinger, E., Cessac, B., Streit, L.: Expectation-driven interaction: a model based on Luhmann's contingency approach. J. Artif. Soc. Soc. Simul. **9**(4) (2006). Article no. 5. http://jasss.soc.surrey.ac.uk/9/4/5.html
4. Borch, C.: Systemic power: Luhmann, and analytics of power. Acta Sociol. **48**(2), 155–167 (2005)
5. Brasil: Institui o Programa Territórios da Cidadania e dá providências. Decreto de 25 de fevereiro (2008)
6. Buckley, W.: Society - A Complex Adaptive System: Essays in Social Theory. Gordon and Breach Publishers, Amsterdan (1998)
7. Castellani, B., Hafferty, F.W.: Sociology and Complexity: A New Field of Inquiry. Springer, Berlin (2009). https://doi.org/10.1007/978-3-540-88462-0
8. Castelfranchi, C.: The micro-macro constitution of power. ProtoSociology **18–19**, 208–268 (2003)
9. Cliff, A.D., Ord, J.K.: Spatial Autocorrelation. Pion, London (1973)
10. Dittrich, P., Kron, T., Banzhaf, W.: On the scalability of social order: modeling the problem of double and multi contingency following Luhmann. J. Artif. Soc. Soc. Simul. **6**(1) (2003). Article no. 3. http://jasss.soc.surrey.ac.uk/6/1/3.html
11. Ferrarese, E.: Niklas Luhmann, une Introduction. Pocket, Paris (2007)
12. Fischer, K., Florian, M., Malsch, T.: Socionics: Scalability of Complex Social Systems. Springer, Berlin (2005). https://doi.org/10.1007/11594116

13. Fleischmann, A.: A model for a simple Luhmann economy. J. Artif. Soc. Soc. Simul. **8**(2) (2005). Article no. 4. http://jasss.soc.surrey.ac.uk/8/2/4.html
14. Foucault, M.: Power/knowledge: Selected Interviews and Other Writings, 1972–1977. Pantheon Books, New York (1980)
15. Fullsack, M.: Communication emerging? On simulating structural coupling in multiple contingency. Constr. Found. **8**(1), 103–110 (2012)
16. Fullsack, M.: Modeling social interaction. A proposal oriented on Luhmann. Syst. Connect. Matter Life Cult. Technol. **1**(3), 39–49 (2013)
17. Goldspink, C.: Modelling social systems as complex: towards a social simulation model. J. Artif. Soc. Soc. Simul. **3**(2) (2000). Article no. 1. http://jasss.soc.surrey.ac.uk/3/2/1.html
18. Grant, W.E., Rai, T., Peterson, M.J.: Quantitative modeling of coupled natural/human systems: simulation of societal constrains on environmental action drawing on Luhmann's social theory. Ecol. Model. **158**(1–2), 143–165 (2002)
19. Hardin, G.: The tragedy of the commons. Science **162**(3859), 1243–1248 (1968)
20. Le Moigne, J.-L.: La modélisation des systèmes complexes. Dunod, Paris (1990)
21. Leydesdorff, L.: Anticipatory systems and the processing of meaning: a simulation study inspired by Luhmann's theory of social systems. J. Artif. Soc. Soc. Simul. **8**(2) (2005). Article no. 7. http://jasss.soc.surrey.ac.uk/8/2/7.html
22. Luhmann, N.: Poder, 2nd edn. Editora Universidade de Brasília, Brasília (1992)
23. Luhmann, N.: Social Systems. Stanford University Press, Stanford (1995)
24. Luhmann, N.: Politique et complexité: Les contributions de la théorie générale des systèmes. CERF, Paris (1999)
25. Luhmann, N.: Introduction to Systems Theory. Polity Press, Cambridge (2013)
26. Malsch, T., Schulz-Schaeffer, T.: Socionics: sociological concepts for social systems of artificial (and human) agents. J. Artif. Soc. Soc. Simul. **10**(1) (2007). Article no. 11. http://jasss.soc.surrey.ac.uk/10/1/11.html
27. Ministério do Desenvolvimento Agrário (MDA): Referências para a gestão social de territórios rurais. SDT, Brasília, DF (2005). Série Documentos
28. Moine, A.: Le territoire comme un système complexe: un concept opératoire pour l'aménagement et la géographie. L'Éspace Géographique **35**(2), 115–132 (2006)
29. Moine, A.: Le territoire: comment observer un système complexe. L'Harmattan, Paris (2007)
30. Nassehi, A.: Organizations as decisions machines: Niklas Luhmann's theory of organized social systems. Sociol. Rev. **53**(s1), 178–191 (2005)
31. Pereira, G., Prada, R., Santos, P.A.: Integrating social power into the decision-making of cognitive agents. Artif. Intell. **241**, 1–44 (2016). https://doi.org/10.1016/j.artint.2016.08.003
32. Rempel, M.: Systems theory and power/knowledge. Int. J. Sociol. Soc. Policy **16**(4), 58–90 (1996)
33. Rosen, R.: Anticipatory Systems. Pergamon Press, Oxford (1985)
34. Schluter, M., Baeza, A., Dressler, G., Frank, K., Groeneveld, J., Jager, W., Janssen, M., McAllister, R.R.J., Muller, B., Orach, K., Schwartz, N., Wijermans, N.: A framework for mapping and comparing behavioural theories in models of social-ecological systems. Ecol. Econ. **131**, 21–35 (2017)
35. Shannon, C.E.: A mathematical theory of communication. Mob. Comput. Commun. Rev. (Repr.) **5**(1), 3–55 (1948)
36. Seidl, D., Becker, K.H.: Organizations as distinction generating and processing systems: Niklas Luhmann's contribution to organization studies. Organization **13**(1), 9–35 (2006)

37. Sibertin-Blanc, C., Roggero, P., Adreit, F., Baldet, B., Chapron, P., El-Gemayel, J., Maillard, M., Sandri, S.: SocLab: a framework for the modeling, simulation and analysis of power in social organizations. J. Artif. Soc. Soc. Simul. **16**(4), 1–30 (2013). https://doi.org/10.18564/jasss.2278

38. da Silva, V.L., das Graças Bruno Marietto, M., Ribeiro, C.H.C.: A multi-agent model for the micro-to-macro linking derived from a computational view of the social systems theory by Luhmann. In: Antunes, L., Paolucci, M., Norling, E. (eds.) MABS 2007. LNCS (LNAI), vol. 5003, pp. 52–68. Springer, Heidelberg (2008). https://doi.org/10.1007/978-3-540-70916-9_5

39. da Silva, M.A.S.: The territory as a complex system. In: Furtado, B.A., Sakowski, P.A.M., Tóvolli, M.H. (eds.) Modeling Complex Systems for Public Policies, 1st edn, pp. 363–396. Institute for Applied Economic Research, Brasília (2015)

40. da Silva, M.A.S.: Stylized Spatial-Social Subsystem based on Luhmann's theory (S4Luhmann) model (Version 1.0). CoMSES Computational Model Library (2017). https://www.openabm.org/model/5543/version/2/view. Accessed 30 Mar 2017

41. da Silva, M.A.S., Medeiros, S.S., Manos, M.G.L., Siqueira, E.R.: Modelagem social computacional como instrumento de análise de sistemas sociais territoriais complexos: o caso do Território Sul Sergipano, Brasil. Campo - Território **9**, 55–85 (2014)

42. da Silva, M.A.S., Santos, A.V., Galina, M.H., dos Santos Medeiros, S., de Almeida, M.R.M.: Análise exploratória de simulações sociais computacionais por meio de estatística multivariada e mapas auto-organizáveis. Scientia Plena **12**, 1–18 (2016)

43. Zoya, L., Roggero, P.: La modelización y simulación computacional como metodología de investigación social. Polis **13**(39), 417–440 (2014)

MABS Applications

Schumpeterian Competition, Technology Space, and Patents

Martin H. Barrenechea[✉]

Programa de Pós-Graduação em Economia Aplicada PPEA-UFOP,
Universidade Federal de Ouro Preto UFOP, Rua do Catete 166,
Mariana, MG 35420-000, Brazil
mbarrenechea@icsa.ufop.br

Abstract. A model that describes the innovation process is developed in order to understand the effect of patent policies on an industry where firms interact under Schumpeterian competition. The technology space that is harvested by the firms in this particular case is a grid of 200×200 sites, each site has a level of productivity and a resistance to be discovered and firms have the capacity to explore this space and imitate other discoveries locally and globally. However, even with such an appropriate scenario for a patent system, a negative effect was found on consumers and innovation due to the implementation of a strong patent system compared to the situation where there is no patent system.

1 Introduction

The first model developed by Nelson and Winter (NW henceforth, see [5, chap. 12]) described and translated the theory of schumpeterian competition in algorithms and formulas giving the key insights to understand the long run dynamics of industries with oligopolist structures. Later in other work [10] a new model included adaptive behavior of the firms respect to the investment decisions and an evolutionary description of the birth of industries [10]. In addition to this Winter also analysed patents as the next step in the use of these new evolutionary models. For instance this is different from the classic models in economics that consider just the effects of single innovations like in the evolutionary models of NW. [10] are clearly more sound for the analysis of patent policies, because such models assume the occurrence of several innovations. However the results of various simulations realized in such models revealed that a strong patent system does not have positive effects on social welfare and innovation compared to a situation in which patents are not allowed [11].

To overcome those negative results of the earlier NW models respect to patents, Vallée and Yıldızoglu [9] explored other potential positive effects of

M. H. Barrenechea—I will like to thank three unknown referees, for their patience in reading the early version of this manuscript, their comments and recommendations were very useful. Also I will like to give special thanks to Ronaldo Nazaré and Gertjan Dordmond for their corrections and suggestions on the text.

© Springer International Publishing AG, part of Springer Nature 2018
G. P. Dimuro and L. Antunes (Eds.): MABS 2017, LNAI 10798, pp. 143–155, 2018.
https://doi.org/10.1007/978-3-319-91587-6_10

the patent system, namely it is the case where the NW models represent just an industry in a isolated way. In this scenario, it could be possible that the society would have benefited throughout the economic agents that obtain profits from the firms. Moreover, patents are not merely fixed policies that give incentives to innovators, they could be used strategically against other firms, blocking the development of other competitors. Unfortunately the results of Vallée and Yıldızoglu under such scenarios show that a stronger patent systems will lead to negative results on social welfare and innovation when compared with milder patent systems of [9].

In general one can think that patents could block the research and development of other firms. It would be reasonable to think that this negative effect could be counterbalanced with a compulsory necessity of the other firms to explore other alternatives and techniques, different from the patented ones. Nevertheless in the NW models the innovations happen to come from a random process that produces, if successful, an innovation together with a corresponding size from a log-normal distribution and just the innovation is protected against imitation without considering the effects of the patent breadth[1]. This is an effect that is frequently observed and it derives into expensive legal processes. In the NW models there is no explicit structure about the cumulativeness of the innovation process, instead the structure is modelled as a latent growth rate for the innovations size.

Recently Silverberg and Verspagen have offered several alternatives to make a more explicit theory of how innovations are discovered and used by firms and industries. One trial is the technology-performance space (defined as the cartesian product of a technological space and the performance of innovations, where technology space is conceived as the set of different technologies or techniques arranged by technological proximity). Based on empirical observations and theoretical developments about technology, a model based on the theory of percolation was proposed (see [7]) in such model when a technology-performance space is presented as the space where inventions are discovered. Such space in its simpler form is a half-plane where the horizontal line represents different technologies sorted by technological proximity, and in the other dimension of this plane it is represented the performance of the innovation. In this space a particular innovation is a site, so innovations are arranged by technological type and performance. The use of percolation in the space categorize the sites as excluded or not by nature. This is an interesting point of this model since from these results its is possible to replicate some empirical regularities related to innovation. A new version of this model (see [8]) appears to be more flexible and with a simpler mechanics of construction. With this new model each site can be discovered if enough effort is maintained by the firms. Additionally, firms have the possibility to change columns as a difference of the earlier model.

Based on the model of [8], Goldschlag developed an Agent Based Model for the study of the impact of patents, taking the columns in the technology-

---

[1] Patent breath is the largeness of the protection of a innovation in the sense of similarity with other innovations.

performance space as product innovations and using firms as agents in this space. In such scenario firms obtain temporal monopolistic power and during this time these firms use their own resources to have more exploration throughout R&D on the technology-performance space. Also this model incorporates intellectual protection. The results from simulations show that patents can have a positive effect in the innovative performance, when there is a few monopoly power and when the resistance of the sites in the technology-performance space is high [2].

What is proposed in this manuscript is a model that incorporates some features developed in [8] as the concept of technology space and the resistance of sites. Such concepts are used in the process of innovation and imitation in an industry under a schumpeterian competition[2]. The technology space is basically a grid in a two dimensional space of 200 × 200 sites. This is different of the model of [8] percolation where the term productivity is used instead of the term performance because productivity is a more suitable concept in the realm of economics.

The structure of this article is as follows, in Sect. 2 the model is described, in Sect. 3 the simulation protocol is established and the results of simulations are presented. Finally the Sect. 4 gives the conclusions, recommendations and describes the potential future work.

2   Description of the Model

2.1   Overview

Purpose. The purpose[3] of the model is to explore the consequences of different patent policies on an industry. Such policies impact directly the way the firms discover and imitate new techniques. An important fact that the model explores, in greater detail when compared to other models, is the technology space (TS). Such space resides in a two dimensional grid of 200 × 200 sites with its origin at the center of the two dimensional grid.

Entities. The elements of the TS are sites. Each site has the following variables:

1. **state** (ω)**:** 0 (not discovered, red); 1 (discovered but not viable, yellow); 2 (discovered and viable, green). The variable state describes the state of the site, all the sites starts on the state 0.
2. **resistance** (β)**:** this is a real positive number. Once the resistance of the site is depleted by the efforts of the firms the site changes into the state 1 or 2.

---

[2] Initially in the first attempts of what is done in the paper used the model developed in [8]. Lately in this paper this strategy was changed because the NW models describe competence in a market with a unique good, so the innovations are directed in the production of a such good, called processes innovations, not product innovations as in [8].

[3] The presentation of the model was inspired in the ODD protocol [3].

3. **productivity (α):** this is a real positive number. It represents the productivity per unit of capital when the technique is used in the production of goods.
4. **nprotected (ν):** number of periods left with patent protection.

The other entities are the firms. They explore the technology space to use new techniques for the production of a single good. Each firm has the following variables:

1. **productivity (a):** The best productivity available for the firm.
2. **capital (k):** level of capital.
3. **quantity (q):** quantity supplied to the market.
4. **profit (profit)**
5. **markup (m):** The markup relative to the cost of production c.
6. **share (s):** The share of the firm production on the total production of the market.
7. **(lx1, ly1), (lx2, ly2):** knowledge is saved in coordinates obtained from exploration and imitation.

The coordinates in the grid are scaleless, and each period represents a trimester (tick)[4].

2.2 Processes

Short-Run Behavior. The behavior in the short run is completely based in the model developed in [5, chap. 12]. Hence, there is a fixed number of firms n, each one of them produces a quantity q with the following production function:

$$q = ak, \tag{1}$$

where a is the best productivity available and k is the capital of the firm. The market price is decided by the inverse demand function as follows

$$P = D/Q, \text{if } Q > D/2 \text{ and 2 in all other cases.} \tag{2}$$

where $Q = \sum q_i$ is the aggregate quantity of the good supplied by all firms. The profit is:

$$\text{profit} = p(a - c - r^{in} - r^{im})k, \tag{3}$$

where c is the variable cost of production as a rate of the current capital, r^{in} is the rate of expenditure in innovation per unit of capital, and r^{im} is the imitation rate per unit of capital, and p is the current market price.

---

[4] The choice of the calibration of the parameters yields similar results as in [5, chap. 12].

Imitation. At each period it is identified the site that could be imitated by all the firms, such site has to be discovered and viable (state 2) and it has no patent protection ($\nu = 0$). If there is more than one site the choice of the imitation site is random. The result are coordinates of the site, this site is going to be called candidate for global imitation, its location is common knowledge.

In the same way that the candidate for global imitation, the candidate for local imitation lies to the firm's location neighborhood with radius r, such candidate could be different, because it could be taken from a different neighborhood.

The expected productivity of a candidate for imitation at the point (x, y) is $1.25r^{im}k(1 - \text{distance}(x, y)/150)$, where $\text{distance}(x, y)$ is the distance form the current location of the firm to the potential candidate. Once it is compared this expected productivity of the local candidate against the global candidate for imitation, the firm decides if to imitate locally or imitate globally and the firm makes an imitative effort in order to reach the desired location. The probability that the imitation trial is successful is given by the following expression:

$$\Pr(\text{imitation}) = 1.25r^{im}k(1 - \text{distance}(x, y)/150). \tag{4}$$

If a firm imitates successfully, then the variables lx2 and ly2 of that firm are updated to the coordinates of the imitation site, so that the firm can use this innovation for production.

Exploration. The R&D activities are exerted each period by using a percentage of capital. These resources b are directed to the exploration of the technology space,

$$b = r^{in}k \tag{5}$$

The firm then uses this budget to explore each one of the sites inside a Moore neighborhood around the firm with the same intensity bc for each site (see (6)). The size of the search neighborhood is r Eventually bigger values of r not necessarily mean that the exploration is better in terms in the technology space, because there are less resources for each site compared with the situation of a lower search radius. However the firm could be benefited from bigger search radius, because other firms can weaken the resistance of the surrounding sites.

$$bc = \frac{b}{(2r + 1)^2} \tag{6}$$

The dynamics of the resistance of a site is given for the following equation:

$$\beta_{t+1} = \beta_t - bc * \epsilon.$$

where $\epsilon \sim U(0, 1)$ and bc is the R&D effort by the firm in that site. When a site has its resistance completely weakened the last firm that explores this site can patent the site. It happens just if the site is free and undiscovered. The firm can also claim its breadth (the neighborhood of size ϕ of undiscovered cells). This right is the patent and its exclusion to others have a duration of v periods (patent life).

The required inventive step governs which innovations are protectable, and the breadth governs how different another product must be to avoid infringement – [6, p. 84]

The definition of the duration of a patent is well known and very intuitive. However the breadth is a concept that needs a more detailed explanation. As a definition pointed out by Scotchmer (see above) it is assumed that the breadth of a innovation is immediately translated to a neighborhood in the technology space.

Hence v denotes how many periods the protection is valid and the patent breadth ϕ tells how much extends the right on a neighborhood in the technology space. The sites that belongs to the patent breadth of an innovation have to be undiscovered (state 0). The undiscovered sites inside the breath of a patent that are property of another firm can be discovered, but cannot be used by the firm during the life of the patent to which the breadth belongs, unless the patent belongs to the same firm.

Inside the radius of search, the firm chooses the best location that is discovered and viable and does not have a valid patent as a potential location for exploration. Hence the location is registered by the firm in the variables lx1 and ly1.

Movement. Once the firms have obtained the coordinates of imitation $(lx2, ly2)$[5] and exploration $(lx1, ly1)$, both sites are compared based on the productivity weighted by the sites in radius r that are not property of the other firms (sites without a valid patent or without patents or property of the same firm). The best site under such criterion is chosen as a new place of exploration and the firm moves to this new position, if the imitation site is chosen then $(lx1, ly1) \leftarrow (lx2, ly2)$ $((lx1, ly1)$ is updated to be the point $(lx2, ly2))$ otherwise the locations are maintained, and finally the firm moves to $(lx1, ly1)$.

Capital and the Best Productivity Update. About the dynamics of the capital, it follows almost explicitly the specification in [5], the markup as

$$m = \frac{p_t a_t}{c}, \tag{7}$$

and the market share as

$$s = \frac{q_t}{Q_t} \tag{8}$$

The ratio of desired investment related to capital is $1.03 - \frac{2-s}{\rho(2-2s)}$[6] and the financial restriction is $(1 - 0.03)\pi$ so the investment rate by unit of capital is

$$I(m, s, \text{profit}, 0.03) = \max\left(0, \min\left(1.03 - \frac{2-s}{m(2-2s)}, 0.97\text{profit}/k\right)\right), \tag{9}$$

---

[5] If the imitation trial was not successful the last coordinates are maintained, and a similar procedure is used for the exploration location.

[6] See [4] for a detailed example, about how to calculate conjectures in the case of a duopoly.

where the term 0.03 is the depreciation of capital. Then with such investment the dynamics of firm's capital is

$$k_{t+1} = (I(m, s, \text{profit}, 0.03) + 0.97)k_t \tag{10}$$

The best productivity of a firm a is taken by comparing the productivity levels between the location $(lx2, ly2)$ of imitation and the productivity in the location of exploration $(lx1, ly1)$, choosing always the higher one.

Space Update. Once the resistance of a site has been completely consumed, the site turns to state 1 (discovered and not viable), such innovation could be able to turn state 2 (discovered and viable) if the site is neighbor to a site on state 2, then the neighborhood considered for such evaluation is a Moore neighborhood of size 1. It is also necessary to update the information about the patented sites, because such sites will reduce the number of periods of protection by one in each period (tick).

2.3   Design Concepts

Basic Principles. The basic principle addressed by this model is the assessment of effects of patents on innovation and welfare when innovations lie in a technology space – a set of innovations reordered in a grid by technological proximity–. Thus the patent policies summarized in a patent life and in a patent breadth are easily transformed in rules inside this technology space.

Emergence. In several early models the market inclines to be highly concentrated, which is a result that is also expected in this model because the exploration and imitation depends on the levels of capital. Then it is expected that the activities of research are developed in the end for a small number of firms with a big share of the market.

Adaptation. In this version of the model firms cannot learn. However, they are able to imitate the best non patented technology available inside the technology space. Furthermore, in the knowledge of each firm there are: (i) the imitation location (if a imitation trial became successful); (ii) the exploration location. These two locations that can be used for exploration in next periods.

Objectives. The basic objective of the firms by navigating the technology space is to reach viable sites with the highest productivity.

Sensing. The firms sense the site with the highest productivity available for imitation (site viable and non patented), and the firm also perceives the sites that are viable sites around the exploration and imitation location.

Interaction. Firms interact in two scenarios in the market where prices are determined based in the quantities produced for each firm, and in the technology space where firms discover sites, and harvest resistance of sites.

Observation. In order to analyse the results of the patent policies some variables and statistics are observed:

- Market price.
- Highest productivity and average productivity (weighted by k) used by firms.
- Inverse Herfindahl–Hirschman Index that represents the effective number of firms IHH.
- Consumer's surplus (CS): $D(1 - P/2 + \ln Q - \ln(D/2))$.
- Firms' surplus: $\sum \text{profit}_i$.

2.4   Initialization

At first an artificial topography was created for the productivity. Such productivity was created in a way that exists one hilltop of productivity ta the point $(30, 30)$. This scenario is rugged by a random component and this ruggedness is controlled by a parameter $\delta \in [0, 1]$. When δ is lower, the topography is smoother, see Fig. 1 below to visualize the different topographies. The lightest site represents the site with the highest productivity and the darkest site represents a site with a very low productivity. The topography of productivity is adjusted in such a way to have a maximum α_f and minimum α_0 values of the productivity of the sites.

Fig. 1. Different topographies for the productivity for $\delta = 0$ and $\delta = 1$

All the sites are provided with a resistance level generated from a log normal distribution with mean μ_β and standard deviation σ_β, finally all the sites in the bottom are set its state to 2 (discovered and viable).

Each firm is randomly located in the bottom line of the technology space, and its initial coordinates of imitation and exploration are set to the initial location. The initial values of the best productivity a is fixed to the productivity of the site where the firm is located, and all the firms start with the same capital k_0.

3   Simulation

Here a descriptive analysis is performed using twoway graphs in the cases where we want to observe the trajectory of a run and box plots to summarize the results in the last period of a run[7].

3.1   Baseline

First a scenario is created to describe the dynamics of the model in order to compare the patterns with the classical NW models, this scenario is called baseline. Here the patent life is set to zero(no patents), the number of firms used in all simulations is 32, in each case the model was simulated for $M = 10$ runs and each run has over 200 steps (each step means a trimester), which means 50 years. The other parameters are summarized in Table 1.

Table 1. Baseline parameters

c	μ_β	σ_β	δ	D	r	α_f	α_0	r^{im}	r^{in}
0.16	0.10	0.15	0.60	50	5	0.80	0.16	0.00097	0.0194

The results have the same patterns as the ones in the NW models (see Fig. 2), such patterns are:

1. The industry tends to become highly concentrated as time increases.
2. The prices are decaying over the time.
3. The average productivity and the best productivity are increasing.

What is relevant to observe is the increase of the variance in the last periods, in particular in the productivity. This effect comes as consequence of the topography of the productivity in the technology space.

3.2   Patents

In the case of patents, values of $\{0, 10, 20, 40\}$ were considered for the patent life (PL) and $\{0, 10, 20, 40\}$ as the radius for the patent breadth (PB), the other parameters were maintained as the ones in the baseline setup (see Table 1), thus $M = 10$ runs with 200 steps for each run.

---

[7] In case of ambiguity, some tests for comparisons should be used. Nonetheless, in our analysis we did not confront with such situation.

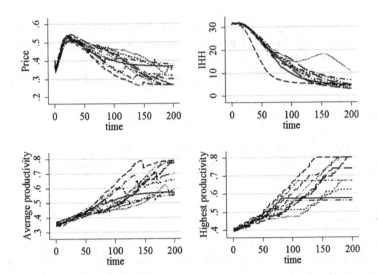

Fig. 2. Results of simulations for baseline parameters

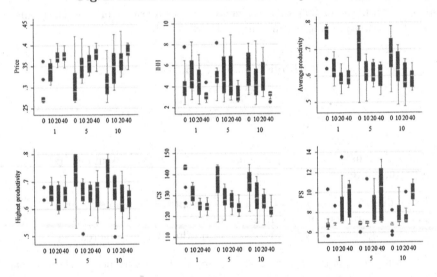

Fig. 3. Situation of the variables in the final step

Figure 3 shows the distributions of different variables under different combinations of duration for the patent (zero, ten or twenty periods) and different radius levels of search of firms in the technology space (1, 5 or 10) for the last step of each run. At first sight there is no evidence that the PB has a significant effect on any relevant variable. For the PL there is an effect that is most visible in prices and the average productivity. Unfortunately the effects are negative because prices are increasing as PL increases: the average productivity decays as the PL becomes longer and finally there no effect on the best productivity of all firms.

It is interesting from a social welfare point of view to see if there is an optimal combination of patent policies. The results in Fig. 3 show that the optimal combination is $PL = 0$ and $PB = 1$, which means no patents at all. The worst scenario is where patent life and breadth are maximum ($PL = 40$ and $PB = 10$). When both scenarios are compared, it is remarkable to notice that:

1. Prices are bigger in $PL = 40, PB = 10$.
2. Concentration as measured by the IHH are almost the same.
3. Average productivity is lower in $PL = 40, PB = 10$ compared with $PL = 0, PB = 1$.
4. The best productivity is lower in $PL = 40, PB = 10$ compared with $PL = 0, PB = 1$.
5. Firms are better off in $PL = 40, PB = 10$ and consumers are better off in $PL = 0, PB = 1$.

It is interesting to observe the dynamics of the variables in both scenarios. These dynamics are shown in the Fig. 4 (see below). The results clearly show a situation consistent with the analysis of the last step. It is pertinent to explain the situation of the Firms' Surplus (FS) that in some cases is negative. This situation comes from the fact that the spending on innovation is based on the level of capital, meaning that even failed companies will continue making R&D

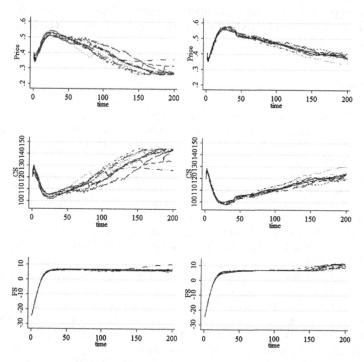

Fig. 4. Price, CS, FS under ($PL = 0, PB = 1$) left and ($PL = 40, PB = 10$) right.

operations. This situation is amplified by the fact that the model does not consider death and birth of firms.

4 Conclusions

A model that encompasses several important points from schumpeterian dynamics and from the technology-performance space developed in [8], in order to analyze several patent policies related to the patent life and patent breadth.

The main objective of a patent system is to promote innovation. However, the findings show that the effects of a strong patent system are negative for social welfare and for innovation, or they do not have the positive effects that defenders of patent systems claim in terms of promotion of innovation.

The only combination of patent life and patent breadth that benefits society in the end is having no patents at all. In contrast it is found that the worst situation for consumers and innovation is a industry with a strong patent system.

There are points that could be expanded, in particular the development of the process of entrance and exit of firms could be included in the model. Another point that is lost in the analysis here is the learning process of firms in order to invest in innovation and imitation.

Regarding the structure of the model there are also several options to explore. A promising development that could be researched is related to the complexity of products (products are made with several different parts). One area that has already been partially explored is the complexity developed by the NK approach that describes this complexity (see [1]).

References

1. Chang, M.: Industry dynamics with knowledge-based competition: a computational study of entry and exit patterns. J. Econ. Interact. Coord. **4**(1), 73–114 (2009)
2. Goldschlag, N.: Percolating patents: balancing the effects of patents on innovation (2014, unpublished)
3. Grimm, V., Polhill, G., Touza, J.: Documenting social simulation models: the odd protocol as a standard. In: Edmonds, B., Meyer, R. (eds.) Simulating Social Complexity. Understanding Complex Systems, pp. 117–133. Springer, Heidelberg (2013). https://doi.org/10.1007/978-3-540-93813-2_7
4. Jonard, N., Yildizoğlu, M.: Technological diversity in an evolutionary industry model with localized learning and network externalities. Struct. Chang. Econ. Dyn. **9**(1), 35–53 (1998)
5. Nelson, R.R., Winter, S.G.: An Evolutionary Theory of Economic Change. Harvard Business School Press, Cambridge (1982)
6. Scotchmer, S.: Innovation and Incentives. MIT Press, Cambridge (2004)
7. Silverberg, G., Verspagen, B.: A percolation model of innovation in complex technology spaces. J. Econ. Dyn. Control **29**(1–2), 225–244 (2005)
8. Silverberg, G., Verspagen, B.: Self-organization of R&D search in complex technology spaces. J. Econ. Interact. Coord. **2**(2), 211–229 (2007)

9. Vallée, T., Yıldızoglu, M.: Social and technological efficiency of patent systems. In: Cantner, U., Malerba, F. (eds.) Innovation, Industrial Dynamics and Structural Transformation, pp. 407–424. Springer, Heidelberg (2007). https://doi.org/10.1007/978-3-540-49465-2_21

10. Winter, S.: Schumpeterian competition in alternative technological regimes. J. Econ. Behav. Organ. **5**(3–4), 287–320 (1984)

11. Winter, S.: Patents and welfare in an evolutionary model. Ind. Corp. Chang. **2**(1), 211 (1993)

KILT: A Modelling Approach Based on Participatory Agent-Based Simulation of Stylized Socio-Ecosystems to Stimulate Social Learning with Local Stakeholders

Christophe Le Page[1,2]([✉]) and Arthur Perrotton[3,4]([✉])

[1] CIRAD, UPR Green, 34398 Montpellier, France
christophe.le_page@cirad.fr
[2] CIRAD, UPR Green, University of Brasilia, Brasília, Brazil
[3] CIRAD, UMR Astre, 34398 Montpellier, France
arthur.perrotton@cirad.fr
[4] Center for Applied Social Sciences, University of Zimbabwe,
Harare, Zimbabwe

Abstract. A new approach is introduced under the slogan « Keep It a Learning Tool » (KILT) to emphasize the crucial need to make the purpose of the modelling process explicit when choosing the degree of complicatedness of an agent-based simulation model. We suggest that a co-design approach driven by early-stage and interactive simulation of empirical agent-based models representing stylized socio-ecosystems stimulates collective learning and, as a result, may promote the emergence of cooperative interactions among local stakeholders.

Keywords: Participatory agent-based simulation · Social learning
Stylized landscape · Role-playing game · Companion modelling

1 Introduction

An agent-based simulation is said to be "participatory" as soon as some decisions of the agents are entrusted to the participants. A typology of simulations has been proposed by Crookall and his colleagues [1]. They distinguished two types of simulations depending on who controls it, and where the focus is. When the simulation is mainly controlled by the computer, the focus of interaction can be set on computer-participant interactions (participants observe the simulation run in the manner of a cinema audience), or on participant-participant interactions (participants can intervene while the simulation runs or at intervals provided during the run). In any of these cases, the flexibility of the simulation remains limited. A second type is when the simulation is mainly controlled by the participants. The focus of interaction can then be set on

This paper has already been published in: © Springer International Publishing AG 2017 G. Sukthankar and J. A. Rodriguez-Aguilar (Eds.): AAMAS 2017 Visionary Papers, LNCS 10643, pp. 31–44, 2017. https://doi.org/10.1007/978-3-319-71679-4_3

© Springer International Publishing AG, part of Springer Nature 2018
G. P. Dimuro and L. Antunes (Eds.): MABS 2017, LNAI 10798, pp. 156–169, 2018.
https://doi.org/10.1007/978-3-319-91587-6_11

computer-participant ("flight simulator" for which generally only one user interacts continuously with the simulation), or on participant-participant. In that last case, participants will be confronted with concrete situations, acted out by the organizers of the participatory simulation workshops, which they must react to.

This type of interactive participatory agent-based simulation is very similar to what is called a computer-assisted role-playing game in the framework of the companion modeling approach [2–4]. As pointed out by Barreteau [5], there is a striking correspondence between the features of an agent-based simulation and a role-playing game session: agent/player, role/rule, game-turn/time-step, game board/interface. This similarity is due to the fact that, from a formal point of view, a role-playing game is a kind of multi-agent system: it is composed of interacting entities, evolving in a shared environment, each one seeking to achieve a specific goal. Apart from the simulation of agents' decisions, the computerization may also support the following features: (i) recording the decisions of human agents, which enables computing performance indicators (results of their actions) and "replaying" the session during the debriefing; (ii) simulating the dynamics of the resources; (iii) visualizing the updated state of the resources and the positioning of the agents, possibly according to points of view specific to each type of players [6].

In computer science, participatory agent-based simulation represents a fertile ground for improving the techniques of Artificial Intelligence related to supervised learning such as inverse reinforcement learning or support vector machines [7]. Introducing assistant agents with learning abilities can help eliciting the behavior of human participants and also supporting them to make decisions during the course of the simulation [8]. Participatory agent-based simulation sessions have been successfully used as an experimental framework to extract interaction patterns in negotiated (written) elements between participants [9].

By integrating the HubNet module into the NetLogo platform, which allows interconnecting several identical user interfaces to the same simulation, Wilensky and Stroup [10] paved the way for using participatory simulation to facilitate the learning of complex systems to students. One of the first applications of HubNet is called Gridlock[1]. It is a simulation of car traffic in real time where each student controls a traffic light while the teacher controls the global variables, such as speed limit and number of cars. The group is challenged to develop strategies to improve traffic and discuss the different ways of measuring the traffic quality [11]. Another example of the educational potential of interactive multi-agent simulations is given by the experiment on the spread of a contagious disease conducted with US high school students [12]. A network of miniature communicating computers (tags) allows simulating the spreading of a virus among the participants, each of them wearing a tag as a bracelet, only one being initially infected. Participants are challenged to meet as many people as possible without getting sick. To stimulate experiential learning, students were told nothing about how the virus moved from one tag to another, the degree of contagiousness, the possibility for latency.

In such an immersive configuration, the space of interactions does not have to be "re-presented" to the participants. In most of the applications of participatory agent-based

---

[1] http://ccl.northwestern.edu/netlogo/models/HubNetGridlockHubNet.

simulation anyway, space has to be explicitly represented into the model. This is of particular importance when the target system is a socio-ecosystem. The distribution of a participative multi-agent simulation on several computers is an efficient way of staging information asymmetry between participants. It is then interesting to observe if participants take the initiative to share certain information - initially private - with others. When the objective is to improve the mutual understanding between the participants, it becomes critical to encourage direct interaction between them and to stimulate exchanges. Representing a common visualization space and a support to materialize the decisions of the players with pawns and tokens, a large game board (so that everyone can sit around) is a configuration that answers perfectly to this need. For instance, the environment of the *SAMBA* model, developed in Vietnam [13, 14], consists of a rectangular support filled with cubes, each of the six faces representing a land cover. Players then manipulate the cubes directly to signify the changes in land use corresponding to their actions. But when the simulation includes ecological and/or hydro-physical processes not directly under the control of the players, manually updating the environment by an operator is a tedious operation that causes dead times for the participants.

Using a digital game board provided by the projection on a horizontal flat surface of the computerized representation of the environment was recently tested in rural Zimbabwe. Before presenting the participatory agent-based simulation approach that was conducted with local actors to foster social learning, we propose a review of the applications of participatory agent-based simulation in the field of socio-ecological science, distinguishing its uses with scholars and with stakeholders. We stress the importance to clarify two fundamental features that are interconnected: the degree of realism of the model and the purpose of the modelling process.

2   Abstract, Stylized and Realistic Representations of Space in Agent-Based Models of Socio-Ecosystems

The representation of the environment can range from purely abstract landscapes to realistic ones integrating spatial data from geographical information systems. In the case of an abstract world, the environment of the model does not refer to any particular landscape, like in the *ReHab* participatory simulation tool [15], where harvesters have to collect a resource in an imaginary landscape that is also a nesting and breeding ground for a migratory bird under the protection of rangers (see Fig. 1a).

In an intermediate case, the implicit reference to a given socio-ecological system results in equivalent proportions in the distribution of the modalities of each landscape characteristics (primarily the land use) and possibly also in the similarity of the space configuration, with the integration of typical spatial patterns. For instance, in the *BUTORSTAR* model, the impacts on avifauna of the management of reed beds resulting from decisions made by farmers, reed collectors, hunters and naturalists are simulated in a stylized representation of the Camargue wetland [16]. Similarly, in the *SylvoPast* gaming tool [17] featuring conflicts of interest between a forester and a shepherd in the context of fires' prevention in the Mediterranean region, the proportions of the different types of vegetation cover (see Fig. 2b) are based on empirical data, so that the stylized environment of the model represents an archetypical grazed Mediterranean forest.

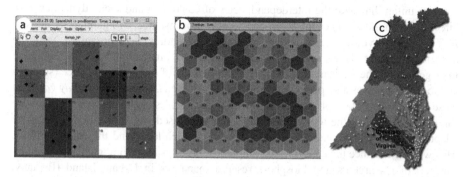

Fig. 1. The three types of environment in participatory agent-based simulation: (a) abstract, like in the *ReHab* game [15]; (b) stylized, like in the *SylvoPast* game [17]; (c) realistic, like in the uva bay game [18].

It is also the case of the *NewDistrict* interactive and asymmetric agent-based simulation [19] where the impacts of peri-urban development on biodiversity are investigated in a stylized landscape. Three ecological processes are simulated (bee colonization, bird migration and water quality), with participants playing the roles of mayor, building contractor, farmer, forester and ecologist, each one equipped with a specific computer interface representing the landscape according to a point of view specific to its activity.

Recent technological advances [20, 21] have reinforced a trend that emerged some fifteen years ago [22–24] to move towards spatially-explicit agent-based models representing realistic landscapes by associating them with GIS. Extensions to integrate spatial data from GIS have been added to the main existing platforms (NetLogo, Mason, RePast). New platforms have been developed focusing mainly on these aspects: GAMA [25] and MAGéo [26]. This type of data-intensive models are becoming more and more popular, due to the increased availability of data, the computing power of computers and the increasing demand from policy-makers and managers for policy and scenario analysis [27]. A recent and emblematic example is the *uva bay game*, a large-scale agent-based participatory simulation of the Chesapeake Bay socio-ecosystem [18]. The game allows players to take the roles of stakeholders, such as farmers, developer, watermen, and local policy-makers, make decisions about their livelihoods or regulatory authority and see the impacts of their decisions on their own personal finances, the regional economy, fish and crab populations and overall bay health. Figure 1c shows the locations of the players (white dots) in one of the 8 watersheds represented in the model.

3   Involvement of Local Stakeholders: Adjusting the Degree of Complicatedness of the Model to Its Purpose

All the examples presented in the previous section were firstly developed to be used with students, for educational purpose. It is quite common to note a dual use of participatory agent-based simulation in the field of socio-ecological science: either support to the implementation of experiential learning in classrooms to teach students who are unfamiliar with the interdependencies of ecological and social dynamics, or a direct use with the actors of the socio-ecosystems. For instance, two gaming sessions of *BUTORSTAR* involving stakeholders of Étang de Vendres were organized, with the aim of increasing their capacity to adopt modes of interactions favoring adaptive management of the environment [28]. This duplication of the target audience (students and local actors) was also performed with *SylvoPast*, *NewDistrict* and *uva bay game*. In these three cases, the tool used with students and local stakeholders was strictly the same. In other cases, the tool initially designed to be used with stakeholders has to be adapted to meet the educational needs of both schoolchildren and the general public. This was for instance the case for the computer-assisted role-playing game designed by a group of researchers and biosphere reserve managers in Ushant Island (Brittany, France) to investigate consequences of land-use changes and fallow land encroachment on landscape, traditional activities and biodiversity [29, 30].

Even when the tools are similar, there is a shift in the purpose of conducting participatory simulation with stakeholders, who are definitively knowledgeable, rather than students. Generally, simulation is viewed as a mean to support experimentation by conducting *what-if* analysis that are not pre-determined, and not anymore as a mean to gain experience [31]. It does not make much sense to discuss the appropriate degree of complicatedness of a model supporting participatory agent-based simulation with stakeholders without specifying the type of stakeholders to be involved and without clarifying the purpose of their involvement [32]. Most commonly, the stakeholders involved are policy-makers and/or managers and the purpose is to gain insight about the functioning of the target socio-ecosystem as a basis for policy and scenario analysis related to agriculture and natural resource management [33].

In such a context of use, the *KIDS* ("Keep it Descriptive Stupid") approach [34] is undoubtedly relevant: models should be as complicated as necessary to answer the specific research question, with mid-levels of complicatedness providing the highest benefit per unit of modeling effort, which is reflected by the existence of what was called the "Medawar zone" [35]. On the other hand, the popular admonition *KISS* ("Keep It Simple, Stupid") that enjoins modelers to fight against their propensity to endlessly refine their model [36] is especially valid for theory-building and education purposes. A common idea is that choosing an intermediate posture in between these two zones of efficiency (see Fig. 2) may jeopardize the achievement of one purpose or the other. The empirical details in such models may hinder the theory building purpose and the stylized components may limit their applications in policy support. [32].

Yet we believe there is a *raison d'être* for this type of intermediate stylized empirical agent-based models, which is to stimulate social learning through their co-design with local actors. Social learning has become a central concept in discourse on management issues related to the complexity of socio-ecosystems. Yet the theoretical and practical development of the concept is problematic [37, 38]. Most publications attempt to define its meaning, or to account for its realization in a given situation. Referring to the theory of communicative action [39], the different definitions of social learning emphasize the role of dialogue and intercommunication between group members in facilitating the perception of different representations and the development of collective problem-solving skills [40]. In this perspective, the relational dimension of learning is essential [41].

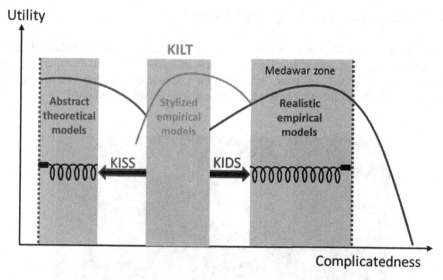

Fig. 2. Utilities of agent-based models according to their complicatedness. The red, pink and blue lines represent the utility functions of the abstract theoretical models, the stylized empirical models and the realistic empirical models. The black springs within the areas of effective use of abstract theoretical models and realistic empirical models symbolize the retraction force exerted by the *KISS* and *KIDS* principles [adapted from 32] (Color figure online)

We advocate that, to fulfill its role of intermediate object allowing exchanges of viewpoints among participants, the model must be connected to reality in a stylized form so that each user can find ways to project features of the socio-ecosystem that make sense for him. To mark the specificity of this approach, we introduce the acronym *KILT* for Keep It a Learning Tool!

The *KILT* approach consists in initiating the process with an over-simplified stylized yet empirically grounded model that enables tackling the complexity of the target socio-ecosystem with a tool that has the status of a sketch. It provides the main features of the final version; however, it is clearly unfinished: there remains an important work of progressive shaping and improvement so that it acquires its final form and becomes usable with people who were not involved in its design.

In this approach, participatory simulation is used from an early stage of the process, as a strategic method to facilitate the co-design. A first version of a stylized agent-based model, deliberately simplistic, is designed by a group of 2–3 researchers. Handled as a participatory simulation tool (the actions of the agents are decided by the participants), it is introduced to a group of local actors to gather their suggestions to adjust it so that it enables discussing an issue related to the target system that was collectively formulated. A group of co-designers is then set up and the model is fine-tuned through a series of successive workshops. Once the design of an operational version is achieved, the tool is introduced to the other kinds of local actors as a support for communication.

To illustrate such a process, we will now present a recent implementation that took place in Zimbabwe.

4   Kulayijana: "Teaching Each Other"

A companion modelling process has been thought to create a fair and balanced communication arena in which local communities and protected area managers would exchange constructively on issues related to the coexistence between human populations and wildlife in the periphery of Hwange National Park, Zimbabwe.

Fig. 3. The virtual game board of the *Kulayinjana* agent-based model [42]

Co-designed with a group of 11 villagers, the agent-based model represents the interactions between agricultural activities, livestock practices and wildlife. The model runs in an abstract virtual landscape that does not integrate specific details of the area, but shares fundamental features with two adjacent areas: a communal area and a forest. To motivate the participation of local actors involved in the co-design of the simulation tool, we chose to initiate the process by crash-testing with them a voluntarily simplistic version, not including some factors that clearly impact the result of their activities, especially crop losses due to extreme climatic events or crop raiding by elephants. During the first test of the game, these on-purpose omissions led to overly positive results of the players, who had all "enriched" dramatically. Although this was very pleasing to everyone, all participants acknowledged it was clearly unrealistic. Drawing on this, the participants engaged in a process of refining the game to make it more realistic while remaining "playable." This process lasted more than a year, with a set of iterative co-design workshops to test and improve the successive versions.

In the context of workshops organized in rural areas in countries such as Zimbabwe, the use of a computer is not always simple. In terms of ease of use, a non-computerized game is much more interesting, and as mentioned above, the use of a physical game board usually improves the direct interaction among the participants.

During the co-design process, we therefore introduced a computer-free version with a game board. In this configuration, it was necessary to manually carry out the updates related to crops and fodder growth processes, losses of crop production due to climatic hazards and raiding by elephants, cattle predation by lions, water levels in ponds according to the input of rainfall data, which considerably slowed down the game and made its use very tedious. The local actors themselves felt that this mode of operation was not suitable and requested the return of the computer support. This challenging request was addressed by the use of a short focal projector allowing the horizontal projection of the computerized environment. With the stylized environment projected on a horizontal support, the players were able to position the artefacts making it possible to materialize their actions: the positioning and guarding of their cattle, the sowing and harvesting on their five plots, and the collective guarding of their communal paddock at night to prevent crop raiding by elephants (cf. Fig. 3).

The final version of the role-playing game was tested and validated with other villagers who were not involved in its co-design. In February 2016, a game session involving protected area managers from the study area was co-facilitated by 3 local members of the co-design team. One of them expressed his feelings before this event: *"It's our game, we are proud of what we have done. It shows our life, what we need and what we have to live with [wildlife]. I hope they will like the game and see ways we can play together."* At the end of the session, one of the managers said:" *This game is great, it could be useful for me to understand better the way they [the villagers] use my forest, and if we could play together and discuss, we could produce good management plans*" [42].

5   Discussion

The case study in Zimbabwe suggests that the horizontal projection of the environment on a physical support serving as a digital game board is an innovation that greatly benefits the implementation of participatory agent-based simulation in stimulating interactions. Other applications are currently underway. In the Poitevin marsh, such type of interactive multi-agent simulation is used to discuss with local stakeholders the relevance of agri-environmental public policies as incentives for farmers to adopt practices favoring the conservation of biodiversity [43]. In the flood plains of the Brazilian Amazon, it is used to better understand how populations adapt their practices to the drastic changes in the hydrographic regime currently observed [44].

In contexts where power asymmetries are strong, strengthening the capacities of the least favored actors constitutes a prerequisite to enable their fair inclusion in concertation processes [45]. Involving them in the co-design of a simplified but still meaningful representation of the socio-ecosystem taking the form of a computer-simulation tool requires some specific attention. Involving heterogeneous participants (here researchers and local actors) in a balanced co-design process is challenging. The rewards, in terms of learning, make the effort worthwhile [46]. Such a process exhibits features that may foster social learning: small group work, multiple sources of knowledge, egalitarian atmosphere, repeated meetings, open communication, unrestrained thinking [47]. The interviews conducted with the 22 local farmers who participated to the three workshops organized to test the "*Kulayijana*" tool indicated that it was found useful (75%) or very useful (25%), that it served as an opportunity to think (40%), learn (28%) and open new perspectives (12%). The self-learning dimension, which was also highlighted by the members of the co-design team, was therefore confirmed by the players [42].

Because social learning entails individual learning, measuring it is very challenging [47]. Scholz [48] recently proposed an analytical framework to monitor and compare the results of participatory approaches with respect to social learning, adding to the definition proposed by Reed [38] in looking for a convergence in the direction of individual learning. Most of the existing work aiming at assessing to what extent participatory modeling can support social learning is based on the use of conceptual diagrams (causal loop diagrams; stock/flow diagrams, cognitive maps), through a statistical analysis of the distributions of concepts' categories in the individual diagrams and in a diagram collectively built [49–51]. Involving local actors in activities like drawing relationships among conceptual entities can be abstruse, especially for those who only had access to rudimentary education. In such a context, we believe it is more suitable to use a concrete playable model.

Visual representations easily grasped by the participants can facilitate socially constructing shared meaning [52, 53]. The constructionist philosophy of learning advocates for mixing media in the model construction: translating one media into another can illuminate one media model formulation by seeing it in terms of another way of formulating it [54]. In the Zimbabwean case presented above, the introduction of a non-computerized version of the model at some stage of the co-design process (see Fig. 4) contributed to reinforce the sense of ownership of the computerized version by mitigating the black-box effect inherent to the use of such high-tech tool.

Fig. 4. Non-computerized (left) and computerized (right) versions of the Kulayinjana model

Providing detailed realistic representations may tend to keep the local actors focusing on some particular features that could distract them from taking a critical distance needed to debate issues in depth and not just superficially. Moreover, tackling conflict situations requires stepping back from the peculiarities on which the existing tensions could easily crystalize. On the contrary, purely abstract representations are likely to appear completely unrelated to the practical difficulties faced by the local actors. A stylized representation constitutes an interesting compromise between these two extremes.

The *KILT* approach does not fall within the scope of the two classical orientations of science, namely theory-oriented science and policy-oriented science (see Fig. 5).

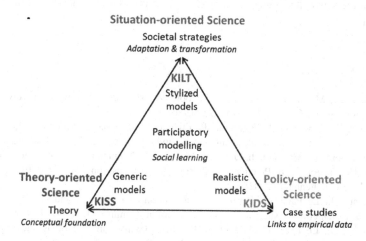

Fig. 5. The scientific orientation inherent to the KILT approach (adapted from [55])

Theory-oriented science -for which the KISS approach is well suited- is intended to consolidate generic knowledge. Policy-oriented socio-ecological science, which aims at supporting policy-makers by assessing the effects of various management rules, will mainly gain from modeling processes implemented according to KIDS principles. Issues arising from local stakeholders could be more properly dealt with by the KILT approach, where the social learning could foster mutual understanding and common agreement leading to collective action.

6   Conclusion

Deeper work is needed to investigate if and why the co-design with local actors of stylized models through the early use of participatory agent-based simulation triggers more effectively social learning. Difficulties arise from the complexity and context-dependence of processes influencing social learning. Moreover, the existing approaches to measuring social learning focus on cognitive learning while neglecting the social-relational dimensions of learning. With the *KILT* approach, the focus is specifically set on how interactive settings of participatory agent-based simulation processes could facilitate social learning. Among the features that account for fostering social learning in collaborative natural resource management, small group work, repeated opportunities to interact, open communication and unrestrained thinking are highlighted [56].

When a small group of researchers from different disciplines engage with local actors in the co-design of stylized models, it has to be very clearly stated that the main purpose is to foster communication through social learning. If any participatory modelling process can potentially lead to such an effect, it is still not so common to set it as the core goal [57]. This situation-oriented science hinges on a transdisciplinary practice in the sense that societies do not know the boundaries that science imposes on them [58].

References

1. Crookall, D., Martin, A., Saunders, D., Coote, A.: Human and computer involvement in simulation. Simul. Gaming **17**, 345–375 (1986)
2. Bousquet, F., Barreteau, O., D'Aquino, P., Etienne, M., Boissau, S., Aubert, S., Le Page, C., Babin, D., Castella, J.-C.: Multi-agent systems and role games: collective learning processes for ecosystem management. In: Janssen, M.A. (ed.) Complexity and Ecosystem Management. The Theory and Practice of Multi-agent Systems, pp. 248–285. Edward Elgar Publishing, Cheltenham (2002)
3. Barreteau, O., Le Page, C., Perez, P.: Contribution of simulation and gaming to natural resource management issues: an introduction. Simul. Gaming **38**, 185–194 (2007)
4. Barreteau, O., Le Page, C., D'Aquino, P.: Role-playing games, models and negotiation processes. J. Artif. Soc. Soc. Simul. **6**(2), 10 (2003)
5. Barreteau, O.: The joint use of role-playing games and models regarding negotiation processes: characterization of associations. J. Artif. Soc. Soc. Simul. **6**(2), 3 (2003)
6. Le Page, C., Abrami, G., Barreteau, O., Becu, N., Bommel, P., Botta, A., Dray, A., Monteil, C., Souchère, V.: Models for sharing representations. In: Etienne, M. (ed.) Companion modelling. A participatory approach to support sustainable development, pp. 69–96. Quæ, Versailles (2011)
7. Berland, M., Rand, W.: Participatory simulation as a tool for agent-based simulation. In: Icaart 2009: Proceedings of the International Conference on Agents and Artificial Intelligence, pp. 553–557 (2009)
8. Guyot, P., Honiden, S.: Agent-based participatory simulations: merging multi-agent systems and role-playing games. J. Artif. Soc. Soc. Simul. **9**(4), 8 (2006)
9. Guyot, P., Drogoul, A., Honiden, S.: Power and negotiation: lessons from agent-based participatory simulations. In: Fifth International Joint Conference on Autonomous Agents and Multiagent Systems (AAMAS-2006), pp. 27–33 (2006)
10. Wilensky, U., Stroup, W.: Learning through participatory simulations: network-based design for systems learning in classrooms. In: Proceedings of the Computer Supported Collaborative Learning Conference (CSCL 1999), pp. 667–676. Lawrence Erlbaum Associates, Mahwah (1999)
11. Wilensky, U., Stroup, W.: NetLogo HubNet Gridlock HubNet model. Center for Connected Learning and Computer-Based Modeling, Northwestern University, Evanston, IL (1999)
12. Colella, V.: Participatory simulations: building collaborative understanding through immersive dynamic modeling. J. Learn. Sci. **9**, 471–500 (2000)
13. Boissau, S., Lan Anh, H., Castella, J.C.: The SAMBA role play game in Northern Vietnam. Mt. Res. Dev. **24**, 101–105 (2004)
14. Castella, J.C., Trung, T.H., Boissau, S.: Participatory simulation of land-use changes in the Northern Mountains of Vietnam: the combined use of an agent-based model, a role-playing game, and a geographic information system. Ecol. Soc. **10**(1), 27 (2005)

15. Le Page, C., Dray, A., Perez, P., Garcia, C.: Exploring how knowledge and communication influence natural resources management with REHAB. Simul. Gaming **47**, 257–284 (2016)
16. Mathevet, R., Le Page, C., Etienne, M., Lefebvre, G., Poulin, B., Gigot, G., Proréol, S., Mauchamp, A.: ButorStar: a role-playing game for collective awareness of reedbed wise use. Simul. Gaming **38**, 233–262 (2007)
17. Etienne, M.: SYLVOPAST a multiple target role-playing game to assess negotiation processes in silvopastoral management planning. J. Artif. Soc. Soc. Simul. **6**(2), 5 (2003)
18. Rates, C.A., Mulvey, B.K., Feldon, D.F.: Promoting conceptual change for complex systems understanding: outcomes of an agent-based participatory simulation. J. Sci. Educ. Technol. **25**(4), 610–627 (2016)
19. Becu, N., Frascaria-Lacoste, N., Latune, J.: Distributed asymmetric simulation—enhancing participatory simulation using the concept of habitus. In: The Shift from Teaching to Learning: Individual, Collective and Organizational Learning Through Gaming Simulation, pp. 75–85 (2014)
20. Heppenstall, A., Crooks, A., See, L.M., Batty, M. (eds.): Agent-Based Models of Geographical Systems. Springer, Heidelberg (2012). https://doi.org/10.1007/978-90-481-8927-4
21. Crooks, A.: Agent-based models and geographical information systems. In: Brunsdon, C., Singleton, A. (eds.) Geocomputation: A Practical Primer, pp. 63–77. SAGE, London (2015)
22. Ligtenberg, A., Bregt, A.K., Van Lammeren, R.: Multi-actor-based land use modelling: spatial planning using agents. Landscape Urban Plan. **56**, 21–33 (2001)
23. Gimblett, H.R.: Integrating Geographic Information Systems and Agent-based Modeling Techniques for Simulating Social and Ecological Processes. Oxford University Press, Oxford (2002)
24. Brown, D.G., Riolo, R., Robinson, D.T., North, M., Rand, W.: Spatial process and data models: toward integration of agent-based models and GIS. J. Geogr. Syst. **7**, 25–47 (2005)
25. Taillandier, P., Vo, D.-A., Amouroux, E., Drogoul, A.: GAMA: a simulation platform that integrates geographical information data, agent-based modeling and multi-scale control. In: Desai, N., Liu, A., Winikoff, M. (eds.) PRIMA 2010. LNCS (LNAI), vol. 7057, pp. 242–258. Springer, Heidelberg (2012). https://doi.org/10.1007/978-3-642-25920-3_17
26. Langlois, P., Blanpain, B., Daudé, E.: MAGéo, une plateforme de modélisation et de simulation multi-agent pour les sciences humaines. Cybergeo Eur. J. Geogr. (2015). [In line] Systèmes, Modélisation, Géostatistiques, document 741, uploaded on 02 October 2015. https://doi.org/10.4000/cybergeo.27236
27. Schlüter, M., McAllister, R.R.J., Arlinghaus, R., Bunnefeld, N., Eisenack, K., Hölker, F., Milner-Gulland, E.J., Müller, B., Nicholson, E., Quaas, M., Stöven, M.: New horizons for managing the environment: a review of coupled social-ecological systems modeling. Nat. Res. Model. **25**, 219–272 (2012)
28. Mathevet, R., Le Page, C., Etienne, M., Poulin, B., Lefebvre, G., Cazin, F., Ruffray, X.: Des roselières et des hommes. ButorStar: un jeu de rôles pour l'aide à la gestion collective. Rev. Int. Géomatique **18**, 375–395 (2008)
29. Gourmelon, F., Chlous-Ducharme, F., Kerbiriou, C., Rouan, M., Bioret, F.: Role-playing game developed from a modelling processRole-playing game developed from a modelling process: A relevant participatory tool for sustainable development? A co-construction experiment in an insular biosphere reserve. Land Use Policy **32**, 96–107 (2013)
30. Gourmelon, F., Rouan, M., Lefevre, J.-F., Rognant, A.: Role-playing game and learning for young people about sustainable development stakes: an experiment in transferring and adapting interdisciplinary scientific knowledge. J. Artif. Soc. Soc. Simul. **14**(4), 21 (2011)
31. Ören, T.I.: Uses of simulation. In: Sokolowski, J.A., Banks, C.M. (eds.) Principles of Modeling and Simulation, pp. 153–179. Wiley, Hoboken (2008)

32. Sun, Z., Lorscheid, I., Millington, J.D., Lauf, S., Magliocca, N.R., Groeneveld, J., Balbi, S., Nolzen, H., Müller, B., Schulze, J., Buchmann, C.M.: Simple or complicated agent-based models? A complicated issue. Environ. Model Softw. **86**, 56–67 (2016)

33. Lusiana, B., van Noordwijk, M., Suyamto, D., Mulia, R., Joshi, L., Cadisch, G.: Users' perspectives on validity of a simulation model for natural resource management. Int. J. Agric. Sustain. **9**, 364–378 (2011)

34. Edmonds, B., Moss, S.: From KISS to KIDS – *an 'anti-simplistic' modelling approach*. In: Davidsson, P., Logan, B., Takadama, K. (eds.) MABS 2004. LNCS (LNAI), vol. 3415, pp. 130–144. Springer, Heidelberg (2005). https://doi.org/10.1007/978-3-540-32243-6_11

35. Grimm, V., Revilla, E., Berger, U., Jeltsch, F., Mooij, W.M., Railsback, S.F., Thulke, H.-H., Weiner, J., Wiegand, T., DeAngelis, D.L.: Pattern-oriented modeling of agent-based complex systems: lessons from ecology. Science **310**, 987–991 (2005)

36. Axelrod, R.: Advancing the art of simulation in the social sciences. In: Conte, R., Hegselmann, R., Terna, P. (eds.) Simulating Social Phenomena, pp. 21–40. Springer, Heidelberg (1997). https://doi.org/10.1007/978-3-662-03366-1_2

37. Kilvington, M.J.: Building capacity for social learning in environmental management, vol. Ph.D. Lincoln University, Canterbury, New Zealand (2010)

38. Reed, M., Evely, A., Cundill, G., Fazey, I., Glass, J., Laing, A., Newig, J., Parrish, B., Prell, C., Raymond, C.: What is social learning? Ecol. Soc. **15**(4), r1 (2010)

39. Habermas, J.: The Theory of Communicative Action, vol. I. Beacon, Boston (1984)

40. Daré, W., Van Paassen, A., Ducrot, R., Mathevet, R., Queste, J., Trébuil, G., Barnaud, C., Lagabrielle, E.: Learning about interdependencies and dynamics. In: Étienne, M. (ed.) Companion Modelling, pp. 233–262. Springer, Dordrecht (2014). https://doi.org/10.1007/978-94-017-8557-0_10

41. Bouwen, R., Taillieu, T.: Multi-party collaboration as social learning for interdependence: developing relational knowing for sustainable natural resource management. J. Community Appl. Soc. Psychol. **14**, 137–153 (2004)

42. Perrotton, A., de Garine Wichatitsky, M., Valls-Fox, H., Le Page, C.: My cattle and your park: co-designing a role-playing game with rural communities to promote multi-stakeholder dialogue at the edge of protected areas. Ecol. Soc. **22**(1), 35 (2017)

43. Hardy, P.-Y., Souchère, V., Dray, A., David, M., Sabatier, R., Kernéis, E.: Individual vs collective in public policy design, a cooperation example in the Marais Poitevin region. In: Sauvage, S., Sánchez-Pérez, J.M., Rizzoli, A.E. (eds.) 8th International Congress on Environmental Modelling and Software, Toulouse, France (2016)

44. Bommel, P., Bonnet, M.-P., Coudel, E., Haentjens, E., Kraus, C.N., Melo, G., Nasuti, S., Le Page, C.: Livelihoods of local communities in an Amazonian floodplain coping with global changes. From role-playing games to hybrid simulations to involve local stakeholders in participatory foresight study at territorial level. In: 8th International Congress on Environmental Modelling and Software, pp. 1140–1147 (2016)

45. Barnaud, C., Van Paassen, A.: Equity, power games, and legitimacy: dilemmas of participatory natural resource management. Ecol. Soc. **18**(2), 21 (2013)

46. Druckman, D., Ebner, N.: Onstage or behind the scenes? Relative learning benefits of simulation role-play and design. Simul. Gaming **39**, 465–497 (2008)

47. Muro, M., Jeffrey, P.: A critical review of the theory and application of social learning in participatory natural resource management processes. J. Environ. Plan. Manag. **51**, 325–344 (2008)

48. Scholz, G.: How participatory methods facilitate social learning in natural resource management. An exploration of group interaction using interdisciplinary syntheses and agent-based modeling. Osnabrück, Germany (2016)

49. Vennix, J.A.M.: Group Model Building: Facilitating Team Learning Using System Dynamics. Wiley, Chichester (1996)
50. Mathevet, R., Etienne, M., Lynam, T., Calvet, C.: Water management in the Camargue Biosphere Reserve: insights from comparative mental models analysis. Ecol. Soc. **16**(1), 43 (2011)
51. Scholz, G., Austermann, M., Kaldrack, K., Pahl-Wostl, C.: Evaluating group model building exercises: a method for comparing externalized mental models and group models. Syst. Dyn. Rev. **31**, 28–45 (2015)
52. Black, L.J.: When visuals are boundary objects in system dynamics work. Syst. Dyn. Rev. **29**, 70–86 (2013)
53. Black, L.J., Andersen, D.F.: Using visual representations as boundary objects to resolve conflict in collaborative model-building approaches. Syst. Res. Behav. Sci. **29**, 194–208 (2012)
54. Wilensky, U., Papert, S.: Restructurations: reformulations of knowledge disciplines through new representational forms. In: Constructionism 2010, Paris (2010)
55. Schlüter, M., Müller, B., Frank, K.: How to use models to improve analysis and governance of social-ecological systems-the reference frame MORE (2013)
56. Schusler, T.M., Decker, D.J., Pfeffer, M.J.: Social learning for collaborative natural resource management. Soc. Nat. Res. **16**, 309–326 (2003)
57. Brugnach, M.: From prediction to learning: the implications of changing the purpose of the modelling activity. In: Proceedings of the iEMSs Fourth Biennial Meeting: International Congress on Environmental Modelling and Software (iEMSs 2010). International Environmental Modelling and Software Society, pp. 547–553 (2010)
58. de Sartre, X.A., Petit, O.: L'interdisciplinarité comme méthode de compréhension des interactions entre natures et sociétés. In: Hubert, B., Mathieu, N. (eds.) Interdisciplinarités entre Natures et Sociétés, pp. 367–386. P.I.E. Peter Lang, Bruxelles (2016)

Multi-agency Problem in Financial Markets

Nuno Trindade Magessi[(✉)] and Luis Antunes[(✉)]

BioISI/MAS/Universidade de Lisboa, Lisbon, Portugal
nmaggessi@hotmail.com, xarax@ciencias.ulisboa.pt

Abstract. Multi-Agency problem occurs in Financial Markets, when multiple companies face agency problems at the same time, in different companies. It happens, when different shareholders' types entering in conflict in order to maximise their benefits. This article explores the agency conflict between controlling shareholders and minor shareholders. This type of conflict arises from arbitrary power that sometimes major shareholders have, over small ones. In order to understand this multilateral conflict occurring in different companies, at the same time, it was created a multi-agent model where different agents' type interact each other in an artificial financial market. The interaction occurs under the assumptions of a game theory, which means that multiple games happen among shareholders in different companies at the same time. In this specific study, we also added the agent who retaliates to the incursions of other agents. This article analyses the type of agents that constantly "wins the fights" in distinct scenarios previously simulated. After several simulations, it could be concluded that the initial structure of shareholders in a companies has impact in how the multiple games end up. Another important result that was achieved is about the gap between the value to be distributed among shareholders and consequent agency costs. Shareholders give more relevance to the value rather than agency costs that they can face out. This means that if the gap is negative because of the value, the shareholders may abandon the market and the same doesn't happen, when it comes from a raise of the agency costs.

1 Introduction

One of the issues behind corporate governance is the conflict between managers and shareholders which generates the so called agency costs [1–3]. The problem first arises, from the discretionary power existent in one agent type in deterrence of other agents and second, in information asymmetry had by executive managers about the company. The conflict happens under the assumptions of agency theory [1, 4]. The agency theory is an approach that explains the relationship between principals and agents in corporate governance context and concerned with problems associated to the misalignment of interests or different risk aversion levels among company stakeholders. The most common agency relationship and problems, in corporate governance arise between shareholders (principal) and company executives (agents), in terms of different goals and interests [1–4].

This situation may happen because the principal isn't aware of the agents' actions or is prohibited by resources from acquiring the information. For example, company executives may have a desire to expand a business into other markets. This will

© Springer International Publishing AG, part of Springer Nature 2018
G. P. Dimuro and L. Antunes (Eds.): MABS 2017, LNAI 10798, pp. 170–183, 2018.
https://doi.org/10.1007/978-3-319-91587-6_12

sacrifice the short-term profitability of the company for prospective growth and higher earnings in the future. However, shareholders that desire high current capital growth may be unaware of these plans or even their goals. Meanwhile, the conflicts can also happen between shareholders with high percentage of capital and the ones with a lower percentage in the capital structure of the company. In fact, this is another source for agency problem with subsequent agency costs. The conflicts could come up even from the relation among the shareholders with the majority of the capital.

In the case of this work, the interest is to find out what is the group of shareholders that have more tendencies to grow inside of a financial market context, where they can face multiple agency problems. Clearly, the objective of this study is to analyse the agency problem with subsequent agency costs between shareholders, also conditioned to the agency conflict between executive managers (agents) and shareholders (principal). Fundamentally, when the agents involved can move and invest in multiple companies which belong to an artificial financial market that was created for this specific effect. A very common case is where one of the major or minority investors achieves or not, what they have defined as a target or move away into another company in order to continue getting benefits from the discretionary power they have. Another important add-on of this works and normally neglected by literature is the retaliation effect that many times occurs in those conflicts.

To tackle this problem, it was built a multi-agent model where agents make their decisions using the approach of game theory to solve their dilemma of maximising their benefits.

This article is organised as follows: in the next section, it is reviewed the relevant literature about agency theory and subsequent agency costs in terms of the impact they have in corporate governance. In Sect. 3, it is described the multi-agent model that was developed in order to unravel the proposed problem. Section 4 shows the obtained results. Finally, on Sect. 5, it is drawn our conclusions and introduce future steps for this research.

2 Advances of Agency Theory in Corporate Governance

An agency dilemma, in general terms, is the relationship between two parties, where one is a principal and the other is an agent who represents the principal in transactions with a third party [5]. Agency relationships occur when the principals hire the agent to perform a service on the principals' behalf. Principals commonly delegate decision-making authority to these agents. Because contracts and decisions are made with third parties by the agent that affect the principal, agency problems can arise [1, 6]. Another central issue dealt with, by the agency theory is to handle the various levels of risk between a principal and an agent. There is a contrasting risk desire, where executive managers representing the principal take decisions more focused in short term results and the major shareholders are more interested on long run profitability. Of course, some minor shareholders (e.g. speculators) are more aligned with executive managers, in terms of risk.

In some situations, an agent could use resources of a principal. Therefore, although the agent is the decision-maker, they are incurring little to no risk because all losses will be the burden of the principal. This is most commonly seen when shareholders con-tribute with financial support to an entity that corporate executives use at their dis-cretion. The agent may have a different risk tolerance than the principal because of the uneven distribution of risk.

It is important to point out that agency theory handles multiple and distinct situ-ations in which one party acts on the behalf of the other [7]. For example, financial institutions are given the responsibility of generating shareholder wealth. However, its business practice forces it to incur risk by issuing loans – some of which are outside the comfort level of the shareholders.

Recently, and to reflect on the conflict there was a division of the problem in three categories: good, bad, and ugly [8]. Agents are bad when they use their positions to get unwarranted leisure prerequisites at the expense of their principals (companies), its shareholders or both. The modern agency costs paradigm was conceptualised on the duty of executive managers in maximising shareholder value [1, 9]. Sometimes this value is designed thinking on short-run and causing harms to the companies, in long run.

In terms of good, the agency cost paradigm analyses the problem of managerial enrichment, clarifying the bad agents with a message about the purpose of their work which should not be working for themselves, but looking for a solution. It is an alert to managers when they are performing badly. In what concerns to the bad, someone would say short-term-shareholder value have become clear. For example, the role of takeovers and other transactions, where the principal intuits include reductions in research and development costs or tax savings which are relocated to other business areas. "These may not be as unambiguously bad as the bad agents' behavior in acting for themselves, but the bad, ambiguous though it may be, may ultimately prove more costly" [8].

Finally, the ugly, where agency costs were supposed to go down if managers put their attention fundamentally on the increasing share price. In this sense, it was given more relevance on paying for performance[1] than on fixed salaries. But it has proven exceedingly difficult to define performance, and gaming of performance measures is scarcely uncommon. So, the ugly is how some managers have reacted to the agency cost paradigm's making them more focused on the shareholder value and by increasing their own value first and foremost.

It's clear that dividends distribution is the crux of matter from a fraught relationship between executive managers and shareholders sustained on conflicting interests. The pay out of dividends to shareholders could generate strong conflicts that have received little attention in the past [3, 10] but now is much explored on literature. The distri-bution of dividends to shareholders diminishes the value under managers' control, thereby reducing their own power, and increasing the monitoring of the capital markets which occurs when the company must raise new capital [11, 12].

The decision of financing internal projects flees this monitoring and for certain financial resources will be unavailable or available only at high explicit prices.

---

[1] A case where performance was defined as an increase in share price, and a share price was considered to accurately reflect performance.

Executive managers have incentives to bring growth beyond the optimal size to the companies they managed. The main reason is the fact that growth increases the managers' power by increasing the value under their control. Besides it is reflected on the increase of their compensations. It was discovered a positive correlation between compensation and growth [13].

The tendency of rewarding intermediate managers through the promotion rather than yearly bonuses also provokes a strong organizational bias toward growth. The number of new positions offered is substantial high in comparison to reward systems based on required promotions [14].

The problems surrounding corporate governance emerge wherever contracts are incomplete and then some agency problems arise [15]. This author has described and evaluated several governance mechanisms in public companies. One of his conclusions was to find that in many cases a market economy can achieve efficient corporate governance by itself. This brought some implications in terms of designing policies. First, he argued the case for statutory rules which in his opinion, they are weak and education has been useless on companies. Adopt an evolutionary perspective is the best choice to make changes in corporate governance. Second, the Cadbury recommendations should be seen as general rules with relative importance for corporate governance. Some of the big corporations have already mechanisms (e.g. takeover mechanism) that help them to ensure their good management. The Cadbury recommendations are not substitutes for these mechanisms. Thus, the existing mechanisms can operate freely to provide appropriate checks and balances on managerial behaviour.

As we can see, the literature is fruitful of those theories suggests several incentives and monitoring methods that may control opportunistic behaviour among managers [16]. This author has established ten hypotheses concerning those incentives and monitoring methods regarding the congruence of managerial and shareholder interests.

A recent work has studied hedge fund activism where substantial abnormal returns occur but fails to answer the question whether these returns cover the large costs of the activist campaigns [17]. This author provided benchmarks for monitoring costs and evaluates the net returns of activism. He modelled the activism as a sequential decision process consisting of demand negotiations, board representation and proxy contest and estimated the costs of each distinct stage. A campaign ending in a proxy fight has average costs of $10.71 million, as he estimated. He concluded that the proxy contest is the most expensive stage, followed by demand negotiations. The estimated monitoring costs consume more than two-thirds of gross activist returns implying that the net returns to activism are significantly lower than previously thought. Even though the mean net return is close to zero, the top quartile of activists earns higher returns on their activist holdings than on their non-activist investments, he concluded. This generates agency problems with future retaliations.

After this review about the advance in corporate governance, we can verify that the main agency conflict in concentrated ownership environments occurs between controlling and the minority shareholders.

It was clear that ownership and respective structure is crucial for the determination of the relevant agency costs taking place in a given company. In companies characterized by dispersed capital structures, it is more important to measure the costs of the executive managers versus shareholders' relationship. However, these companies are specific cases outside of the general norm [18]. In markets that are composed by companies with concentrated ownership and capital structures, it becomes crucial to measure the costs of the controlling shareholders versus minority shareholders' relationship. It happens because of the existence of a permanent probability that the former will try to extract private benefits of control [19, 20].

Consequently, we can see that the multiple agency problem is a subject that is not covered in the literature of corporate governance and need to be study.

3 The Multi-agency Model

The Multi-Agency Model is a multi-agent model built under the Netlogo software [21] to analyze, on the one hand, the impact of agency costs between the principal (shareholders) and the executive managers represented by the agents. On the other hand, the conflict between the large shareholders who have the majority of the capital in a company and those shareholders who have a minority part of the capital. In fact, big shareholders have a discretionary role over the company managers influencing them to take measures against to shareholders with a few part of the capital [3]. The main goal of big shareholders is to expropriate the small ones from the company. However, there is a possibility in this model for retaliation among the involved agents during the time stipulated for the simulation.

To proceed with the implementation of this multi-agency model, it was developed under the scope of game theory. It means that, agents play a kind of game against each other and make decisions using a game theoretical reasoning.

This model has also the objective of understanding which type of agents is more representative in the market.

3.1 Multi-agency Model Parameters

The Multi-Agency Model is composed by a set of parameters that characterises some aspects of Agency Theory. The model is split on the parameters who affect all the type of shareholders, even the retaliators and the executive managers who manage the companies.

3.1.1 Companies Parameters

Companies are represented by patches in the multi-agent environment which is the simplification of a financial market. Companies are dependent from their performance, which is managed by executive managers who assume the accountability of the company towards the owners of capital. These agents are the decision-makers who take the high level decisions. In this sense, the performance is displayed by four colours: green, yellow, red and black. According to this, the companies have a green colour (patches are green) when they achieved a good performance and increased their value in the market attracting the investment of other investors, who are shareholders in other companies in the market. These companies have the capability and are in conditions to distribute dividends among their shareholders.

Companies who have a yellow colour (yellow patches) are companies which had a sufficient performance with restricted conditions to distribute dividends, partially distributed by the various owners of capital. This situation could arise simply from the performance of the company, where executive managers are responsible for it or executive managers were influenced to prejudice the minority shareholders, by the ones who have a great share of the company. Companies which present a red colour (red patches) are companies which had a bad performance because the executive managers only look for their own benefits and interests instead of the owners of the capital. In this case, there is no dividends distribution.

Finally, we have the case of companies with black colour (black patches). These are the companies who entered in bankruptcy as a result of bad management or the conflicts and agency costs provoked by all stakeholders.

The initial cash-flow generated by each company (patch) to shareholders is settled at the beginning of the simulation, by the user. The initial cash-flow is given by the parameter "initial_cash-flow". This parameter represents the maximum of cash-flow that each company can have, at beginning of the simulation. According to this, the cash-flow generated for each income is random using this parameter as a cap of randomness. The decision of distributing dividends is dependent from a fixed threshold and given by the parameter "cash-flow_distribution_threshold". The distribution is also dependent from a threshold that relates cash-flow versus the time period of its generation and it is given by "cash-flow_time_threshold".

3.1.2 Shareholders Parameters

Shareholders have the role of principal agent normally designated on agency theory. In this model, we have three types of principal agents who form the structure of capital in the companies:

a. Major shareholders: these are the shareholders who have the biggest participations of the company's capital with discretionary power over others shareholders and executive managers. It's the type of agents with capacity to influence the board management and expropriate the small shareholders from the capital structure of the company. The number of big owners of companies' capital is given by the parameter "initial_major_shareholders" and it is established and controlled by the user of the model. The weight on the capital structure of the company is settled randomly above a floor of 10%. These agents have a red colour in the model;

b. Minority shareholders: These are the shareholders with a small participation on the capital of the company with no discretionary power over the board of managers and no capacity to influence their management. The number of small owners of company capital is given by the parameter "initial_minority_shareholders" and is established and controlled by the user of the model. The weight on the capital structure of the company is settled randomly below a cap of 10%. These agents have a black colour in the model;

c. Retaliators shareholders: This is the group of shareholders who suffered some attacks to their position on the structure of the company's capital. The number of retaliators is settled at the beginning of the simulation and it is given by the parameter "init_retaliators". This is also controlled by the user of the model. These agents have a blue colour in the model;

3.1.3   Game Parameters

The game played by the agents in each company is dependent of the value of income and the agency costs or costs of the conflict. Both values are given by two parameters: "Value"[2] and "Agency_costs". Those parameters act as sensitivity influence on the agent's decision. Companies generated income for a period of time and can hold it for another period of time or distributed. On the other hand, shareholders search in the market for opportunities in order to maximize their wealth and for that reason they will look for companies with good performance, in order to enter in their capital.

3.2   Explaining Multi-agency Model

The Multi-Agency model is a model based on evolutionary game theory. This theory was first applied to evolutionary processes [22]. Game theory is based on sub-groups of interacting agents, drawn from a financial market population, with certain payoffs occurring between the agents. These payoffs depend on the behavioural strategies of each of the interacting agents. In this case of corporate governance, where big shareholders of a company fight against others with the same dimension or against the ones who have a small share in the capital structure of the company, where two behavioural strategies exist in a financial market composed by investors in stocks and subsequent companies with respective executive managers. In one hand we have the minority shareholder strategy, which is cooperative and, on the other hand we have the big shareholders' strategy, which is more competitive and exploitative.

From one side, we have the shareholders with a minor representation on the company capital, who wants to increase their participation on the capital of the company and let the management board create more value. From other side we have the shareholder with a large representation of the capital with arbitrary to influence the executive managers in order to expropriate the small owners of capital and send them off from the company.

Table 1.   Strategic payoffs of the theoretical game

Strategic positions	Meets a major shareholder	Meets a minor shareholder
If a major shareholder	$Pi = Pj = V - AC/2 - I$	$Pi = V - I; Pj = -I$
If a minor shareholder	$Pi = -I; Pj = V - I$	$Pi = Pj = V - I$

Table 1 represents the inherent strategies of this theoretical game, when the principal agent, in this case shareholders, independent of their dimension, encounters a company with good performance and consequently high value for them, they can access it by investing on it. The shareholders can work together with the executive managers, in putting the company creating value.

If two minor shareholders enter in the capital structure of the company and cooperate, then they will share the value created and the income generated according

---

[2] Value is the discounted cash-flows for shareholders.

their participation in the company, Pi, j V (where V = value of cash-flows). However, if a major shareholder and a small one invest together on a company, the major shareholder grabs everything, so the minor shareholder loses its investment and the major shareholder gets V minus the investment done. The catch comes if two major shareholders invest and interact on the management of the company; they both try to grab the value of the company where they invested for them, fighting against each other at an agency's cost equals to C. Consequently, on average, they get Pi, j V − AC/2) − I. Depending on the value of the company, V, and the cost of fighting or conflict, AC, major shareholders can go to the expropriation of minor shareholders taking them off from the capital structure of the company or a stable polymorphism can exist, where the level of both types of shareholders balances, though not necessarily at 50% each in global financial market.

In this model, it was also added a third strategy, the "retaliator". Retaliators act like minor shareholders when confront shareholders with same dimension and with other retaliators. However, retaliators act like major shareholders against major shareholders. In this sense, retaliators thus have an advantage over major shareholders because they will only pay the agency cost of fighting, AC, if they interact with a major shareholder, but won't pay that cost, if interacting with a minor shareholder or another retaliator. Major shareholders, however, will pay the cost AC, if they interact with another major shareholder or retaliator. A financial market composed by financial agents with all these three strategies can have a number of different outcomes, depending on whether minor shareholders go expropriated (see Fig. 1).

It is evident that actual payoff however depends on the probability of meeting a major or a minor shareholder, which in turn is a representation of the percentage of major and minor shareholders in the total investors of the financial market when a particular conflict takes place. But those financial investors take decisions dependent of the results from all previous conflicts and interactions before the actual conflict. In reality we are in front of a continuous iterative process where the resultant financial investors of the previous conflict were transformed in the input investors to the next conflict in the same company or moving out to another country. If the associated agency cost of losing AC is greater than the value of winning V the mathematics ends in an evolutionarily stable strategy situation having a mix of the two strategies, where the number of major shareholders is given by Pi, j V/AC. The number of investors in this financial market will turn back to this equilibrium point if any new major or minor shareholder makes a temporary perturbation in the financial markets.

All the investors' type major or minor shareholders wander from company to company in a somewhat random search for good performers companies. Both investors change their heading plus or minus 45°. Each move has opportunity costs associated to the fact of leaving a company. Instead, they can get income from the investment done in new companies. If they arrive alone, then they get all the income available for them but if there is another shareholder, then they get a payoff depending on the three types of agents mentioned before. Up to two investors' type can occupy the same company. This is only to simplify the model, since in reality there can be more shareholders. If the wealth of an investor reaches a certain level, he moves and also invests into another company. Instead if its wealth reaches zero, he simply leaves the financial market. The reason that an investor gets income if his alone is that otherwise, in situations where

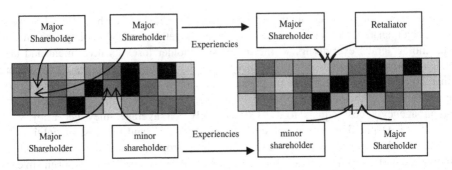

Fig. 1. Multi agency games-1st run and 2nd run (Color figure online)

there is a net cost for major shareholders interacting with other major shareholders and there are two strategies, major and minor shareholders, then the major shareholders would become fixed, and then all leave the financial market.

It is important to not forget that companies require a certain amount of time before they recover their value. This controls the investors' movements and investments in financial market.

4   Simulation Results and Analysis

The results reported in this section were obtained conducting the described experiments using version 5.0.4 of the NetLogo framework [21]. NetLogo is a programmable modelling environment for simulating natural and social phenomena. It is particularly well suited for modelling complex systems and developing them over time.

At this stage of research, the main goal is strictly committed with the scope of this article. In this section, we will only hint the obtained results, and present the respective analysis. The simulations contemplated firstly, an analysis of the initial repartition of shareholders. After these analyses, it was simulated variations on the value parameter which influences the dynamic of the game between agents in each company they pass. Finally, it was simulated oscillations on the agency costs incurred by agents. At this time, it was not simulated the agency problem between executive managers and the different type of shareholders. The main reason for that was the fact that it is outside of the programmed scope.

For this exercise it was simulated 1300 days corresponding to five years of 260 days.

4.1   Initial Number of Agents by Shareholders Type

When we start to analyse the initial number of investors that participate in this artificial financial market, it is verified when the controlling shareholders are less than minority shareholders, the proportion of shareholders with short positions in the company have tendency to decrease during the established period. The same happens to retaliators. A result that derives from the concentration of capital in the companies that compose the market However, when we analyse the big shareholders, we verify an increase of their proportion. The number of investors investing on this market increases to 1236 participants. (see Table 2 and Figs. 2 and 3)

Table 2. Output results for variations in proportions of the agents

Controlling shareholders < Minority shareholders					
Simulation	Minor = 80	Major = 20	Retaliators = 50	Cycles	Investors
Begin	53.3%	13.3%	33.3%	0	150
End	15%	69.8%	15.1%	1300	1236
Controlling shareholders > Minority shareholders					
Simulation	Minor = 20	Major = 80	Retaliators = 50	Cycles	Investors
Begin	13.3%	53.3%	33.3%	0	150
End	30.8%	0.0%	69.2%	1300	2072

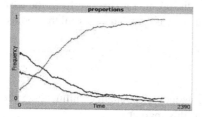

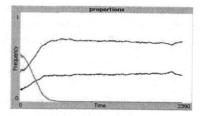

Fig. 2. Controlling   shareholders < Minority shareholders

Fig. 3. Controlling   shareholders > Minority shareholders

The situation inverts when the Controlling shareholders are in majority at the beginning. As we can see, this type of shareholders simply disappears remaining the retaliators with 69.2% of the total investors in the market and small investors with 30.8% of total presences. Meanwhile, it could be checkout that the number of participants in the market increases from 1236 to 2072.

4.2 Value Variation

The next step was to simulate variations on the variables belonging to the payoffs of the played game in each company. The simulation has started by increasing the Value parameter from \$40 M to \$100 M which is greater than agency costs parameterised value. The output results reveal that Major shareholders are more present in this market with a proportion of 45.7% followed by retaliators with a proportion of 38.2%. It is demonstrated by the numbers that this type of agents increases proportionally rather the ones with less representativeness, which decrease. It is also important to mention that this simulation provokes a substantial increase in the number of investors (3672)

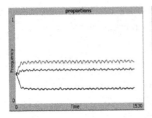
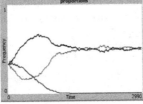
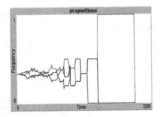

Fig. 4. Increasing value from $40 M to $100 M

Fig. 5. Decreasing value from $40 M to $20 M

Fig. 6. Decreasing value from $40 M to $10 M

playing on financial market (see Table 3 and Figs. 4, 5 and 6).

Nevertheless, the obtained results are completely different when the value parameter is equal or less than agency costs. If both parameters have the amount in the game, we can verify that small shareholders become with more proportion after 5 years in the market. The same happens with the big shareholders.

On the contrary retaliators have tendency to disappear. Finally, we have the case when the value is less than the agency costs. In such a case we can verify all the agents' types leave the market very soon after 126 days.

4.3 Agency Costs Variation

Now is time to analyse what happens when the agency cists changes influencing the dynamic of the game played in each company of this market.

According to the results, if the agency costs increase up to the amount of value, the major shareholders have the biggest proportion in the market, followed by the small shareholders of the companies. In this scenario there is no propensity for retaliation (see

Table 3. Output results for variations in value parameter

Increasing value from $40 M to $100 M (>Agency costs)					
Simulation	Minor = 50	Major = 50	Retaliators = 50	Cycles	Investors
Begin	33.3%	33.3%	33.3%	0	150
End	16.1%	45.7%	38.2%	1300	3672
Decreasing value from $40 M to $20 M (=Agency costs)					
Simulation	Minor = 50	Major = 50	Retaliators = 50	Cycles	Investors
Begin	33.3%	33.3%	33.3%	0	150
End	53.6%	46.1%	0.4%	1300	545
Decreasing value from $40 M to $10 M (<Agency costs)					
Simulation	Minor = 50	Major = 50	Retaliators = 50	Cycles	Investors
Begin	33.3%	33.3%	33.3%	0	150
End	0.0%	0.0%	0.0%	196	0

Table 4 and Figs. 7, 8, 9 and 10).

Table 4. Output results for variations in agency costs parameter

Simulation	Minor = 50	Major = 50	Retaliators = 50	Cycles	Investors
Increasing agency costs from $20 M to $40 M (=Value)					
Begin	33.3%	33.3%	33.3%	0	150
End	48.8%	51.2%	0.0%	1300	1524
Increasing agency costs from $20 M to $50 M (>Value)					
Begin	33.3%	33.3%	33.3%	0	150
End	60.0%	40.0%	0.0%	1300	1645
Decreasing agency costs from $20 M to $10 M (<Value)					
Begin	33.3%	33.3%	33.3%	0	150
End	3.8%	0.0%	96.2%	1300	2061
Decreasing agency costs from $20 M to $0 (<Value)					
Begin	33.3%	33.3%	33.3%	0	150
End	0.0%	67.4%	32.6%	1300	2069

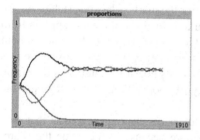

Fig. 7. Increasing agency costs from $20 M to $40 M

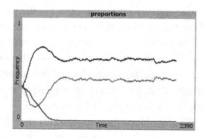

Fig. 8. Increasing agency costs from $20 M to $50 M

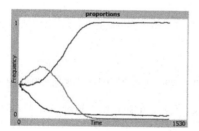

Fig. 9. Decreasing agency costs from $20 M to $10 M

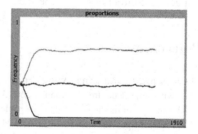

Fig. 10. Decreasing agency costs from $20 M to $0

In the scenario where the agency costs go above the value there is no retaliation and the proportion of minor shareholders is more representative than major shareholders. Now in the case of decreasing agency costs retaliators assume the biggest proportion and major shareholders when the agency costs are zero. In this specific case investors with minority participation end up by disappearing.

An important point is to reference that a decrease of agency costs it has less impact than an increase of value regarding the attractiveness in participating on this market.

5   Conclusion and Future Work

In this work, under the multi-agent based systems methodology and game theoretical approach, it was developed a model to study multiple agency problems. The obtained results have revealed a couple of interesting findings. First of all, the preponderance of the initial proportion of investors that arrived firstly into the financial market. As more is the number of controlling shareholders at the beginning of simulation the less they are at the end. This reflects a constant fight and exhausting derivative of the payoffs that forces them to share the value of the investment with agency costs. Another important finding from the results is that, as higher is the gap between the value of the company and the agency costs the higher is the propensity for the markets become stable. A case where the number of investors increase in the market. However, if the gap appears from a reduction of agency costs the small shareholders who cooperate become without expression in financial market like the big shareholders except for the case where it is no agency costs. So the fact of not having agency costs doesn't mean that is beneficial for the small shareholders who have the strategy of cooperation. This is the opposite from what is defended by literature.

Shareholders give more relevance to the value rather than agency costs that they can face out. This means that if the gap is negative because of the value the shareholders may abandon the market and the same doesn't happen, when it comes from a raise of the agency costs.

Future research will take in consideration the possibility of the different shareholders to have participations in different companies and play at the same time the respective conflicts using game theory again.

References

1. Jensen, M., Meckling, W.: Theory of the firm: managerial behavior, agency costs, and ownership structure. J. Finan. Econ. **3**, 305 (1976)
2. Fama, E., Jenson, M.: Agency problems and residual claims. J. Law Econ. **26**, 327–349 (1983). https://doi.org/10.2139/ssrn.94032. SSRN 94032
3. Jensen, M.: The takeover controversy: analysis and evidence. Managerial Economics Research Center, Working Paper No. 86-01, University of Rochester (1986)
4. Ross, S.: The economic theory of agency: the principal's problem. Am. Econ. Rev. **63**(2), 134–139 (1973)
5. Eisenhardt, K.: Agency theory: an assessment and review. Acad. Manag. Rev. **14**(1), 57–74 (1989). http://www.jstor.org/stable/258191

6. Shapiro, S.: Agency theory. Ann. Rev. Sociol. **31**, 4.1–4.22 (2005)
7. Pendergast, C.: The provision of incentives in firms. J. Econ. Lit. **37**, 7–63 (1999). https://doi.org/10.1257/jel.37.1.7
8. Hill, C., McDonnell, B.: The agency cost paradigm: the good, the bad, and the ugly. Seattle U. L. Rev. **38**, 561 (2015)
9. Alchian, A., Demsetz, H.: Production, information costs, and economic organization. Am. Econ. Rev. **62**, 777 (1972)
10. Donaldson, G.: Managing Corporate Wealth. Praeger, New York (1984)
11. Rozeff, M.: Growth, beta and agency costs as determinants of dividend payout ratios. J. Financ. Res. **5**, 249–259 (1982)
12. Easterbrook, F.: Two agency-cost explanations of dividends. Am. Econ. Rev. **74**, 650–659 (1984)
13. Murphy, K.: Corporate performance and managerial remuneration: an empirical analysis. J. Acc. Econ. **7**, 11–42 (1985)
14. Baker, G.: Compensation and Hierarchies. Harvard Business School, Boston (1986)
15. Hart, O.: Corporate governance: some theory and implications. Econ. J. **105**(430), 678–689 (1995). Blackwell Publishing for the Royal Economic Society
16. Oviatt, B.: Agency and transaction cost perspectives on the manager-shareholder relationship: incentives for congruent interests. Acad. Manag. Rev. **13**(2), 214–225 (1988). https://doi.org/10.5465/amr.1988.4306868
17. Gantchev, N.: The costs of shareholder activism: evidence from a sequential decision model. Publicly Accessible Penn Dissertations, 442 (2011). http://repository.upenn.edu/edissertations/442
18. La Porta, R., Shleifer, A., Lopez-de-Silanes, F., Vishny, R.: Corporate ownership around the world. J. Finan. **57**, 471–517 (1999)
19. Nenova, T.: The value of corporate voting rights and control: a cross-country analysis. J. Finan. Econ. **68**, 325–351 (2003)
20. Dyck, A., Zingales, L.: Private benefits of control: an international comparison. J. Finan. **59**(2), 537–600 (2004)
21. Wilensky, U.: NetLogo: Center for Connected Learning and Computer-Based Modeling. Northwestern University, Evanston (2012)
22. Maynard-Smith, J., Price, R.: The logic of animal conflict. Nature **246**(5427), 15–18 (1973). https://doi.org/10.1038/246015a0

Benchmark for Coalitions at Multiagent Systems in a Robotic Soccer Simulation Environment

Eder Mateus Nunes Gonçalves$^{(\boxtimes)}$ (iD), Diana Adamatti (iD),
and Telmo dos Santos Klipp

Center for Computational Sciences, Universidade Federal do Rio Grande - FURG,
Rio Grande, RS, Brazil
edergoncalves@furg.br, dianaada@gmail.com, voidtsk@gmail.com

Abstract. This paper presents a benchmark for multiagent systems specific to the simulator Soccerserver 2D, an environment to develop teams of robotic soccer, providing metrics and evaluation procedures for multiagent organization schemes, more specifically, coalitions formation. This benchmark has considered a MAS with two main levels, at least: (i) individual level, where agents are implemented from requisites of a social structure and considering its individual capabilities (roles, skills, etc); (ii) a social level, where all the social aspects of the MAS are specified (organization, plans, goals, etc.) and where the individual level of each agent instantiates these social knowledge to act in the system. The method proposed here has applied at social level, once it measures the quantity and quality of coalitions that arise in the environment.

Keywords: Benchmark · Coalitions · Robotic soccer · Soccerserver

1 Introduction

To conceive a MAS, at least three dimensions must be considered: organization, communication and the agents themselves. Each dimension has specific properties and, consequently, it has specific evaluation mechanisms and criterion [7].

According to [20], an agent is evaluated from the consequences of its actions. When inserted in a Multiagent System (MAS), to evaluate is a difficult job, once there are many agents acting simultaneously in the environment. Also, the whole system has structured from an architecture with multiple levels, in a hierarchical or even non-hierarchical structure, integrating different techniques (decision trees, machine learning, knowledge-based-system), models (like BDI systems) and many others features. Nevertheless, in not critical environments, it will be expected the best possible behavior to agents, not necessarily the correct one.

In this scenario, an important question arises: how to evaluate each specific component of a MAS?

© Springer International Publishing AG, part of Springer Nature 2018
G. P. Dimuro and L. Antunes (Eds.): MABS 2017, LNAI 10798, pp. 184–196, 2018.
https://doi.org/10.1007/978-3-319-91587-6_13

To act in complex environments[1], different features, in different levels, are demanded: (i) real-time responses to the environment; (ii) to acknowledge the environment state; (iii) to plan in an individual and social context in short and long-term. There are some methods to evaluate the overall agent behavior, even empiric ones. However, to evaluate and test each of these features in an isolated way is a complex issue.

Such problem occurs in the *Soccer Server* simulator [4], an environment where a robotic soccer team can be implemented as MAS. Soccer Server is the platform used by annual Robocup world championship [15] to support development of new technologies in intelligent distributed systems, specially in software issues [17]. For a team with good performance in Soccerserver, players/agents must present some fundamental features, such that, considering an ascending behavior complexity: (i) to be able to pass, to kick, to move to different positions in a quick way; (ii) to identify the most efficient position to play, to intercept the ball in a defense situation; (iii) to coordinate actions with teammates; (iv) to know the team collective strategies. To integrate these features in a single agent, different techniques/modules must be instantiated, and they can be structured in multiple decision levels with different requisites. However, the normal procedure is to evaluate the team as a whole, considering its performance on the environment. Individually, each module/level/technique can have a incorrect performance measure.

In a more general view, a MAS has, at least, two main levels: (i) individual level, where agents are implemented from requisites of a social organization and considering its individual capabilities (roles, skills, etc); (ii) a social level, where all the social aspects of the MAS are specified (organization, plans, goals, etc.) and where the individual level of each agent instantiates this knowledge to act in the system.

This paper presents a method to evaluate the performance of organizational structures in teams of robotic soccer in Soccer Server simulator, which corresponds to the social level of MAS. Under this perspective, it is considered that in a game, the social level is structured as a organizational model based on teams, i.e., a number of cooperative agents which have agreed to work together toward a common long-term goal [9]. However, to present some group behavior pattern, in the game, each team uses *coalitions* as sub-organizational structures, in short periods of time. Coalition is a goal-directed and short-lived organizational structure, formed with a defined purpose and dissolved when that need no longer exists [10]. In a match, coalitions must emerge when executing some plays, in offensive or defensive formations, or another group behavior pattern. As main goal, this paper define a set of indicators to evaluate the organizational structure of a MAS as a team in the Soccer Server environment, specifically the emerging coalitions. An important feature about the method proposed is that is not considered any information or data about agent's internal structure,

---

[1] Here, we consider a complex environment those in the [20] sense: partially observable, stochastic, dynamic and unknown.

architecture, model and even its interactions. The whole method consider only externally observed aspects of agents behaviors.

The paper is in this way structured. In the next section, some related works about evaluation on agents and MAS are described. In section refsec:model the approach proposed is presented, and in Sect. 4 the model validation process is described and complemented with some quantitative data. Finally, Sect. 5 presents the main conclusions about this paper, and perspectives of future developments about evaluation on specific MAS components.

2   Related Work

According to [16], it is a difficult task to validate and test an agent, and for consequence a MAS, because its conceptual essence, i.e., it is hard to measure features like autonomy, flexibility, social skills, and dependent-context behavior. In a broader sense, this means: (i) it is hard to distinguish which behavior to test; (ii) behaviors can be executed randomly; (ii) how to track actions; and (iv) how to treat failure considering the context.

In [11], it is described another difficulties about agent and MAS evaluations: (v) with a few agents, it is possible to generate an intractable number of data; (vi) it is hard to preview the agents interactions; (vii) communication occurs in the knowledge level; (viii) autonomy permits that an agent acts contrary to goals or rules defined to the group.

However, there are some approaches that try to carry out some kind of strictly assessment. In [18], an evolutionary method guide agents improvement through *soft-goals*, which are qualitative features inferred from requisite analyses. Besides that, the method also act in the environment to evaluate the agent capacity to adapt in a new context. This evolutionary approach does not consider agent internal processes, even social features among agents. But only its adequacy according to optimization parameters.

In [21] has presented a test approach which mainly consider the role that an agent play. A role embeds a notion of responsibility where a role can include one or more responsibilities. A test is about goals, roles and responsibilities hierarchically.

An interesting way to evaluate new techniques and models on artificial intelligence in general is through standard problems. In a long-term, these problems guide developments in a research area and define benchmarks to evaluate its contributions. IBM Deep Blue is a result of a standard problem, which integrate techniques and algorithms that in 1997 defeat the human world champion in chess, forty years later after the initial challenge [12].

In [22], it was proposed a challenge where teams coordination strategies must be created without a priori knowledge about internal structures of agents, defined as *ad hoc team setting* problem. In [2], it has presented an approach to evaluate and compare strategies for ad hoc teamwork considering different scenarios in a common environment, the popular pursuit domain.

Currently, Robocup is a standard platform to develop and test new techniques, models and algorithms on artificial intelligence [17]. The main goal is to build teams of robotic soccer that are organized through different categories, where each one is dedicated to specific problems. Since 1996, Robocup organizes competitions around the world, where different teams from different locations found a place to test its contributions. However, when using the competition results as the only way to evaluate the contributions proposed, one can lead to misleading conclusions. One problem with this kind of benchmark is the absence of methods to isolate some specific aspects of a solution to a modular analysis. In this sense, even a team with a poor performance on competitions can present some outstanding technique as a component of an agent.

There are some attempts to minimize this situation. In [13] has proposed the agent behavior modeling challenge, in order to emphasize the opponent modeling approaches. This feature provides a basis to the adaptation of an agent to an environment in complex domains. Most approaches work to establish relationships between actions, like kick, pass, dribble, move, with specific events on the game. In this sense, [3] presents a solution based on graphs, where is possible to analyze sequences of actions, game states and team strategies adopted. In [19] was proposed an approach to understand agents actions including mechanisms to generate *logs* about its internal states. These logs are organized into different agent's abstraction levels and permit to analyze the conditions where decision-make was executed.

Considering tools and techniques to analyze teams in the organization level, as the model proposed in this paper, there are some important works to be discussed.

In [1] was proposed an approach to extract tactical plans from teams in a structure named *set-play*. A set-play is a high level description for a plan, where is represented the needed steps to be executed and its preconditions, the agent set and its respective roles. This method is used in the software *SoccerScope2*, a tool to analyze and evaluate matches from Soccer Server. [14] uses data mining techniques and algorithms to analyze logs from Soccer Server 2D. Most decisions are based on ball, players positions and distances, which permit to preview its movements. [5] proposes a method to identify cooperative behavior among players only considering positions and movements. Behaviors are structures as oriented graphs, which represent pairs of players, where is possible to infer a network pattern.

In summary, even all techniques and approaches presented above ignore details about agent internal architecture or about a formal social organization, some conjectures about these issues must be made. It is necessary to conceive a conceptual framework about agents and its organizations to define metrics to evaluate its performance, individually and collectively. So, this conceptual framework aid to define an external view of individual and social behavior and, considering also environment specific features, is possible to evaluate each component/module/level of an agent and its organization.

3   An Approach to Recognize and Evaluate Coalitions

In this section, we present a method to measure the number of coalitions and their size in teams of robotic soccer which play in Soccerserver. We claim that the number of coalitions identified in a match measure the performance of the social level in a MAS. It is a measure which consider the agent behavior, i.e., the consequence of its actions in the environment. Nothing about internal aspects is considered.

In an external perspective of performance, a soccer team has the concept of *teams* as organizational paradigm. According to [10], a team consists of a number of cooperative agents which have agreed to work together toward a common goal. In a soccer match, a team organization is maintained for the whole match. To different situations, a team can make specific formations to achieve particular goals. To do this, coalitions with a small group of players is arranged to achieve specific goals with short-term duration. According to this view, when a sequence of coalitions are executed and succeeded, the team goal is attended. Coalitions are subsets of agents organized dynamically, goal-directed and with short life. A coalition has a specific purpose and can be dissolved once that need no longer exists. They are organized from populations of cooperative agents. The group coordinate their activities according the coalition's purpose.

[8] claims that social aspects of a team has as premises the practice, training, coaching, and something that people on soccer world calls *team spirit*. We understand that this team spirit can be measured through coalitions formations identified during a match.

Specifically in this paper, we describe how to identify and evaluate coalitions to attack strategies. This approach is based on identifying passes, an individual basic behavior, in a "give and go" way between two or three agents/players. Figure 1 describes these two type of plays: (a) a "give and go" pass with two players (GG2) and; (b) a "give and go" pass with three players (GG3).

To identify instances of these types of play, we use software that analyses matches through log files to detect this individual basic behaviors: *SoccerScope2* and *Statistics* [6]. The whole method is described on Fig. 2.

The algorithm implemented to identify these types of plays has as requisites:

- to determine the time interval of passes sequence to each team;
- inside these intervals, which type of plays occur and which players participate;
- to identify if occur some event that can invalidate a play: wrong pass, lost ball possession, faults, etc.
- to determine which events occur after play: a goal, a lost goal, goal chance, kick to goal, etc.

The algorithm implemented to detect coalitions as GG2 and GG3 plays, and included in Statistics software is presented in Algorithm 1.

Evaluate plays means that is necessary to know what happens after its execution, i.e., it is necessary to identify which game events take place, what players

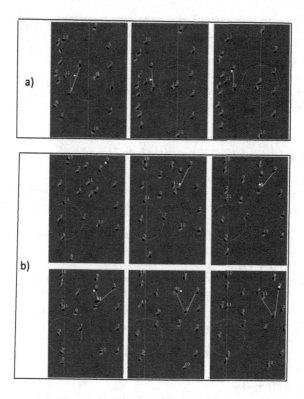

Fig. 1. Features of a "give and go" pass with: (a) two players; (b) three players.

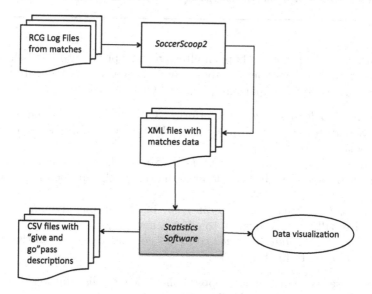

Fig. 2. Components and software used to identify and evaluate coalitions on Soccer Server 2D.

Algorithm 1. Algorithm to detect coalitions on Soccer Server

---

for $passe = i \in dados$ do

 if $passe.getAttribute("team") = time\_atual$ then

  $passer(i) = pass.getAttribute("kick")$;

  $receiver(i) = pass.getAttribute("reception")$;

  $pass(i) = addPass(passer(i), receiver(i))$;

 else

  $t\_events['opponentkick'] =$

  $pass.getAttibute("kick").getAttribute("team")$;

for $i = 0$ to $passador - 2$ do

 if $receiver(i+1).num == passer(i).num \lor receiver(i).num == passer(i+1).num \lor TrueChainPass(receiver(i).team, passer(i+1).team, t\_events)$

 then

  $list\_GG2 = add.GG2(team\_current, pass(i), pass(i+1))$;

  $calculeMovementOnField(team\_current, passer(i),$

  $receiver(i+1))$;

  $goalpattern(team\_current, domain, pass(i+1), pass)$;

  $passpattern(team\_current, pass(i+1), pass, t\_events)$;

 if $receiver(i+2).num == passer(i).num \lor receiver(i).num == passer(i+1).num \lor TrueChainPass(receiver(i).team, passer(i+2).team, t\_events)$

 then

  $list\_GG3 = addGG3(team\_current, pass(i), pass(i+1), pass(i+2))$;/

  $calculeMovementOnField(team\_current, passer(i),$

  $receiver(i+2))$;

  $goalpattern(team\_current, domain, pass(i+2), pass)$;

  $passpattern(team\_current, pass(i+2), pass, t\_events)$;

---

was involved, and what plays happen after previous plays until lost ball possession. Also to define some metrics about GG2 and GG3, it is requisite to know why this kind of play is important. GG2 and GG3 plays is about:

- *to maintain ball possession* - to perform GG2 and GG3 plays makes difficult to adversary to recover ball possession. Without the ball, it is impossible to reach goal;
- *to search and open space on the field* - to execute short pass in a specific area of the field force the adversary team to move, which can open new spaces in the goal direction;
- *to aid to get out from adversary covering* - inside this play dynamic is fruitful to receive ball with more space to effect a new play.
- *a better way to evolute to attack position* - coordinate actions in the sense of a good position to finalize a play.

From these requisites, it is proposed the following distribution to evaluate GG2 and GG3, considering its full performance:

- to advance to attack field - $+0,5$

- to retreat to defense field - 0
- when the consequent event of a direct action, i.e., when the play action of the last player involved in the GG2 or GG3 is:
  - wrong pass - -1
  - received foul - $+0,7$
  - performed foul - $-0,5$
  - goal chance - $+1$
  - shoot to goal - $+1,5$
  - scored goal - $+7$
- when the consequent event of a indirect action, i.e., the play occur after the last play action of a player involved in GG2 or GG3:
  - wrong pass - $-0,2$
  - performed foul or offside - $-0,1$
  - received foul - $+0,2$
  - corner kick - $+0,2$
  - goal chance - $+0,3$
  - shoot to goal - $+0,6$
  - scored goal - $+2$

The values attributed to each play type consider its importance to a match, i.e., how well a team is defending and attacking. The values were set in a heuristic method.

4 Tests and Results

The database used to test the method proposed in the previous section was the official repository of Robocup, more specifically, the teams that participated of Robocup 2014 2D Simulation League, held in Brazil. In that occasion, the final classification was that presented in Table 1[2].

Initially, it was necessary to verify and validate the algorithm, i.e., if it was capable to identify and to count coalitions, GG2 and GG3 plays, in a match. This checking process was made observing games and a specific signal was emitted each time a coalition was happening, in a visual approach. The observer must infer about the correct tracking of a GG2 or GG3 play when the signal was emitted.

A demonstration of this procedure is illustrated in Fig. 3. It presents the coalitions identified and tracked in a match between WriteEagle and Gliders. Figure 3 describes all coalitions identified by Algorithm 1 implemented in the Statistics software to the WriteEagle team. For each coalition, the algorithm must infer about the subsequent play, and score points according the table described in the previous section. Figure 3 indicates 39 GG2 and 7 GG3 plays, counting 46 coalitions. Considering respective tracking for each play, the model proposed indicates 36 points for WriteEagle.

---

[2] Once team *tokA1* was not available, it was not considered in experiments.

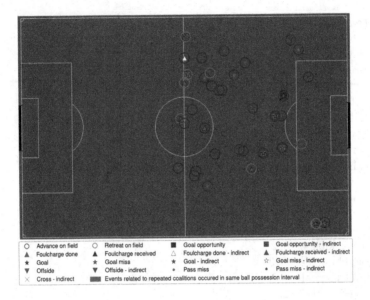

○	Advance on field	○	Retreat on field	■	Goal opportunity	■	Goal opportunity - indirect
▲	Foulcharge done	▲	Foulcharge received	△	Foulcharge done - indirect	▲	Foulcharge received - indirect
★	Goal	★	Goal miss	★	Goal - indirect	☆	Goal miss - indirect
▼	Offside	▼	Offside - indirect	•	Pass miss	•	Pass miss - indirect
✕	Cross - indirect	▨	Events related to repeated coalitions occured in same ball possession interval				

Fig. 3. Coalitions identified to WriteEagle team in a match against Gliders

Once the algorithm was verified, it was necessary to understand what means coalitions in the team performance. In this sense, it was proposed an experiment using tests set where each team played against all other teams, and it has its coalitions and score sized. To each set is considered only one team against all others teams. To each set, the results is tabulated to this only one team. The test is repeated for each team. Table 1 summarizes these tests sets.

The most obvious evidence from Table 1 is that a good social organization is not the only requisite for good performance in matches and competitions. The team with better performance on coalitions stayed on 6th position on 2014 2D competition, and the team with the worst performance on coalitions stayed on 13th position in Simulation League. It is also important to note that Helios2014 reached 4th position on Simulation League with a score on coalitions equal a 37,65.

To better understand the importance of coalitions during matches, it must be understood the context when happens, i.e., to track plays after the coalitions. According Ri-One team test set, it has 178,40 points, which indicates a good incidence of coalitions. However, when Fig. 4 is presented, it is evident the excessive presence of plays where is made a retreat on field. Besides the team is able to maintain ball possession, this is not converted on goals or, at least, goals chances.

Figure 5 describes how teams coalitions behavior can be analyzed through advances or retreats on field. It is possible to infer that teams using coalitions to advance on field has better performance. Good balance between advances and retreats on the field means a good team global performance on competitions.

Table 1. General results of tests sets for each team

Final position	Team	Coalitions	GG2	GG3	Advance on field	Retreat on field	Score
1	WriteEagle	655	541	114	445	211	368, 45
2	Gliders2014	262	218	44	193	69	139, 20
3	Oxsy	351	284	67	253	98	243, 25
4	HELIOS2014	244	179	64	140	99	37, 65
5	CYRUS2014	615	502	113	371	244	201, 00
6	YuShan2014	638	565	73	514	124	376, 05
7	Infographics	156	137	19	93	63	72, 20
8	UFSJ2D	145	129	16	119	26	74, 05
9	FCP_GPR_2014	126	115	11	89	37	59, 60
10	Ri-one2014	554	469	85	234	320	178, 40
11	HfutEngine	222	202	20	135	87	95, 35
12	AUT-Parsian	66	55	11	50	16	18, 30
13	HERMES	217	185	32	168	49	54, 65
14	Enigma	234	213	21	142	92	73, 10

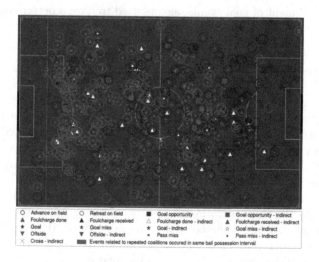

○	Advance on field	○	Retreat on field	■	Goal opportunity	■	Goal opportunity - indirect
▲	Foulcharge done	▲	Foulcharge received	△	Foulcharge done - indirect	▲	Foulcharge received - indirect
★	Goal	★	Goal miss	★	Goal - indirect	☆	Goal miss - indirect
▼	Offside	▼	Offside - indirect	•	Pass miss	•	Pass miss - indirect
✕	Cross - indirect	■	Events related to repeated coalitions occured in same ball possession interval				

Fig. 4. Coalitions of Ri-one team test set

These results prove the paper main argument: different levels/modules/ techniques has different impact on the multiagent final performance. It is necessary a good balance between these levels/modules/techniques to develop a good team. Tests set indicates that for a better use of coalitions, they must impose territorial advance on the field, and creation of goal events. However, for

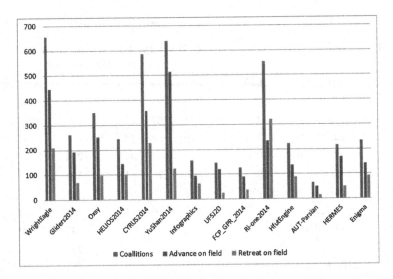

Fig. 5. Coalitions features considering advances or retreats on field for each team test set.

a better improvement of goal events, agents need to have a better adjustment of its individual level, specially kick to goal behaviors.

5   Conclusions

In this paper, we propose a method to evaluate teams social organization, which we consider is carry out through coalition's incidence in an environment as Soccer Server simulator. So important as to form coalitions, it is to perceive which consequences they generate to team subsequent plays. In this sense, it was proposed an algorithm to identify and track coalitions, that are acknowledged as "give and go" plays, with two players (GG2) and three players (GG3). The model also consider the subsequent events after these plays, to dimension the importance of coalitions for the team performance.

Experiments was implemented with two main goals: (i) to verify the algorithm in tasks of identifying and tracking GG2 and GG3 plays; (ii) to dimension the importance these coalitions to team performance.

The results obtained proved that social components in a team is not the only structure necessary to generate a good team. Each level/module/technique in multiagent and agent architecture/model has partial impact in the global performance.

For now, the method proposed has a strong dependency of the environment. Results obtained does not permit arguing about general statements in the evaluation of multiagent systems, in any of their dimensions, in a general sense. Future works are related with the generalization of these assessment mechanisms.

References

1. Almeida, F., Abreu, P.H., Lau, N., Reis, L.P.: An automatic approach to extract goal plans from soccer simulated matches. Soft. Comput. **17**(5), 835–848 (2013)
2. Barrett, S., Stone, P., Kraus, S.: Empirical evaluation of ad hoc teamwork in the pursuit domain. In: Proceedings of 11th International Conference on Autonomous Agents and Multiagent Systems (AAMAS), May 2011
3. Bezek, A.: Modeling multiagent games using action graphs. In: Proceedings of Modeling Other Agents from Observations (MOO 2004) (2004)
4. Chen, M., Foroughi, E., Heintz, F., Huang, Z.X., Kapetanakis, S., Kostiadis, K., Johan Kummeneje, I.N., Obst, O., Riley, P., Timo Steffens, Y.W., Yin, X.: RoboCup Soccer Server: for Soccer Server Version 7.07 and later, May 2001. www.robocup.org
5. Cliff, O.M., Lizier, J.T., Wang, X.R., Wang, P., Obst, O., Prokopenko, M.: Towards quantifying interaction networks in a football match. In: Behnke, S., Veloso, M., Visser, A., Xiong, R. (eds.) RoboCup 2013. LNCS (LNAI), vol. 8371, pp. 1–12. Springer, Heidelberg (2014). https://doi.org/10.1007/978-3-662-44468-9_1
6. da Cunha Abreu, P.M.H.: Artificial intelligence methodologies applied to the analysis and optmization of soccer teams performance. Master's thesis, Faculdade de Engenharia da Universidade do Porto - Universidade do Porto (2011)
7. da Rosa, A.M., Gularte, A., Jung, M., Gonçalves, E.M.: Two different perspectives about how to specify and implement multiagent systems. In: Anais do VII Workshop-Escola de Sistemas de Agentes, seus Ambientes e Aplicações, pp. 141–144 (2013)
8. Drogoul, A., Collinot, A.: Applying an agent-oriented methodology to the design of artificial organizations: a case study in robotic soccer. Auton. Agents Multi-agent Syst. **1**(1), 113–129 (1998)
9. Fox, M.S.: An organizational view of distributed systems. IEEE Trans. Syst. Man Cybern. **11**(1), 70–80 (1981)
10. Horling, B., Lesser, V.: A survey of multi-agent organizational paradigms. Knowl. Eng. Rev. **19**(04), 281–316 (2004)
11. Houhamdi, Z.: Multi-agent system testing: a survey. Int. J. Adv. Comput. **2**(6), 135–141 (2011)
12. Hsu, F.-H.: IBM's deep blue chess grandmaster chips. IEEE Micro **19**(2), 70–81 (1999)
13. Iglesias, J.A., Ledezma, A., Sanchis, A.: The RoboCup agent behavior modeling challenge (2010)
14. Karimi, M., Ahmazadeh, M.: Mining RoboCup log files to predict own and opponent action. Int. J. Adv. Res. Comput. Sci. **5**(6), 27–32 (2014)
15. Kitano, H., Asada, M., Kuniyoshi, Y., Noda, I., Osawa, E.: RoboCup: the robot world cup initiative. In: The First International Conference on Autonomous Agent (Agents 1997) (1997)
16. Miles, S., Winikoff, M., Cranefield, S., Nguyen, C.D., Perini, A., Tonella, P., Harman, M., Luck, M.: Why testing autonomous agents is hard and what can be done about it. In: AOSE Technical Forum (2010). http://www.pa.icar.cnr.it/cossentino/AOSETF10/docs/miles.pdf
17. Nardi, D., Noda, I., Ribeiro, F., Stone, P., von Stryk, O., Veloso, M.: RoboCup soccer leagues. AI Mag. **35**(3), 77–85 (2014)
18. Nguyen, C.D., Miles, S., Perini, A., Tonella, P., Harman, M., Luck, M.: Evolutionary testing of autonomous software agents. Auton. Agents Multi-agent Syst. **25**(2), 260–283 (2012)

19. Riley, P., Stone, P., Veloso, M.: Layered disclosure: revealing agents' internals. In: Castelfranchi, C., Lespérance, Y. (eds.) ATAL 2000. LNCS (LNAI), vol. 1986, pp. 61–72. Springer, Heidelberg (2001). https://doi.org/10.1007/3-540-44631-1_5
20. Russel, S., Norvig, P.: Artificial Intelligence, A Modern Approach. Alan Apt (1995)
21. Sivakumar, N., Vivekanandan, K.: Agent oriented software testing-role oriented approach. Editorial Preface 3(12) (2012)
22. Stone, P., Kaminka, G.A., Kraus, S., Rosenschein, J.S., et al.: Ad hoc autonomous agent teams: collaboration without pre-coordination. In: AAAI (2010)

The Agent Rationality in the Doom Loop of Sovereign Debt: An Agent-Based Model Simulation of Systemic Risk Emergence Process

Paulo Sérgio Rosa[1](✉), Célia G. Ralha[2](✉),
and Ivan Ricardo Gartner[1]

[1] Department of Management, University of Brasília (UnB), Brasília, DF, Brazil
psrosabsb@gmail.com, irgartner@unb.br
[2] Computer Science Department, Institute of Exact Sciences,
University of Brasília (UnB), Brasília, DF, Brazil
ghedini@unb.br

Abstract. This article explores the financial systemic risk emergence process using an agent-based simulation model representing the investor attitudes towards risk. The multidisciplinary theoretic base is compound of portfolio selection, sovereign debt securities and agent rationality literature. Following the 2007/8 world financial crisis, the sovereign debt crises in the European countries have been attracting researches, showing a "diabolic loop" between sovereign debt and the banking credit risk fragility, which can be followed by systemic crises. Modern financial systems rely heavily, mainly at times of political-economic uncertainty, on availability of safe assets (risk-free assets) to choose asset portfolios and also to use them as collateral in markets operations. In order to analyze the relations between financial rationality and investments on bonds of the Brazilian sovereign debt, this article uses a bottom-up approach, based on agent rationality, and simulates portfolio selection by neutrals, risk-seeking and risk-averse investors, all of them concrete classes of an investor abstract class. The main findings confirm that rational choices of investments are likely to be at the base of the doom loop that involves sovereign debt and institutional investors. The findings have important implications to policy makers regarding systemic risk issues, among others public policies.

Keywords: Agent-based simulation · Emergent behavior · Financial system
Sovereign debt · Systemic risk

1 Introduction

In the period from the late 1990s to 2008, the government securities (bonds) issued by European states such as Italy and Spain showed all the characteristics of a risk-free asset, which serves as an important reference point in theoretical economic and finance models. The ratio of sovereign debt to GDP for advanced economies has risen from about 50% in 2007 to 80% in 2012 [7].

In 2011, one of the greatest concerns was the systemic risk of the European banking system, where the contagion fears spread among the euro area investors, resulting in

© Springer International Publishing AG, part of Springer Nature 2018
G. P. Dimuro and L. Antunes (Eds.): MABS 2017, LNAI 10798, pp. 197–210, 2018.
https://doi.org/10.1007/978-3-319-91587-6_14

financial instability [4]. The euro-area sovereign debt crisis spotlighted the nexus between government and banks and its powerful effects on lending and economic activity [3]. A "diabolic loop" between sovereign risk and bank risk amplified the crisis [10].

Some researches in the computational intelligence field applied to economics and finance use agent-based models to study complex systems like financial markets and systemic risk [6, 22, 23]. This article analyzes the emergence of systemic risk regarding the mentioned doom loop of the sovereign debt, using a simple agent-based model with three types of agents: neutrals, risk-seeking and risk-averse investors. Those investors choose portfolios of assets on a monthly basis, following rational options. According to the literature, agent-based models are adequate to study complex systems like financial markets.

Our hypothesis is that risk-averse investors, who choose mainly safe asset to compound their portfolios, have better performance than neutrals and risk-seeking investors, who choose greater proportions of risky assets from the capital market. Therefore, this rational risk attitude is the precondition for the "diabolic loop" [10] that has its foundation on the sovereign bonds attractiveness.

Using Brazilian market data from 2006 to 2016, we analyzed the rational choices of investors with different risk appetite, based on the portfolio selection theory [17, 18, 20]. The results show that risk-averse investors have better performance than neutrals and risk-seeking investors, mainly at times of political and economic uncertainties.

Following this introduction, we present in Sect. 2 a review of the related work, and in the Sect. 3 the methodology of the study, with the high-level research model and the main algorithms. In the Sect. 4, we discuss the results and in the Sect. 5, we conclude.

2   Financial Systemic Risk and Portfolio Selection

In this section we review the literature related to the sovereign debt, systemic risk, and the problem of portfolio selection.

2.1   Sovereign Debt and Systemic Risk

A safe financial asset can be thought as one that is liquid and offers a minimal risk of default [8]. In other words, an asset that can be easily converted into cash and has a very low probability of not being paid by its issuer. This type of asset is usually called a risk-free asset, being a cornerstone in the financial markets as it sets the basis for the interest rates operations. One of the most used risk-free asset around the world is the U.S. Treasury bonds, issued by the U.S. government as a sovereign debt security. Nonetheless, the American bond was for the first time downgraded from "AAA" (the best quality that a bond can have) to "AA+" (one level below AAA) in 2011, reflecting the political risks and rising debt burden.

One of the greatest challenges to the European Union is the scarcity of safe assets in the euro-area [8, 9], because of the growth rate in the Eurozone developing countries during the last two decades that has increased the demand for safe assets. The financial crisis of 2007/8 showed a movement toward assets deemed virtually risk-free, as a process of flight to quality for capital reallocation. It is stated by [8] that European policymakers have treated Greek and Dutch bonds as identically safe, even though the tradable prices are widely different.

It is also important to note the bank regulatory framework regarding bonds of sovereign debt. Following prudential Basel criteria, bank regulators require banks to manage the risk in their assets in proportion to their own capital. Therefore, banks tend to hold a substantial part of sovereign debt in their balance sheets, having a zero risk-weight to this class of asset in calculating capital requirements. To economize on capital [13], particularly during crises when capital is scarce and sovereign risk are elevated, banks are incentivized to hold government debt securities.

Euro area banks hold € 1.9 trillion of euro sovereign bonds. From those, just three members are rated maximum quality (triple-A): Germany, the Netherlands and Luxembourg. The face value of the EU governments bonds stood at € 2.6 trillion in 2015 (25% of euro area GDP), meanwhile the sovereign debt of the United States stood at USD 19 trillion (105% of US GDP) [10].

The Brazilian outstanding bonds was USD 937 billion in September 2016 (49% of Brazilian GDP), with 95% of the total bonds stock issued in its own currency, yielding a real return of 5.95% per year to the investors [19]. Financial institutions, pension funds and mutual investment funds hold each one around a quarter of the government securities. The mean value of the secondary market stood at USD 10 billion on a daily basis.

The Doom Loop of Sovereign Debt

A design of European Safe Bonds is proposed in [8–10] considering the securitization of sovereign bonds of euro area nation-states as a diversified portfolio. This proposal is a response to the open issue stated by the authors as the "diabolic loop" (Fig. 1).

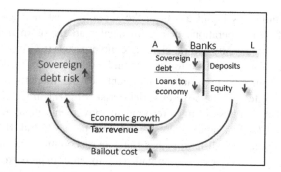

Fig. 1. The sovereign-bank diabolic loop. Source: [10]

The threat is due to empirical observations of preferences of banks to hold claims on their own sovereign, particularly during crises. According to [1], in the stress-test data released by European regulators in 2010, banks of Greece, Ireland, Portugal, Spain and Italy held on average more than 60% of their government bonds in their own government bonds.

This home bias creates a potent diabolic loop between sovereign risk and bank risk [10]. Considering an initial economic shock, it would affect the sovereign risk that could reduce the market value of the bonds and cause, consequently, a loss in the bank book and market equity value. After that, two propagations channels would follow. The first loop operates via a bailout (bank rescue by government) channel: the reduction in the solvency of banks raises the probability of a bailout, leading to an increasing sovereign risk and lowering bond prices. The second loop appears in the real economy: the reduction in the solvency of banks owing to the fall in sovereign bond prices prompts them to cut lending, reducing real activity, lowering tax revenues, and increasing sovereign risk further.

This cyclical effect amplified the euro area sovereign debt crisis after 2009 [10]. In Ireland, Spain, Greece, Italy, Portugal and Belgium the debt dynamics threatened banks solvency and the domestic governments' guarantees became less credible.

Systemic Risk

Systemic risk refers to the potential bankruptcy events of multiple banks, in a domino effect, that can cause huge losses to investors, governments and to the whole economy. There are four types of systemic risk [2]: panics, banking crises due to asset price falls, contagion and foreign exchange mismatches in the banking system. The sovereign defaults are classified in the second type, as a part of the diabolic loop. The sovereign debt crises tend to be more costly than banking crises, which in turn tend to be more costly than currency crises [15].

In 2011, one of the greatest concerns was the systemic risk of the European banking system [4], where the contagion fears spread among the euro area investors resulting in financial instability. To measure the systemic risk of European banks, [4] calculates a total distress insurance premium around € 500 billion, largely due to sovereign default risk.

Beyond their utility as liquid assets in the economy, risk-free assets serve as an important part of daily operations in the financial markets, as in the Repo Market, where those assets are used by central clearing counterparties (CCP) in trade operations collateralized with a security. Due to the size and connections of CCPs, they are also monitored as systemically important components of the modern financial markets infrastructure. The effect of the sovereign debt crisis of 2011 in CCPs is analyzed by [5], showing that repo rates strongly respond to movements in sovereign risk, indicating significant CCP financial distress. The European Central Bank (ECB) also accepts sovereign bonds of all its member states in discounting operations [8].

In 2009, the ECB hosted a workshop gathering together experts from central banks and international organizations in the fields of financial stability and payment system to focus on the financial sector as a network of financial agents [12]. The report states that policy makers were looking for new analytical tools that help to better identify, monitor and address sources of systemic risk. To tackle this shortcoming, agent-based modelling was considered a recent alternative approach, relying on algorithms and simulations, where simple decision-make rules can generate complex behavior at the system level. Some research have been applied to investigate the dynamic of financial markets using agent-based model [6, 22, 23].

Our research aims to investigate the emergence of systemic risk regarding the diabolic loop mentioned by [8–10], using an agent-based approach to model three types of agents: neutrals, risk-seeking and risk-averse investors.

2.2 Portfolio Selection

The quantification of the tradeoff between risk and expected return is one of the important problem of modern financial economics [11]. In spite of the common sense that suggest that risky investments such as stock market will generally yield higher returns than investments free of risk, it was only during the decade of 1960 that academic researchers developed seminal works comprising portfolio theory [17, 18, 20]. The main concern was economic agents who act under uncertainty and could make use of sufficient computer and database resources in order to obtain diversification of investments to reduce uncertainty and maximize their expected utility function. The existence of uncertainty is essential to the analysis of rational investment behavior [18].

A survey with 274 asset managers in Brazil [16] showed that the Markowitz's portfolio theory [18] and the Capital Asset Price Model are part of the current practices regarding performance attribution, risk management and portfolio selection, similarly to European asset managers' practices. Therefore, this set of rationality rules will drive the agents' investment decision process in this study.

Investors would optimally hold a mean-variance efficient portfolio: a mix of assets with the highest expected return for a certain level of variance. Given a vector ω of weights or investments proportions of each of the n assets to compound the portfolio, the expected return and the risk of this portfolio are respectively:

$$E(R) = \sum_{i=1}^{n} R_i \omega_i \tag{1}$$

$$V(R) = \sum_{i=1}^{n} \sum_{j=1}^{n} \omega_i \omega_j \sigma_{ij} \tag{2}$$

where R_i is the return of asset i and σ_{ij} is the covariance between the returns of assets i and j.

A portfolio p is the minimum-variance portfolio of all portfolios with mean return μ_p if its portfolio weight vector is the solution to this optimization:

$$\min \omega' \Omega \omega$$
$$\text{s.t. } \omega' \mu = \mu_p \text{ and } \omega' \iota = 1 \tag{3}$$

where ι is a vector of ones, μ is the vector of expected returns, and Ω is the variance-covariance matrix of returns.

Solving the Eq. (3) gives ω_p [11]:

$$\omega_p = g + h\,\mu_p \tag{4}$$

$$g = \frac{1}{D}\left[B\left(\Omega^{-1}\iota\right) - A\left(\Omega^{-1}\mu\right)\right] \tag{5}$$

$$h = \frac{1}{D}\left[C\left(\Omega^{-1}\mu\right) - A\left(\Omega^{-1}\iota\right)\right] \tag{6}$$

$$A = \iota'\Omega^{-1}\mu,\ B = \mu'\Omega^{-1}\mu,\ C = \iota'\Omega^{-1}\iota,$$
$$D = BC - A^2 \tag{7}$$

The efficient frontier of portfolios suggested by Markowitz [18] was improved with the introduction of a risk-free asset in the model known as Capital Asset Price Model (CAPM), given an opportunity to invest a proportion α of the resources in the risky assets and the proportion $(1-\alpha)$ in the risk-free asset [17, 20].

The factors β measure the sensibility of return of each asset in relation to the return of a market portfolio, which is an ideal portfolio of all invested wealth,

$$\beta_i = \frac{\sigma_{im}}{\sigma_m^2} \tag{8}$$

where m refers to the market portfolio.

Therefore, the expected return of any asset would be calculated as a function of its sensibility coefficient (β_i), of the risk-free asset return (R_f) and of the expected return of the market portfolio (R_m):

$$E(R_i) = R_f + \beta_i\left[E(R_m) - R_f\right] \tag{9}$$

Figure 2 shows that with a risk-free asset, all efficient portfolios lie along the "security market line" from the risk-free asset through the portfolio q that is the tangency or

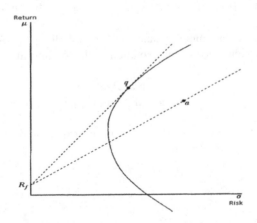

Fig. 2. Efficient frontier with a risk-free asset. Source: [11]

market portfolio [11]. From the point R_f to q there is a continuum of choices to the vector ω, with $0 \leq \alpha \leq 1$. Specifically for the tangency portfolio, the proportion α is equal to one, and beyond this point, the investor would be willing to borrowing at a risk-free rate of interest and reinvesting this amount in risky assets.

The tangency portfolio weights ω_q can be obtained as follows [11]:

$$\omega_q = \frac{1}{\iota' \, \Omega^{-1} \left(\mu - R_f \iota \right)} \cdot \Omega^{-1} \left(\mu - R_f \iota \right) \tag{10}$$

3   The Agent-Based Model

According to [24], an agent can have the property of calculative rationality in its decision-making process and make use of utility functions. Intelligent agents are able to perceive their environment and act according to their repertoire of actions. A sequence of interleaved environment states and agents' actions is defined as a run $r : e_1 \xrightarrow{a_1} e_2 \xrightarrow{a_2} e_3 \xrightarrow{a_3} \ldots \xrightarrow{a_i} e_i$. An agent makes a decision about what action to execute knowing the history of the environment transformation. The agents are modelled as functions that map runs to actions: $Ag : R^E \rightarrow AC$, where R^E represents any current environment state during a run and $AC = \{a_1, a_2, a_3, \ldots, a_n\}$ is the set of agent actions.

The different attitudes toward risk are influenced by the utilities functions and their respective outcomes. A risk-averse agent prefers a "sure thing" to a risky situation with the same expected value. In the other hand, a risk-seeking agent would prefer to engage in opportunities with major gains, in spite of the low probability, instead of high probability of relative minor gains, having both situations the same expected value. The risk-neutral agent is in the middle of the risk spectrum and its main concern is about the expected value, being indifferent about the risk. Figure 3 shows the high-level ontology model of this research.

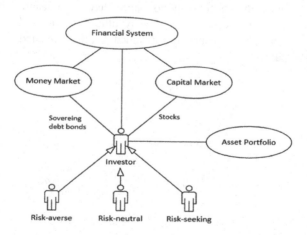

Fig. 3. Conceptual model – high-level ontology

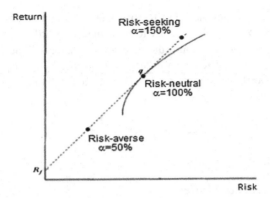

Fig. 4. Type of investors and risky assets weights

Following [21] in order to avoid making assumptions about the utility curve of each investor, and considering the absence of parameters in the literature, we fixed the quantities of risky assets that each investor will hold in the portfolio simulations (Fig. 4). The risk-averse agent will hold 50% of risk-free asset, the risk-neutral investor will hold the market portfolio, and the risk-seeking agent will borrow money at the risk-free interest rate to buy more risky assets. This definition is an attempt to equalize the three risk attitudes in the security market line spectrum, having the market portfolio in the middle point.

At the beginning of each month $t \in$ [Jan/2006, Jan/2016], the agents update their beliefs, perceiving the current asset prices in the environment state $e_t \in E = \{e_1, \ldots, e_{120}\}$ and proceed the actions $a_m \in AC = \{$portfolio performance evaluation, portfolio rebalance$\}$. To execute the action a_2, each agent $A_k \in Ag = \{$Risk-averse, Risk-neutral, Risk-seeking$\}$ selects the assets weights $\omega_{k,t}$ considering its risk attitude: $\alpha_{k=1} = 50\%, \alpha_{k=2} = 100\%, \alpha_{k=3} = 150\%$. Each agent starts the simulation with a $\$100.00$ portfolio value.

To identify whether the portfolios performances have significantly differences, the Sharpe and Treynor measures are used for hypothesis testing [14], with the null hypothesis of equivalent performance. It is assumed that the simulated observations are normally distributed:

$$Z_{Sin} = \frac{\widehat{Sh}_{in}}{\sqrt{\hat{\theta}}} \sim N(0, 1) \tag{11}$$

$$\widehat{Sh}_{in} = s_n \bar{r}_i - s_i \bar{r}_n \tag{12}$$

$$\theta = \frac{1}{T} \left[2\sigma_i^2 \sigma_n^2 - 2\sigma_i \sigma_n \sigma_{in} + 0.5 \, \mu_i^2 \sigma_n^2 + 0.5 \, \mu_n^2 \sigma_i^2 - \frac{\mu_i \mu_n}{2\sigma_i \sigma_n} \left(\sigma_{in}^2 + \sigma_i^2 \sigma_n^2 \right) \right] \tag{13}$$

3.1   Algorithms

This subsection describes the main procedures to simulate the model proposed in this study: the actions $a_m \in AC$ = {portfolio performance evaluation, portfolio rebalance}. The first procedure is responsible for the performance attribution of the portfolios held by the agents. Based on the prices time series, it calculates the returns on each asset of the sample and, after that, calculates the current value of the portfolios. It is the same procedure to all of the agents.

Algorithm 1 - Action a_1 :Portfolio performance evaluation at time t

1: **for** each asset $x_i \in$ market portfolio **do**
2:    $\mu_{i,t} \leftarrow \frac{Price_{i,t}}{Price_{i,t-1}} - 1$
3: $\mu_{Rf} \leftarrow$ Riskfree yield$_t$
4: **for** each agent $A_k \in Ag$ **do**
5:    calculate the return of the $portfolio_{k,t}$
6:    calculate the new value of the $portfolio_{k,t}$

The second algorithm is in charge of the agent assessment about the assets he will choose. It distributes the agent wealth among the risky assets and the risk-free asset, having in account the agent preferences and the state environment at t.

Algorithm 2 - Action a_2 :Portfolio rebalance at time t

1: **for** each agent $A_k \in Ag$ **do**
2:    $\alpha_k \leftarrow$ preference for risky assets
3:    $Rf_k \leftarrow 1 - \alpha_k$
4:    calculate the new weight vector $\omega_{k,t}$, using the six asset $x_i \in$ market portfolio
5:    calculate the new value to invest (or to borrow) in the risk-free asset
6:    calculate the new value to invest in each asset $x_i \in$ agent portfolio, according to $\omega_{k,t}$

3.2   Data and Simulation Setup

We use real data from the Brazilian stock exchange (BM&FBOVESPA – São Paulo) for the period Jan-2006 to Jan-2016. The stock closing prices are adjusted for dividends payment and splits operations.

In a way to simulate a reasonable diversification of investments (different sectors of the economy), we choose six stocks as a proxy to the simulated market portfolio. This choice was a result of a deliberate selection of the two blue chips companies – Petrobras (PETR4) and Vale do Rio Doce (VALE5) – plus four other randomly selected stocks from distinct sectors: transport – Gol Linhas Aéreas (GOLL4); financial intermediaries – Banco do Brasil (BBAS3); energy – CPFL Energia (CPFE3); and retail – Lojas Americanas (LAME4).

The use of this fixed list of assets is a limitation of this study. This shortcoming could be addressed by using the entire list of the BM&FBOVESPA index of stocks, proceed that would also allow more runs in the simulation and the validation of the results.

To proxy the returns of the government securities (risk-free asset), we use a very tradable Brazilian financial instrument and commonly used in researches of this type, the Certificado de Depósito Interfinanceiro (CDI) that has a return very close to the government bonds yield. The BM&FBOVESPA Stock Exchange Index (IBOV) was also collected as a market benchmark.

Due to the fixed list of assets above described, the simulation setup is based on singletons instances of each agent acting as representative agents of each class. More instances would lead to same results for each agent type, as new instances of agents would have the same risk appetite.

4 Results and Discussion

Initially, the environment state e_1 was set with the prices observed from Jan-2001 to Jan-2006 in order to generate the current expected returns and the respective assets risks for the portfolio selection action a_2 at $t = 1$. The returns time series have the past returns on a monthly basis for each one of the assets chosen for the simulation (PETR4, VALE5, GOLL4, BBAS3, CPFE3, LAME4, and CDI).

Subsequently, the agents' beliefs are updated at every new state until the simulation reached the final state e_{120} at Jan-2016. At every new state, each agent executes action a_1 (portfolio performance evaluation) to calculate its portfolio value and action a_2 (portfolio rebalance) to redefine the amount of investment in each asset.

Figure 5 shows the security market line and the efficient frontier related to the environment state at $t = 01/2008$, a few months before the great impacts of the sub-prime crisis. At that time, an investor with 50% of risky assets in its portfolio would have an expected return of 1.9% and a portfolio risk close to 3.3%, while an investor with 100% of risk-free asset would have a return of 0.88% ($\sigma = 0\%$ in this case). The increasing expected return for the risk-neutral investor in relation to the risk-averse portfolio is around 1%, nonetheless the increasing in risk is about 3.3%. The same applies to the risk-seeking investor, who would increase its expected return to 3.9%, facing a greater risk of 9.93%.

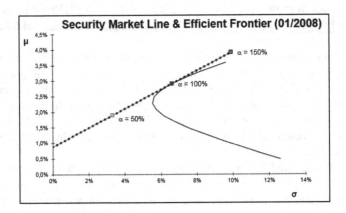

Fig. 5. Portfolios expected return and risk

Table 1. Correlations of portfolio returns

Agents portfolio	ρ_{ij}
A_1, A_2	0.83
A_1, A_3	0.35
A_2, A_3	0.81

Agent $A_k \in Ag =$ {Risk-averse, Risk-neutral, Risk-seeking}

The correlations between the portfolio values along the simulation period are in Table 1. It shows a quite strong correlation between the performance of the agents 1 and 2, and the agents 2 and 3, while the performance of the risk-averse and risk-seeking agents has a low correlation.

Figure 6 presents the results of each agent rationality driving its portfolio selection. It is notable the effect of the 2007/8 financial crisis in all of the three agent's portfolios, with a minor impact for the most conservative risk attitude. From t = 01/2006 to t = 06/2008, the risk-seeking agent had the best performance, reaching almost 200% of return in the period. The volatility of its returns continues after the deep falling prices at t = 12/2008, when all of its past accumulated return vanished. After twelve months (t = 12/2009), the risk-seeking agent recovered its portfolio value and then started a descendent trend until the end of the simulation, with a negative accumulated return at t = 01/2016.

Almost the same movements apply to the risk-neutral investor, with a lower impact on its portfolio value because of its lower exposure to risky assets. At t = 09/2014, its portfolio raised up to 200% of the initial value, the leading value in the simulation. Nevertheless, it lost 50% of the value by the last environment state e_{120}, showing the exposure effect to risky asset, even in a less proportion than in the risk-seeking investor portfolio.

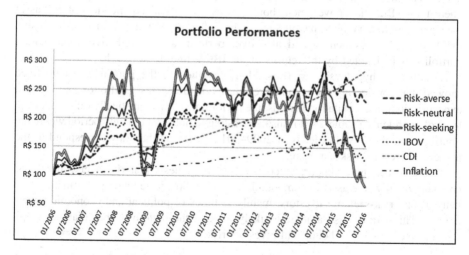

Fig. 6. Performances of initial R$ 100 value portfolios (Brazilian Real)

Table 2. Hypothesis test

Periods	$\mu_{A=1}$	$\sigma_{A=1}$			Results
	$\mu_{A=2}$	$\sigma_{A=2}$	$\widehat{Sh}_{1,2}$	p-value$_{1,2}$	
	$\mu_{A=3}$	$\sigma_{A=3}$	$\widehat{Sh}_{1,3}$	p-value$_{1,3}$	
2006–2008	36%	3.7%			
	21%	7.5%	0.02	0.0000[***]	Rejects H_0
	−0.1%	11.2%	0.04	0.0000[***]	Rejects H_0
2009–2011	55%	4.1%			
	75%	8.1%	0.01	0.0000[***]	Rejects H_0
	90%	12.2%	0.03	0.0000[***]	Rejects H_0
2012–2015	1%	3.7%			
	−36%	7.4%	0.01	0.0000[***]	Rejects H_0
	−63%	11.2%	0.02	0.0000[***]	Rejects H_0
2006–2015 full period	131%	3.8%			
	54%	7.7%	0.08	0.0000[***]	Rejects H_0
	−17%	11.5%	0.15	0.0000[***]	Rejects H_0

*** Significance level of 1%

H_0: The performances are equivalent

Regarding the risk-averse rationality, Fig. 6 shows less accentuated variations in this portfolio value along the simulation history. Actually, the risk-averse portfolio selection rationality achieved the most valuable portfolio at t = 01/2016, suggesting that a more conservative risk attitude would have been the optimal approach to wealth management in the context of the analyzed data.

Another performance is quite interesting to note in the graph. The CDI line represents a total risk-averse investor, who would choose only risk-free assets to invest, like sovereign debt. In the long run, a CDI investment, which is a proxy to post-fixed interest rate Brazilian government bonds, wins the virtual competition of the asset managers, with a notably payoff above the inflation of the period. An exclusive risk-free asset investment would also over perform a real well diversified market portfolio, as is denoted by the returns of the IBOV line in the graph.

Finally, the hypothesis test (Eqs. 11–13) applied to the portfolios performance showed that considering the cumulative returns of the agents' portfolios and the risk exposure along the simulation periods, the performances are statistically different at 1% level of confidence (Table 2). It is also interesting to note that the only period where the returns are in a crescent order is in 2009–2011, in a way that they correspond to the associated crescent risk exposure.

These results give support to confirm our hypothesis that risk-averse investors, choosing mainly safe asset to compound their portfolios, have better performance than neutrals and risk-seeking investors, mainly at times of political and economic uncertainties. This rational risk attitude is likely to be at the bottom of the "diabolic loop" [10] between sovereign bonds and investors risk.

5 Conclusions

Safe assets, generally called risk-free assets, have become an important class of assets to investors around the world. Besides being a liquid font of cash, their usefulness are also related to regulatory capital requirements to financial institutions that follows Basel prudential criteria, as a zero weight financial instrument.

The development of financial models, like the Capital Asset Price Model, found in the risk-free asset an important piece to portfolio selection approaches.

Using a bottom-up approach and Brazilian financial market data from 2006 to 2016, this study has analyzed the rationality of three types of agents, regarding their risk attitude that drives portfolio selection processes. Among the risk attitudes, the risk-averse agent who invested half or its wealth in risk-free assets like sovereign bonds has reached the most successful result. Furthermore, portfolios of solely risk-free assets best performed all of the simulated choices.

The results has confirmed our hypothesis that risk-averse investors, acting rationally in order to manage their asset portfolios, are likely to be at the bottom of a "diabolic loop" between sovereign bonds and investors (bank) risk. Their demand for sovereign bonds feeds the cyclical problem, even at times of falling interest rates in medium-advanced economies. Nonetheless, the conclusion is restrict to the context studied reflecting the country data of the sample.

This brings important issues to the policy makers in charge of systemic risk monitoring, banks regulation, fiscal and public budget constraints, and the development of the capital markets. The interconnectedness of financial institutions that hold significant part of sovereign debt in their portfolios can contribute significantly to the doom loop and consequently to the emergence of systemic risk crises. The relative high interest rates and the regulatory incentives to this behavior contribute to the rational choices of risk-averse investors. The growing ratios of the sovereign debt to GDP place an additional concern to governments, which may deal concomitantly with economic downturns.

Regarding the agent-based methodology, the process of programming, testing and executing the software components of the model may be time-consuming, especially when the framework starts from the scratch. Despite this, it can also be worth building or extending a framework to promote new research questions, even in the broad area of the social science.

Future studies could insert corporate governance actors – important agents to the credibility of the stock markets – in the agent-based model, in order to cope with the classical principal-agent problem.

References

1. Acharya, V., Rajan, R.G.: Sovereign debt, government myopia, and the financial sector. Rev. Financ. Stud. **26**(6), 1526–1560 (2013)
2. Allen, F., Carletti, A.: What is systemic risk? J. Money Credit Bank. **45**(1), 121–127 (2013)
3. Altavilla, C., Pagano, M., Simonelli, S.: Bank exposures and sovereign stress transmission. In: Working Paper no. 11. European Systemic Risk Board (2016)

4. Black, L., Correa, R., Huang, C., Zhou, H.: The systemic risk of European banks during the financial and sovereign debt crises. J. Bank. Finan. **63**, 107–125 (2016)
5. Boissel, C., Derrien, F., Ors, E., Thesmar, D.: Systemic risk in clearing houses: evidence from the European repo market. In: Working Paper no. 10. European Systemic Risk Board (2016)
6. Bookstaber, R.: Using agent-based models for analyzing threats to financial stability. In: Working Paper 3. U.S. Department of the Treasury-Office of Financial Research (2012)
7. Bowdler, C., Esteves, R.P.: Sovereign debt: the assessment. Oxf. Rev. Econ. Policy **29**(3), 463–477 (2013)
8. Brunnermeier, M.K., Garicano, L., Lane, P., Pagano, M., Reis, R., Santos, T., Thesmar, D., Van Nieuwerburgh, S., Vayanos, D.: European Safe Bonds (ESBies). The Euronomics Group (2012). www.euro-nomics.com
9. Brunnermeier, M.K., Garicano, L., Lane, P., Pagano, M., Reis, R., Santos, T., Thesmar, D., Van Nieuwerburgh, S., Vayanos, D.: The sovereign-bank diabolic loop and ESBies. Am. Econ. Rev. Pap. Proc. **106**(5), 508–512 (2016)
10. Brunnermeier, M.K., Langfield, S., Pagano, M., Reis, R., Van Nieuwerburgh, S., Vayanos, D.: ESBies: safety in the tranches. The Euronomics Group (2016). www.euro-nomics.com
11. Campbell, J.Y., Lo, W., Mackinlay, A.C.: The Econometrics of Financial Markets. Princeton University Press, Princeton (1997)
12. European Central Bank: Recent Advances in Modelling Systemic Risk Using Network Analysis (2010). www.ecb.europa.eu
13. European Systemic Risk Board: Report on the regulatory treatment of sovereign exposures (2015). www.esrb.europa.eu
14. Jobson, J.D., Korkie, B.M.: Performance hypothesis testing with the Sharpe and Treynor measures. J. Finan. **36**(4), 889–908 (1981)
15. Laeven, L., Valencia, F.: Systemic banking crises database. IMF Econ. Rev. **61**(2), 225–270 (2013)
16. Lee, S.C., Eid Jr., W.: Teoria e Prática na Construção, Gestão de Riscos e Mensuração de Desempenho de Portfólios. In: Proceedings of the XL EnANPAD, Brasil, 25–28 Sep 2016 (2016)
17. Lintner, J.: The Valuation of Risk Assets and the Selection of Risky Investments in Stock Portfolios and Capital Budgets. Rev. Econ. Stat. **47**(1), 13–37 (1965)
18. Markowitz, H.: Portfolio selection. J. Finan. **7**(1), 77–91 (1952)
19. Secretaria do Tesouro Nacional. Relatório Mensal da Dívida Pública Federal – Setembro (2016). www.tesouro.fazenda.gov.br
20. Sharpe, W.F.: A theory of market equilibrium under conditions of risk. J. Finan. **19**(3), 425–442 (1964)
21. Shoham, Y., Leyton-Brown, K.: Multiagent Systems: Algorithmic, Game-Theoretic, and Logical Foundations. Cambridge University Press, Cambridge (2009)
22. Terna, P.: Systemic Risk in Artificial Worlds, Using a New Tool in the ABM Perspective. Universidade de Torino (2009)
23. Thurner, S.: Systemic financial risk: agent based models to understand the leverage cycle on national scales and its consequences. In: Working Paper FGS no. 1. OECD (2011)
24. Wooldridge, M.: An Introduction to Multiagent Systems. Wiley, Hoboken (2009)

InterSCSimulator: Large-Scale Traffic Simulation in Smart Cities Using Erlang

Eduardo Felipe Zambom Santana[1](✉), Nelson Lago[1], Fabio Kon[1],
and Dejan S. Milojicic[2]

[1] Department of Computer Science, University of São Paulo, São Paulo, Brazil
{efzambom,lago,kon}@ime.usp.br
[2] HP Laboratories, Palo Alto, USA
dejan.milojicic@hpe.com

Abstract. Large cities around the world face numerous challenges to guarantee the quality of life of its citizens. A promising approach to cope with these problems is the concept of Smart Cities, of which the main idea is the use of Information and Communication Technologies to improve city services. Being able to simulate the execution of Smart Cities scenarios would be extremely beneficial for the advancement of the field. Such a simulator, like many others, would need to represent a large number of various agents (e.g. cars, hospitals, and gas pipelines). One possible approach for doing this in a computer system is to use the actor model as a programming paradigm so that each agent corresponds to an actor. The Erlang programming language is based on the actor model and is the most commonly used implementation of it. In this paper, we present the first version of InterSCSimulator, an open-source, extensible, large-scale Traffic Simulator for Smart Cities developed in Erlang, capable of simulating millions of agents using a real map of a large city. Future versions will be extended to address other Smart City domains.

Keywords: Simulation · Smart Cities · Erlang · Actor model
Scalability

1 Introduction

The growth of cities population around the world brought numerous challenges to their management and operation, especially in big cities. These metropolises, such as São Paulo, Rio de Janeiro, New York, Mexico City, and Tokyo, have to deal with many problems in different areas such as traffic, air pollution, public transportation, health, and education. One approach to tackling these problems is the concept of Smart Cities [1] that proposes the use of Information and Communication Technologies (ICT) to find solutions to deal with the city problems.

There are already some Smart Cities experiences around the world [2–4] with initiatives in different domains. However, deploying a complete environment to

© Springer International Publishing AG, part of Springer Nature 2018
G. P. Dimuro and L. Antunes (Eds.): MABS 2017, LNAI 10798, pp. 211–227, 2018.
https://doi.org/10.1007/978-3-319-91587-6_15

test Smart City Applications and Platforms is still a great challenge due to costs and political issues. Moreover, current Smart Cities experiences have been deployed in small to medium cities. Deploying such infrastructure in a metropolis such as São Paulo, with 11 million inhabitants, will be much more complicated.

The use of simulators can be a good alternative to support large-scale Smart Cities tests and experiments. These tools can simulate different scenarios with various solutions in many city domains such as traffic, public transportation, and resource utilization. Two main challenges arise from the use of simulators. First, the scale: to simulate an entire city, current tools demand high computational power and a long time to simulate large scenarios. Second, the usability of the tools is important because simulator users are not computer scientists. Hence, a Smart City simulator must be both scalable and user-friendly.

To tackle these two main challenges, we are developing InterSCSimulator, an agent-based Smart City simulator which offers a simple to use scenario definition with massive scalability. To achieve scalability, we used Erlang, a language developed to ease the implementation of large-scale parallel and distributed applications. To offer good usability, we studied different simulators with similar purposes such as MATSim [5] and Mezzo [6]. This paper presents the first version of InterSCSimulator which is already able to simulate large-scale traffic scenarios. Our experiments show that InterSCSimulator supports more than 4 million vehicles in a single simulation using a real map of a large city: we already tried the simulator using the maps of São Paulo, New York, and Paris.

Our simulator uses the concept of agents. In our traffic simulations, each vehicle in the simulated city is an agent that can have different behaviors such as start or stop moving, move in a defined path in the city graph, or change its path. Erlang is widely used to implement multi-agent systems [14–16]. Its programming model, called actor model, is very well-suited for this purpose. In Erlang, each application thread is an actor that executes independently of the rest of the application, and the Erlang Virtual Machine can efficiently create and manage millions of actors.

This paper is organized as follows: Sect. 2 presents the requirements to develop traffic simulations in Smart Cities. Section 3 compares InterSCSimulator to other traffic simulators. Section 4 describes the Actor Model and the Erlang language and relates it to the development of multi-agent applications. Section 5 presents the architecture and implementation of InterSCSimulator. Section 6 shows the simulator performance and usability evaluation. Finally, Sect. 7 addresses our conclusions and future work.

2   Requirements

To define the functional requirements for the initial version of our simulator, we reviewed the literature on smart cities domains [2,3] and Smart City simulators. We then opted to begin by using traffic scenarios, which have many implementation challenges such as scalability and usability. To implement traffic scenarios we found four essential functional requirements:

City Road Network: A Smart City simulator has to represent the city road network in a model easy to manipulate algorithmically. A good approach is to create a digraph based on the city map, which can be acquired from many different services such as Open Street Maps (OSM)[1] or Google Maps[2]. The model used must allow large scale simulations with millions of vehicles.

Trips Definition: It is necessary to define all the trips that will be performed during the simulation. To implement this we have two alternatives: creating a tool to generate random trips or converting an origin-destination matrix (when available) for the city we intend to simulate. For examples, in this paper we used the OD generated by the municipality of São Paulo[3].

Vehicles Simulation: All traffic simulators must use a car model to calculate the speed of the cars. There are many models available in the literature, from the simple free model to complex models. In this work, we used a free-flow model, which the vehicle speed is always the maximum speed of the street.

Output Generation: The simulator must generate different outputs to allow the analysis of the results of the simulation. The most common approach is to generate a file with all the events occurred in the simulation, allowing the development of visualization and statistical tools.

Besides the functional requirements, a Smart City simulator also must meet the following non-functional requirements:

Scalability: To simulate Smart City scenarios, it is necessary to manage millions of actors such as cars, people, buildings, and sensors. Therefore, the simulator scenarios have to scale from hundreds to millions of actors. To achieve this, distributed and parallel simulations are almost mandatory.

Usability: Creating descriptions of simulated scenarios for the simulator should be easy, enabling people with no knowledge of the internal implementation of the simulator to develop scenarios with little effort. Thus, the programming model has to be intuitive and independent of the internal implementation of the simulator.

Extensibility: It is unlikely that a simulator will provide all required features for Smart City simulations. The simulator has to be easily extensible, offering simple mechanisms for implementing new actors and changing their behavior, for implementing new metrics, and for the modification of the behavior of the simulator itself. So, it is important not only that the simulator be open source, but also well documented and implemented with high quality, extensible code.

3   Related Work

In our literature and Web searches for Smart City simulators, we did not find any simulator that is capable of simulating large-scale and complex scenarios

---

[1] Open Street Maps—http://www.openstreetmap.org.

[2] Google Maps—http://maps.google.com.

[3] OD Matrix—https://goo.gl/DNM8in.

with multiple actors such as cars, buildings, people, and sensors. We included in this section software that simulates individual agents, such as cars or people, and cites the development of large-scale simulations as one of its objectives.

DEUS (Discrete-Event Universal Simulator) is a discrete-event general purpose simulator, which was used to simulate a Vehicular Ad-Hoc Network (VANET) [7]. In this Java-based, open-source simulator, it is possible to extend the base Node and Event model to implement particular actors to simulate entities such as cars, buildings, people, and sensors. Due to its architecture and non-parallel Java implementation, however, its scalabilityd is weak, which we verified by experiments with almost 10 thousand nodes that we carried out.

Veins is a VANET simulator that integrates [8] OMNET++[4], a well-known discrete-event network simulator, and SUMO (Simulation of Urban Mobility)[5], a microscopic traffic simulator. In Veins, it is possible to simulate traffic scenarios such as traffic jams and accidents. In our experience with it, it was difficult for us to understand the code and architecture and running it in parallel mode was not trivial.

Siafu is a Java agent-based, open-source simulator [9] used to simulate mobile events in a city. The simulator has a user interface to visualize simulation data and can export data sets. In Siafu, the agent creation is manual, so it is more appropriate for small, simple scenarios that can be visualized via a simple graphical representation of the city.

MATSim is also a Java agent-based, open-source simulator [5] that provides a large variety of tools to aid in the development of traffic simulations such as an Open Street Maps converter, a coordinate system converter, and a map editor. Balmer et al. [10] show that MATSim can scale to almost 200 thousand agents. However, due to its architecture and Java implementation as well as the lack of a distributed implementation, it does not have the necessary scalability to simulate an entire city.

Mezzo is a mesoscopic[6] traffic simulation model suited for the development of integrated meso-micro models [6]. Mezzo's most important feature is the output format, which allows easy construction of microscopic simulations after the execution of the mesoscopic simulation. We have not found any information about its implementation. However, tests presented in the paper describing it show just small simulations.

Song et al. [19] implemented a mesoscopic traffic simulator using GPUs (Graphical Processing Unit). Their objective is to use the great computational power of GPUs to process large-scale traffic scenarios in high speed. The results showed a speedup of two times comparing a GPU and a C implementation. However, they found two problems: the communication between the GPU and

---

[4] OMNET++ - https://omnetpp.org.

[5] SUMO—http://sumo.dlr.de.

[6] Mesoscopic Traffic Models simulate each vehicle in transit, but with fewer details than a microscopic model. They often use a density function to determine the vehicle's speed in a street.

the CPU is a bottleneck and, normally, the memory of GPUs is small. Both are problems in the simulation of big scenarios.

DTALite [21] is an agent-based, mesoscopic traffic simulator that, as MAT-Sim, uses a queue model that calculates the speed of the vehicles based on the density of the link. This simulator was tested with the road network of Raleigh in the United States with approximately 1 million trips between 6 and 10 am. The simulator was also extended [22] to improve the capabilities to allow analysis and comparison of different scenarios.

None of the aforementioned simulators can scale to an entire metropolitan area with a map with thousands of streets and millions of vehicles moving in the city. All the simulators are implemented in Java or C++, languages in which the development of parallel and distributed applications is not transparent. Hence, the use of a language better suited for the simple development of parallel and distributed applications can enable the development of very-large-scale traffic simulators.

4   Actor Model

The Actor Model is a powerful model for the development of highly concurrent, distributed software. In this model, each actor is a processing unit, and they can communicate only using asynchronous messages. Each actor has a mailbox which stores the messages until the actor processes them. After processing a message, an actor can change its state, send other messages, or create new actors.

This model diminishes two great problems of concurrent systems: race conditions, as the actors do not share state or resources, and blocking waits, as all the messages between actors are asynchronous. Although the actor model is not a new idea [20], this model is gaining popularity in the last years because of multi-core architectures.

As with the implementation of concurrent applications, the development of distributed software is also very straightforward because there is no difference if two actors are executing in the same or different machines. The unique requirement is that the language based on the Actor Model has to implement a communication model that allows the message exchange of actors running on different machines. Currently, many languages are based on the actor model such as Erlang and Scala [18], and many others have an actor implementation such as Ruby[7], and Java[8].

4.1   Erlang

Erlang is a functional programming language based on the Actor Model developed mainly for the implementation of large-scale, distributed, parallel applications. It was created by Ericsson[9] for use in the development of telecommuni-

---

[7] Celluloid—https://celluloid.io/.
[8] Reactors.io—http://reactors.io/.
[9] Ericsson—https://www.ericsson.com/.

cation applications. Currently, the language is used in various domains such as Internet communication[10], database systems [13], and simulators [11,12].

Most of Erlang characteristics, inherited from the Actor Model, are suitable for the development of large-scale simulators:

Parallelism: The Erlang Virtual Machine allows the creation of a massive number of system threads. In the Erlang programming model, each thread is an actor that can execute functions independently and spontaneously or when it receives a message from another actor.

Distribution: In the Erlang actor model, it makes no difference whether two actors that need to exchange messages are running on the same or different machines. Therefore, the distribution of Erlang applications is very simple and almost transparent to programmers. The unique requirement is the creation of a text file with all the machines where Erlang actors can be deployed.

Fault Tolerance: Each actor in Erlang is independent of the others; therefore an error in an actor does not propagate to the rest of the application.

Communication Protocol: Erlang processes communicate only through messages, which is very useful in the development of parallel applications because that minimizes the necessity of mutual exclusion algorithms.

The Erlang language is frequently used to implement multi-agent systems. The actor model has many similarities with the idea of agents, such as communication mechanisms, multi-thread features, and fault-tolerance [14]. Moreover, each actor can have many different actions triggered by an event that can be the receiving of a message or a timeout. McCabe et al. [17] present a comparison of nine languages used to develop multi-agent systems; Erlang had the third best results, just after OpenMP and C++, but both are low-level languages, making it harder to implement parallel and distributed simulators.

The main Erlang disadvantage for the implementation of a simulator is thread synchronization: because each thread is independent of each other, it is impossible to know the order of the thread execution. Therefore, it is necessary to implement a mechanism to synchronize the execution of the actors. Another problem is the scarcity of proper tools for the development of Erlang applications, such as Integrated Development Environments and testing tools.

In the development of InterSCSimulator, we used Sim-Diasca (Simulation of Discrete Systems of All Scales) [12], a general purpose, discrete-event simulator developed in France by the EDF energy company[11] that has the goal of enabling very large-scale simulations. This simulator is implemented in Erlang, allowing the implementation of massively parallel and distributed simulations. Moreover, Sim-Diasca has a simple programming model enabling fast development of simulation scenarios. Our experiments with Sim-Diasca demonstrated that it scales much better and is much easier to use and extend that the other simulators mentioned in Sect. 3.

---

[10] WhatsApp—https://goo.gl/If6k3d.
[11] EDF—https://www.edf.fr/content/sim-diasca.

5   InterSCSimulator

InterSCSimulator is an Open-Source, scalable, Smart City simulator that has the objective of simulating various, complex, and large-scale Smart City scenarios. This section presents the implementation of the first version of the simulator that already simulates traffic scenarios with cars and buses. The simulator is implemented on top of Sim-Diasca and has all the advantages mentioned above related to the use of the Erlang language.

Figure 1 presents the simulator architecture. The bottom layer is the Sim-Diasca simulator, responsible for the discrete-event simulation activities such as Time Management, Random Number Generation, Deployment Management, and the Base Actor Models. The middle layer is the Smart City Model, which we developed as part of our research and implements the required actors for traffic simulations such as cars, buses, and the streets that represent the city graph. The top layer comprises the scenarios that can be implemented using the Smart City model.

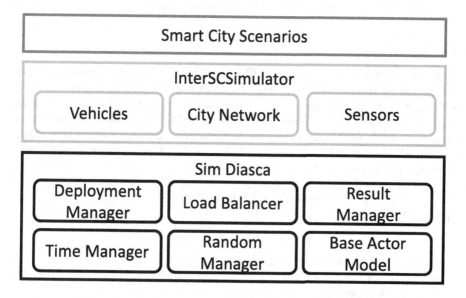

Fig. 1. InterSCSimulator architecture

5.1   InterSCSimulator Components

The InterSCSimulator has four main components: the **Scenario Definition** that receives the input files and creates the city graph and first vehicles; the **Simulation Engine** that executes the simulation algorithms and models and generates the simulation output; the **Map Visualization** that receives the simulation output and creates a visual visualization of the city map and the movement of the vehicles; finally, the **Chart Visualization** that also receives the simulation output and generates a series of charts with information about the simulated scenario. Figure 2 presents the components and their interactions with their inputs and outputs.

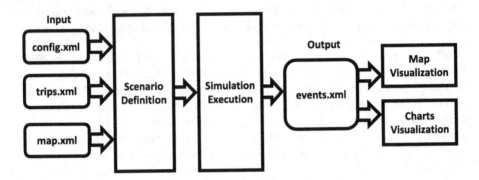

Fig. 2. InterSCSimulator components

5.2 Inputs

InterSCSimulator uses three XML files as inputs. The first, map.xml, is the description of the network of a city. This file can be generated from a region in Open Street Maps (OSM) using a tool that converts the OSM format to an oriented graph using the Erlang's Digraph API. We tested this tool with very large maps such as the entire São Paulo metropolitan area that has more than 80 thousand nodes and 120 thousand links. Listing 1 presents an example of a map file with 3 nodes and 3 links.

Listing 1. XML file with the city network

```
<network>
  <nodes>
    <node id ="1"
    x=" −46.65805" y=" −23.58162" />
    <node id ="2"
    x=" −46.65828" y=" −23.58342" />
    <node id ="3"
    x=" −46.65228" y=" −23.59341" />
    <node id ="4"
    x=" −46.43228" y=" −23.23341" />
  </ nodes>
  <links>
    <linkid="35985" from="1" to="2"
    length="100" freespeed="40" />
    <linkid="35985" from="2" to="3"
    length="200" freespeed="40" />
```

```
<linkid="35985" from="3" to="1"
length="80" freespeed="50" />
<linkid="35985" from="1" to="4"
length="120" freespeed="50" />
</ links>
</ network>
```

The file is divided into two sections. The first section describes the nodes of the graph which are street crossings in the city map; the second section contains all the links which represent stretches of the city streets. Note that many links can represent a single street.

The second XML file has all the trips that must be simulated. Each trip has the origin and destination nodes in the graph and the simulation time when the trip will start. Optionally, the trip can have a fixed path, mainly to simulate buses, or it may be up to the simulator to calculate the best path from the origin to the destination (using algorithms of the Erlang Digraph API[12]). Listing 2 presents a stretch of the trip file.

Listing 2. XML file with the trips to simulate

```
<scsimulator_matrix>
    <trip origin="247951669" destination="60641382"
        type="car" start_time="28801" />
    <trip origin="60641382" destination="247951669"
        type="car" start_time="63001" />
    <trip origin="4511105625" destination="2109902387"
        type="car" start_time="16201" />
    <trip origin="247951669" destination="60641382"
        type="car" start_time="54001" />
    <trip origin="246650787" destination="247951670"
        type="car" start_time="54001" />
    <trip origin="247951670" destination="246650787"
        type="car" start_time="66601" />
    <trip origin="246650787" destination="63451382"
        type="car" start_time="48001" />
    <trip origin="246654787" destination="45341382"
        type="car" start_time="54001" />
    <trip origin="542350787" destination="54341234"
        type="car" start_time="12001" />
    <trip origin="246650787" destination="62345478"
        type="car" start_time="52001" />
</scsimulator_matrix>
```

Finally, the third file contains some important parameters to the simulation such as the total time of the simulation, the path to the map and trip files, the output file path, and the charts that have to be generated at the end of the simulation.

---

[12] Erlang Digraph API—http://erlang.org/doc/man/digraph.html.

With the three files loaded (map, trips, and configuration), a Simulation Scenario is created. This component is responsible for the creation of all Erlang actors necessary for the simulation. Each vehicle (car or bus) is an actor, and each vertex of the city graph is also an actor that knows all its immediate neighbors. The vehicles are active actors that periodically send messages to some city vertex; these, in turn, are passive actors.

5.3 Simulation Execution

In this first version of InterSCSimulator, the Vehicle actor is the main agent of the simulation. This actor can be a car or a bus moving in the city from an origin to a destination vertex in the city graph. Currently, we do not try to check if a single car performs more than one trip throughout the simulation nor do we try to handle individual passengers, which might use more than one Vehicle in a single trip. This actor has four main behaviors: it may **Start Travel**, when the simulation reaches the start time for the vehicle; **Move**, when the simulation reaches the time of the next movement for the vehicle; **Wait**, when the vehicle has to wait until its next move action; and **Finish Travel**, when the car arrives at its destination. One agent is created to simulate each trip in the trips input file.

Another important actor is Street, which represents each vertex of the city graph. This actor knows its neighbor nodes and the links that connect them. At each movement, a car asks the vertex what is the link that it has to use to follow in its path. The street actor answers with the link and the time the car will take to cross the link. Then the car waits until its next movement. This distributed model of the city graph and the fact that all message exchanges are local allow the simulator to scale very well, as there is no central actor that manages the city graph, which would be a bottleneck.

In this first version we use two models to calculate the speed of the cars a very simple free-flow model to calculate the time that a car will spend in a link: $time = link\_length/vehicle\_speed$. Each link stores the number of cars that are in the street at each moment. If the number of cars in the link is equal to its capacity, then no vehicle can enter the link until at least one car leaves the street. If this happens, then there is a traffic jam in the simulation. We already save the number of cars in the links in each moment to allow the future development of more complex models.

InterSCSimulator can use any map collected from OSM. Figure 3 presents an execution of the simulation using the map of São Paulo. This map has approximately 50 thousand vertices and 120 thousand links; in this simulation, 500 thousand trips with 250 thousand actors were used in a one-day simulation. Each actor goes to work and goes back home at random times. In this graphic visualization, we used OTFVis[13], a visualization tool developed as part of the MATSim project.

---

[13] OTFVis—http://matsim.org/docs/extensions/otfvis.

Fig. 3. Simulation execution over the São Paulo street map

5.4   Outputs

The InterSCSimulator generates an XML output file with all the events that occurred during the simulation. We used the same format as MATSim, which allows us to use OTFVis and other MATSim tools. Listing 3 presents a segment of the output file with the events of two cars saved in an example simulation. The events stored in the file are the same described in Listing 2.

Listing 3. Simulation events file

```
<events version="1.0">
    <event time="4" type="start_trip"
    person="2121" link="5243" legMode="car"/>
    <event time="4" type="start_trip"
    person="2223" link="1002" legMode="car"/>
    <event time="11" type="move"
    person="2223" link="4005" />
    <event time="31" type="move"
    person="2121" link="4005" />
    <event time="38" type="move"
    person="2223" link="2007" />
    <event time="52" type="move"
    person="2223" link="3201" />
    <event time="54" type="move"
    person="2121" link="5002" />
    <event time="58" type="finish_trip"
    person="2121" link="4005" />
    <event time="64" type="finish_trip"
    person="2223" link="5243" />
</events>
```

Besides the file, we also created a service that runs R scripts to make statistical analyses with the data generated at the end of the simulation. These scripts produce a series of charts such as the most used links during the simulation and the biggest trips of the simulation. For example, Fig. 4 shows a graph produced by these scripts which shows the most used links during the simulation.

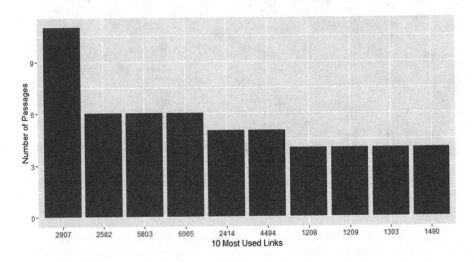

Fig. 4. Top 10 most used links during the simulation

6   InterSCSimulator Evaluation

To evaluate the simulator we tested mainly the scalability, which is our most important feature in comparison to other simulators. We also present some remarks about the usability of the simulator, which is important because people that will use this kind of simulator may not be computer specialists, such as city and traffic managers and traffic engineers.

6.1   Scalability

To test the simulator scalability, we created a scenario based on an Origin-Destination (OD) matrix produced by the subway company of São Paulo[14]. The OD matrix has 170 thousand trips of people in the city, mainly going to or coming back from work. We extrapolated the trip data in this matrix (by simple replication) to create four different synthetic scenarios: 1 million, 2 million, 3 million, and 4 million trips. All the scenarios simulate an entire day in the city. Most of the trips take place during the peak hours in the morning (07:00 to 09:00 am) and in the afternoon (05:00 to 07:00 pm).

---

[14] Origin-Destination Survey—https://goo.gl/DNM8in.

The tests showed that the simulator scales almost linearly with the number of agents. Figure 5 shows two charts, the first with the execution time of the four scenarios (in minutes) and the second with the total amount of memory used (in gigabytes) in the four scenarios. All scenarios were executed on a machine with 24 cores and 200 GB of memory. It should be possible to run the same simulations in a distributed system using a group of machines with more modest resources each.

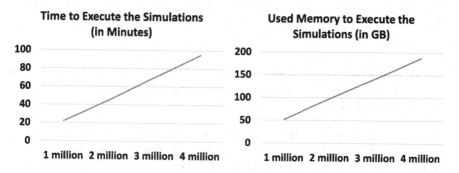

Fig. 5. Execution time and memory used in the four scenarios

Very large simulations usually take many hours or days to complete very large scenarios. With InterSCSimulator, we were able to complete all the four tested scenarios in a comparatively short time: the first scenario simulation took just 22 min, the second 45 min, the third 70 min, and the fourth 95 min. All scenarios simulated 24 h of city traffic and the simulation time grows linearly with the number of simulated agents. The second chart shows that the memory usage growth was also almost linear in the four scenarios. Comparing with the simulators presented in Sect. 3, only the work of [19] has comparable execution times.

Based on the data collected in the four scenarios, we used a linear regression algorithm to estimate the necessary resources to simulate all of the city of São Paulo, currently with 11 million inhabitants, which is our final goal. Table 1 compares the scenarios and shows estimations to simulate the entire city.

The table compares the following characteristics:

Agents: The number of simulated agents in each scenario and the total number of agents to simulate the entire city.

Map Size: The number of nodes in the city graph. In this version, we used just the map of São Paulo, but to simulate all of the city it is also necessary to include parts of the extended metropolitan area.

Memory: The maximum amount of memory used in the simulation and the necessary memory estimated to simulate the entire city.

Events: The number of events that occurred during the simulations and the estimated number of events to simulate the entire city. These events are saved in the output file.

Table 1. Simulated scenarios and estimation

	Scenario 1	Scenario 2	Scenario 3	Scenario 4	Estimation
Agents	1 million	2 million	3 million	4 million	11 million
Map size (Nodes)	50.000	50.000	50.000	50.000	140.000
Memory	51 GB	98 GB	142 GB	196 GB TB	515 GB
Time (Min)	22 m	45 m	70 m	95 m	480 m
Events	70 million	140 million	210 million	280 million	910 million
Output file size	2 GB	4.1 GB	6 GB	8.3 GB	23 GB

Output File Size: The final size of the text file that stores all the simulation events and the estimated size of the file to simulate the entire city. This file can be saved in XML and CSV format.

This data suggests that, if the simulator indeed continues to scale linearly to bigger scenarios, it will be possible to simulate the entire city. We also made some preliminary distributed tests with the simulator on a basic machine. We created three containers using Docker 9 in a machine with 6 cores and 16 GB of memory. As mentioned in Subsect. 4.1, distribution is one of the main Erlang characteristics, and it is very straightforward to execute distributed Erlang applications. Figure 6 compares the same simulation running using one, two, and three containers. The chart shows that, as the number of containers grow, simulation time decreases. We have to investigate further why this happens and also what is the impact of communications among the containers in the simulation.

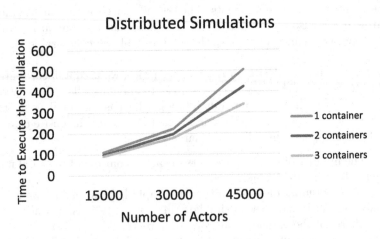

Fig. 6. Execution time of the distributed simulations

6.2 Usability and Extensibility

To verify usability, it is important to analyze how to create the Smart City scenarios. We based our model on MATSim, which requires the creation of a map, a trip, and a configuration file to create the simulation. The map file is based on Open Street Maps, the trip files can be created manually or parsed from an OD matrix, and the configuration file is very simple, with just some options as the input and output folder and the total time of the simulation. Both InterSCSimulator and MATSim provide tools for the creation of these files.

Veins and DEUS have a similar way of defining scenarios using XML files that describe the initial actors and their behavior, but they do not provide any additional tool to facilitate the development of the scenarios. Siafu has a visual interface to define the scenarios, which is good and easy when dealing with small simulations but makes the creation of large simulations with many actors impractical.

Also, extensibility is necessary to allow other researchers to change and add simulation models. InterSCSimulator and DEUS have a very similar programming model. Both provide a base class (Actor in Sim-Diasca and Node in DEUS) that developers can extend to implement the simulation actors. MATSim has many interfaces that new models can extend changing the behavior of the simulation. The Siafu programming model is a little different, and the programmer has to understand all the code of the simulator to use it. In Veins, adding new components to the simulator depends on changing OMNET++ and SUMO and its communication. Therefore, InterSCSimulator, MATSim, and DEUS seem to be more easily extensible than Siafu and Veins.

7 Conclusions

This paper described the development of InterSCSimulator, a simulator that aims to advance the state of the art in the integrated simulation of Smart Cities, offering scalability and a straightforward programming model. In this first version of the simulator, we implemented actors for the simulation of traffic scenarios. The experiments showed that the simulator is scalable, a fundamental requirement to simulate large traffic scenarios; it is reasonable to expect similar performance in other domains. Compared to other simulators, InterSCSimulator is also easy to use and makes it possible to generate charts and an animated simulation with a GUI using the results of the simulations.

We also developed tools to aid in the creation of real scenarios such as an Open Street Maps parser and a parser to read the São Paulo OD Matrix. In our ongoing work, we are experimenting with larger scenarios, going up to the entire vehicle fleet of an enormous city with 11 million inhabitants. To do that, we need to execute the simulator both in larger machines with more cores and in a distributed environment, exploring the parallelism supported by the Actor model of Erlang. However, we anticipate that we will need to address several challenges and bottlenecks before we can achieve that, such as the size of the output file, the maximum number of supported actors in an Erlang virtual machine, and the communication costs in distributed environments.

As future work, we intend to implement other Smart City scenarios such as disaster management and smart grids. We also plan to make large-scale distributed simulations, since we only tested the distribution model of Erlang in small scenarios. Finally, we plan to perform a functional evaluation with city officials and public policy makers to validate the simulated scenarios and improve the simulator usability.

Acknowledgments. This research is part of the INCT of the Future Internet for Smart Cities funded by CNPq, proc. 465446/2014-0, CAPES proc. 88887.136422/2017-00, and FAPESP, proc. 2014/50937-1 and was partially funded by Hewlett Packard Enterprise (HPE).

References

1. Caragliu, A., Del Bo, C., Nijkamp, P.: Smart cities in Europe. J. Urban Technol. **18**, 65–82 (2011)
2. Sanchez, L., Muñoz, L., Galache, J.A., Sotres, P., Santana, J.R., Gutierrez, V., Pfisterer, D.: SmartSantander: IoT experimentation over a smart city testbed. Comput. Netw. **61**, 217–238 (2014)
3. Zanella, A., Bui, N., Castellani, A., Vangelista, L., Zorzi, M.: Internet of things for smart cities. IEEE Internet Things J. **1**, 22–32 (2014)
4. Grimaldi, D., Fernandez, V.: The alignment of University curricula with the building of a Smart City: a case study from Barcelona. Technol. Forecast. Soc. Change **123**, 298–306 (2016)
5. Horni, A., Nagel, K., Axhausen, K.W.: The Multi-Agent Transport Simulation MATSim. Ubiquity, London (2016)
6. Burghout, W., Koutsopoulos, H.N., Andreasson, I.: A discrete-event mesoscopic traffic simulation model for hybrid traffic simulation. In: IEEE Intelligent Transportation Systems Conference (2006)
7. Picone, M., Amoretti, M., Zanichelli, F.: Simulating smart cities with DEUS. In: International ICST Conference on Simulation Tools and Techniques (2012)
8. Darus, M.Y., Bakar, K.A.: Congestion control algorithm in VANETs. World Appl. Sci. J. **21**, 1057–1061 (2013)
9. Nazário, D.C., Tromel, I.V.B., Dantas, M.A.R., Todesco, J.L.: Toward assessing quality of context parameters in a ubiquitous assisted environment. In: IEEE Symposium on Computers and Communication (ISCC), June 2014
10. Balmer, M., Meister, K., Nagel, K.: Agent-Based Simulation of Travel Demand: Structure and Computational Performance of MATSim-T. ETH Zürich IVT Institut für Verkehrsplanung und Transportsysteme, Zürich (2008)
11. Toscano, L., D'Angelo, G., Marzolla, M.: Parallel discrete event simulation with Erlang. In: ACM SIGPLAN Workshop on Functional High-Performance Computing (2012)
12. Song, T., Kaleshi, D., Zhou, R., Boudeville, O., Ma, J.X., Pelletier, A., Haddadi, I.: Performance evaluation of integrated smart energy solutions through large-scale simulations. In: Smart Grid Communications (2011)
13. Anderson, J.C., Lehnardt, J., Slater, N.: CouchDB: The Definitive Guide. O'Reilly Media Inc., Sebastopol (2010)

14. Di Stefano, A., Santoro, C.: eXAT: an experimental tool for programming multi-agent systems in Erlang. In: WOA (2003)
15. Varela, C., Abalde, C., Castro, L. Gulias, J.: On modeling agent systems with Erlang. In: ACM SIGPLAN Workshop on Erlang (2004)
16. Krzywicki, D., Stypka, J., Anielski, P., Turek, W., Byrski, A., Kisiel-Dorohinicki, M.: Generation-free agent-based evolutionary computing. Proc. Comput. Sci. **29**, 1068–1077 (2014)
17. McCabe, S., Brearcliffe, D., Froncek, P., Hansen, M., Kane, V., Taghawi-Nejad, D., Axtell, R.: A comparison of languages and frameworks for the parallelization of a simple agent model. In: Workshop, Multi-Agent-Based Simulation (MABS) (2016)
18. Tasharofi, S., Dinges, P., Johnson, R.E.: Why do scala developers mix the actor model with other concurrency models? In: Castagna, G. (ed.) ECOOP 2013. LNCS, vol. 7920, pp. 302–326. Springer, Heidelberg (2013). https://doi.org/10.1007/978-3-642-39038-8_13
19. Song, X., Xie, Z., Xu, Y., Tan, G., Tang, W., Bi, J., Li, X.: Supporting real-world network-oriented mesoscopic traffic simulation on GPU. Simul. Model. Pract. Theory **74**, 46–63 (2017)
20. Agha, G.A.: Actors: A Model of Concurrent Computation in Distributed Systems. Massachusetts Institute of Technology, Cambridge (1985)
21. Xuesong, Z., Jeffrey, T.: DTALite: a queue-based mesoscopic traffic simulator for fast model evaluation and calibration. Cogent Eng. (2014)
22. Chenfeng, X., Xuesong, Z., Lei, Z.: AgBM-DTALite: an integrated modelling system of agent-based travel behaviour and transportation network dynamics. Travel Behav. Soc. (2017)

Author Index

Printed in the United States
By Bookmasters

Printed in the United States
By Bookmasters